CW00924883

Research Methods for Early Childhood Education

ALSO AVAILABLE FROM BLOOMSBURY

Research Methods for Classroom Discourse, Jenni Ingram and
Victoria Elliott
Research Methods for Education in the Digital Age, Maggi Savin-
Baden and Gemma Tombs
Research Methods for Educational Dialogue, Ruth Kershner,
Sara Hennessy, Rupert Wegerif and Ayesha Ahmed
Research Methods for Social Justice and Equity in Education,
Liz Atkins and Vicky Duckworth
Research Methods for Pedagogy, Melanie Nind, Alicia Curtin and
Kathy Hall
Research Methods for Understanding Professional Learning,
Elaine Hall and Kate Wall
Place-Based Methods for Researching Schools, Pat Thomson and
Christine Hall

Research Methods for Early Childhood Education

ROSIE FLEWITT AND LYNN ANG

BLOOMSBURY ACADEMIC
LONDON • NEW YORK • OXFORD • NEW DELHI • SYDNEY

BLOOMSBURY ACADEMIC
Bloomsbury Publishing Plc
50 Bedford Square, London, WC1B 3DP, UK
1385 Broadway, New York, NY 10018, USA

BLOOMSBURY, BLOOMSBURY ACADEMIC and the Diana logo are trademarks
of Bloomsbury Publishing Plc

First published in Great Britain 2020

Copyright © Rosie Flewitt and Lynn Ang 2020

Rosie Flewitt and Lynn Ang have asserted their right under the Copyright,
Designs and Patents Act, 1988, to be identified as Authors of this work.

All rights reserved. No part of this publication may be reproduced or transmitted
in any form or by any means, electronic or mechanical, including photocopying,
recording, or any information storage or retrieval system, without prior
permission in writing from the publishers.

Bloomsbury Publishing Plc does not have any control over, or responsibility for,
any third-party websites referred to or in this book. All internet addresses given
in this book were correct at the time of going to press. The author and publisher
regret any inconvenience caused if addresses have changed or sites have ceased
to exist, but can accept no responsibility for any such changes.

A catalogue record for this book is available from the British Library.

ISBN: HB: 978-1-3500-1540-1
PB: 978-1-3500-1541-8
ePDF: 978-1-3500-1543-2
eBook: 978-1-3500-1542-5

Series: Bloomsbury Research Methods for Education

Typeset by Deanta Global Publishing Services, Chennai, India
Printed and bound in Great Britain

To find out more about our authors and books visit www.bloomsbury.com
and sign up for our newsletters.

CONTENTS

FIGURES

ABOUT THE
AUTHORS

Rosie Flewitt is Professor of Early Childhood Communication in the Education and Social Research Institute (ESRI), Manchester Metropolitan University, and former Founding Co-director of the Helen Hamlyn Centre for Pedagogy (0–11 years), University College London, Institute of Education. She is an international expert in young children's communication, language and literacy development in mainstream and inclusive education. She has extensive experience in qualitative and participatory research methods, and is renowned for her cutting-edge work bringing multimodal and ethnographic approaches to the study of early communication and literacy. Rosie has led and co-investigated many national and international research projects, and has advised UK and EU policymakers on young children's communication, language and literacy development in a digital age. Rosie is a Fellow of the Royal Society for the Arts (RSA) and board member of the Froebel Trust Research Committee. Recent publications include *The Routledge Handbook of Digital Literacies in Early Childhood* (Erstad, Flewitt, Kümmerling-Meibauer and Pires Pereira 2019), the award-winning *Storytelling in Early Childhood: Enriching Language, Literacy, and Classroom Culture* (Cremin, Flewitt, Marsden and Swann 2017), and *Understanding Research with Children and Young People* (Clark, Flewitt, Hammersley and Robb 2013).

Lynn Ang is Professor of Early Childhood, Department of Learning and Leadership, University College London (UCL), Institute of Education. She is an expert in early learning, early childhood and primary education, and international evidence-based research, particularly in developing countries. She has extensive methodological experience in qualitative and participatory methods, evaluation research, systematic reviews and interdisciplinary research in the fields of early childhood and international development. Her work focuses on social inequality and socially relevant research, and the implications for policy and practice to benefit children and families. She has led and co-led many major research grants and research strands including the first systematic review of international research evidence on early childhood development and peace-building policies across fourteen conflict-affected countries (2015-2016); a five-year study to assess the effectiveness, impact and sustainability of the World Bank Early Learning Partnership (ELP) (2018–22); the Education component of a large Global Challenges Research Funding (GCRF) Research Hub Action against Stunting funded by EPSRC (2019–25); and the Education Endowment Foundation (EEF) funded project 'Manor Park Talks' (2018–20) to embed an evidence-based intervention programme of professional development to improve the outcomes for disadvantaged two-year-olds accessing free early education entitlement in Manor Park, Newham, UK.

SERIES EDITOR'S PREFACE

The idea of the *Bloomsbury Research Methods for Education* series is to provide books that are useful to researchers wanting to think about research methods in the context of their research area, research problem, or research aims. While researchers may use any methods textbook for ideas and inspiration, the onus falls on them to apply something from social science research methods to education in particular, or from education to a particular dimension of education (pedagogy, schools, the digital dimension, practitioner learning to name some examples). This application of ideas is not beyond us and has led to some great research and also to methodological development. In this series though, the books are more targeted, making them a good place to start for the student, researcher or person wanting to craft a research proposal. Each book brings together in one place the range of sometimes interconnected and often diverse methodological possibilities for researching one aspect or sector of education, one research problem or phenomenon. Thus, readers will quickly find a discussion of the methods they associate with that bit of education research they are interested in, but in addition they will find less obvious and more innovative methods and approaches. A quick look at the opening glossary will give you an idea of the methods you will find included within each book. You can expect a discussion of those methods that is critical, authoritative *and* situated. In each text the authors use powerful examples of the methods in use in the arena with which you are concerned.

There are other features that make this series distinctive. In each of the books the authors draw on their own research and on the research of others making alternative methodological choices. In this way they address the affordances of the methods in terms of real studies; they illustrate the potential with real data. The authors also discuss the rationale behind the choice of methods and behind how researchers put them together in research designs. As readers you will get behind the scenes of published research and into the kind of methodological decision-making that you are grappling with. In each of the books you will find yourself moving between methods, theory and data; you will find theoretical concepts to think with and with which you might be able to enhance your methods. You will find that the authors develop arguments about methods rather than just describing them.

Research Methods for Early Childhood Education is an important addition to the literature on early childhood and the literature on research methods in its unique approach to linking the substantive and methodological issues with an international perspective. I will not be including a book on research methods for each sector of the education system in this series because not all the sectors call for particular methods. However, the young age of the children, the diversity of contexts for educating them, and the implications of cultural diversity mean that researchers of early childhood education need particular support with methods. Rosie Flewitt and Lynn Ang are extremely well-placed to help readers with the challenges and they do so knowledgeably and with great clarity. You will find a text that is engaging, current and practically useful as it summarizes the development of the field of early childhood education and its relationship with research and research methods. You will also find the key players, the children and supporting adults, are regarded with respect and as having important active roles to play. *Research Methods for Early Childhood Education* includes a good range of methods and the authors do not shy away from problematizing assumptions or critiquing gaps and shortfalls in contemporary understandings of early childhood.

This book (as with any in the series) cannot be the only book you need to read to formulate, justify and implement your research methods. Other books may cover a different range of methods or more operational detail. The aim for this series, though, is to provide books that take you to the heart of the methods thinking you will want and need to do. They are books by authors who are equally passionate about their substantive topic and about research methods and they are books that will be invaluable for inspiring deep and informed methods thinking.

Melanie Nind
Series editor

GLOSSARY OF RESEARCH METHODS AND APPROACHES

Here, we present some of the central research methods and approaches that are referred to in this book. The glossary is not an exhaustive list but an accessible resource that aims to clarify key ideas that are widely used in research methods.

Action research A systematic approach for practitioners to understand and improve their own practice through a focus on their own practical actions and their own reflections on data about the effects of those actions. This often involves cycles of planning, implementing, recording and analysing a change in process, and usually involves close collaboration between researchers and practitioners.

Audit trail A clear account of how research data are generated in a naturalistic study, which enables readers of the research to track the data sources.

Auto-ethnography An approach that combines life history, ethnography and self-narrative in either an ethnographic study of oneself in the social and cultural context or an autobiographical account that includes ethnographic data. See also ethnography.

Bias Used to describe the act of making prejudiced assumptions or judgements about any aspect of the research process that will distort the research findings.

Case study A research design that centres on in-depth, intensive analysis of a single (or multiple) case within its naturalistic context, valuing its particularity, complexity and relationships with the context. This approach uses multiple methods and perspectives to look at the case holistically. The findings of case studies tend to be indicative of trends and patterns of behaviour, and do not aim to be generalizable.

Child-centred methods Research methods designed or developed to be accessible, attractive and engaging for children, with a view to promoting their active involvement in the research process.

Closed questions Questions where the answers are predetermined or require little more than a simple yes/no response.

Coding The act of organizing data into themes (as in qualitative research) or attaching numerical values to categories (as in quantitative research).

Constructivism A theoretical approach that assumes people construct their own understanding and knowledge of the world through their life experiences and by reflecting on their experiences – 'reality' may therefore be perceived differently by different people.

Control group Used primarily in randomized control trials (RCTs) to describe a participant group that either does not receive an intervention or receives a different intervention to the experimental group, so the effects of the intervention can be measured and compared across different groups.

Conversation analysis An approach to studying audio/video-recorded social interaction and conversation in detail, paying particular attention to the social context and to how the conversation works in terms of turn taking, sequences and functions.

Correlational analysis The use of statistical correlation to evaluate the strength of the relationship between variables.

Covert participation The act of participating in the activity that is being researched, without disclosing one's identity as a researcher.

Credibility Used in qualitative research to describe building readers' confidence in the accuracy of data generation and interpretation; credibility is viewed by some qualitative researchers as more significant than validity or reliability.

Critical discourse analysis An approach that enables researchers to understand how discourse and power are manifested in everyday interaction.

Critical incident analysis A method to focus the researcher on a critical incident or turning point, exploring people's behaviour and experience before, during and after an incident in order to analyse the meaning of the incident for those involved.

Critical reflection Used to describe the process of questioning our understandings by examining and evaluating our assumptions with a view to improving the rigour of research practice and strengthening an argument.

Deductive coding Creating an initial coding list based on themes from a study's conceptual framework, research questions and/or hypothesis. See also *Inductive coding*.

Dependent variable Used in experimental and quasi-experimental research to describe the variable that is being measured and tested.

Descriptive statistics Describing numerical data in summary form with the aim of explaining the data.

Discourse The social and institutional frameworks that predominate in a given culture, society or community, and shape how knowledge and societies are constituted.

Documentary analysis Often used by social science researchers as a supplementary rather than a main method, this involves analysis of documents (pre-existing artefacts or written texts) for what they can reveal about the phenomenon under study.

Educational design research (EDR) An emerging methodological approach aiming to find research-based solutions to complex problems in educational practice and in turn to develop or validate existing theories, for example, about learning processes and/or learning environments. Typically, EDR involves working with practitioners to design an intervention in their classroom and to identify valid design principles (or a local theory) for these interventions.

Emancipatory research Research approach where the subjects of social inquiry take control of the research process to ensure that the process and product of the study brings about social transformation from which they benefit.

Emic Used most frequently in ethnographic research to describe an insider's point of view. See *Etic*.

Empirical research Where knowledge is gained about phenomena by the collection and analysis of primary data through observation or experience in the research field.

Epistemology Used in research to refer to the relationship between truth, belief and what counts as legitimate knowledge. Originates from Greek philosophy and the words *epistēmē* (knowledge) and *logos* (logical discourse).

Equity Used to describe justice and fairness for all, and involves making things equal for everyone.

Ethnographic case study A type of qualitative case study using an ethnographic approach. This sometimes involves a shorter degree of immersion in the context by the researcher than in a full ethnography. The focus is on the case – the individual, event or phenomenon – rather than on the culture of a group. See *Case study* and *Ethnography*.

Ethnography A qualitative research approach that seeks to balance insider (emic) and outsider (etic) perspectives in order to understand social action in a particular community, practice or setting. Ethnographic researchers use methods of progressively focused observation and interview, becoming immersed in the research environment over time and generating complex, detailed data to enable deep descriptions and theorization of the cultural context. See *Thick description*.

Etic Used most frequently in ethnographic research to describe an outsider's (the researcher's) point of view. See *Emic*.

Evaluation research The systematic collection of data about a policy, product or programme with a view to identifying impact and avenues for improvement.

Evidence Data that yield proof or strong confirmation of a theory or hypothesis in a research setting.

Experimental group Used primarily in RCTs to describe a participant group that receives an intervention. Also sometimes known as the *treatment group*. See also *Control group*.

Experimental research Where data are collected and analysed under controlled conditions, and independent variables are manipulated to measure their effect on a dependent variable (the phenomenon under investigation).

External validity The extent to which research findings can be generalized to a wider population.

Factor analysis The use of statistical methods to reduce correlational data to a smaller number of dimensions regarded as the basic variables accounting for the interrelations observed in the data.

Focus group A group interview method where participants are invited to explore a particular topic in group discussion. Participants respond to each other, to activities or stimuli rather than just to the researcher's questions. The researcher aims to facilitate discussion rather than direct it.

Gatekeeper An individual who has the power to control access to a research site, such as a parent, head teacher or teacher.

Generalizability This term describes the extent to which the findings of a research study can be applied to wider populations; it is sometimes referred to as *external validity*.

Group data surgery A method in which a number of researchers and/or participants come together to jointly share, discuss and analyse data.

Hierarchical multiple regression analysis Standard multiple regression is a statistical method used to evaluate the relationship between a set of independent variables and a dependent variable. Hierarchical regression evaluates this same relationship but controls for the impact of a different set of independent variables on the dependent variable.

Hypothesis A predictive statement about measurable phenomena, often used in experimental research to suggest a possible explanation for a phenomenon and its likely cause.

Inclusive research An umbrella term for diverse approaches that respond to the call for democratization of the research process, including participatory, emancipatory and partnership research. The emphasis is on ensuring the relevance of research to the people concerned, so it is beneficial to them, and they are involved in the research process and in decision-making.

Independent variable The variable that is changed or controlled in experimental research to test the effects on the dependent variable. Experimental research that is high in internal validity is able to prove that an independent variable caused a dependent variable.

Inductive research This refers to exploratory research that does not begin with a clear expectation of what the study findings might be and moves from the specific to the building of new theory or concepts.

Internal validity Refers to how well designed a study is and can be said to represent the phenomenon being studied. See also *Credibility*.

Inter-rater reliability Mostly used in quantitative research to refer to the degree of agreement among researchers during data analysis. In statistical analysis, this is sometimes presented as a score that indicates how much consensus there is between analysts in a research team. This approach is also sometimes used in qualitative research, where data extracts are coded by different members of a research team, who then meet and agree a shared coding scheme that relates to the research questions and has agreed definitions for all codes.

Interpretivist research A research approach founded on the belief that individuals create and co-create their social world in a dynamic system of making and sharing meaning with others, within the context of social and cultural discourses and norms.

Inter-semiotic relations The relationships across and between modes in multimodal texts and interaction. See *Semiotic resources*.

Interview The method of asking participants to respond to questions, usually by reflecting on their experiences or views. Interviews may be structured, semi-structured or unstructured and may involve individual participants or participant groups (see also *Focus groups*).

Longitudinal research Where data are generated over an extended period of time. For example, cohort studies in which individuals experiencing the same event are observed at repeated intervals to examine change; panel studies involving a cross-section of a population surveyed at multiple points in time; and qualitative longitudinal research involving multiple visits to the research site, over a relatively long period of time.

Mapping A visual method where participants individually or in groups map out (write or draw) their experiences, often including a space/time dimension. The researcher may record and explore the processes of production of these maps alongside the maps produced.

Modal affordance Used in multimodal research to describe the potentialities and constraints of different modes – what it is possible (or not) to express and represent or communicate easily with the resources of a mode. The affordances of different modes reflect their materiality and their cultural, social and historical use. 'Affordance' originates from Gibson (1986) and is adapted by Kress (2010). See *Mode* and *Multimodality*.

Mode A socially, culturally and historically shaped resource for making meaning – such as, writing and image on the page; moving image and sound on the screen; and speech, gesture, gaze and posture in embodied interaction.

Mosaic approach A combination of participatory and visual methods designed to bring together data generated by young children and adults to help them make sense of their everyday experiences. The resulting mosaic is co-constructed by participants and the researcher.

Multilevel statistics Advanced statistical method for handling clustered or grouped data.

Multimodal analysis An approach that takes into account multiple modes of communication (such as gesture, gaze, action, speech, drawing) and does not assume language is always present in meaning making or is always the most important mode for meaning making.

Multimodality An interdisciplinary approach that understands communication and representation to be about more than language. Multimodality provides a robust framework, concepts and methods for the collection and analysis of visual, aural, embodied and spatial aspects of interaction and environments, and the relationships between these.

Multimodal transcription Representing multimodal data in formats that retain some of the complexity of the ways in which modes of communication interact. Multimodal transcriptions vary but might include photographs or video stills alongside close analysis of gaze direction and/or movement and transcript of language (Flewitt et al. 2014).

Observation A method for recording what can be seen in the research site. Observation can be naturalistic, conducted by participant or non-participant observers. It can be open and responsive to events as they unfold, or it can be systematic and structured, using time sampling, event sampling or pre-prepared schedules.

Ontology Refers to the nature of reality, what can be said to exist and how entities can be categorized. Derives from the Greek words *ontos* (being) and *logos* (logical discourse).

Paradigm A theoretical framing that shapes how the world is seen; each paradigm has a set of values and philosophical assumptions about knowledge. See *Epistemology* and *Ontology*.

Participant observer Used in qualitative research, where the observer takes part in that activities being studied. This gives the observer the opportunity to understand phenomena from an insider perspective, rather than as an outsider.

Participatory action research (PAR) Action research that involves participants in the planning, change and reflection processes, often considering underlying issues of power and social justice as part of a transformatory process. See *Action research*.

Participatory research Research process that involves adults and/or children (the people who are being researched or implicated in the research) in the planning, decision-making and conduct of an empirical study.

Pedagogical documentation A combination of observation, record keeping, analysis and reflection on the pedagogical process (often carried out in collaboration) to inform understanding and action for teachers and researchers. This term is often used in early childhood education.

Phenomenology` A research approach that asks questions about the subjective experience of research participants and how meaning is made in the moments of practice as individuals experience the world. Participants identify what is meaningful to them about particular practices and the researcher explores this with the participants.

Photo questionnaire The use of photos related to the research question as stimuli for focused or open-ended responses from participants.

Population Used in research to describe the group to which a researcher suggests the findings of a study might apply.

Positivism Where researchers attempt to isolate cause-and-effect relationships between social phenomena to find a universal 'truth' that can be applied to broader populations.

Practice-based inquiry A research strategy for practitioners (individually or collectively) to systematically and rigorously study their own practice. Related to action research, this is a way to support the development of knowledge contextualized within specific contexts of practice, emphasizing the role of collaboration and reflection in the inquiry and learning process.

Praxis The notion that practice and theory are inseparable, with theory informing practice and observations of practice informing the development and refinement of theory.

Probability sampling Selecting a participant sample at random from a wide population, so findings can be generalized across that population.

Purposive sampling A non-probability approach where participants are selected on purpose to represent certain predefined traits in a population.

Quasi-experimental design Research that takes an experimental approach without the core ingredient of random assignment of subjects to groups. In education it is often difficult or impossible to randomly select the sample, so quasi-experimental designs are more commonly used than experimental designs as they raise fewer ethical concerns and fit better with real-life contexts.

Qualitative research Concerned with collecting non-numerical data, and often using inductive analysis to describe experiences and to explore the complexity of phenomena in detail; the focus is on the credibility of robust descriptions rather than on generalizability.

Quantitative research Concerned with formulating a hypothesis and collecting numerical data to test the hypothesis, often using deductive analysis to measure, quantify and generalize the study findings.

Questionnaire Administration of a pre-prepared set of (usually written) questions with a view to obtaining data, often for numerical or statistical analysis. Questionnaires can be delivered in paper format or online, and can include qualitative, open-ended questions where participants are invited to use their own words to comment on particular phenomena.

Randomized control trial (RCT) An experimental design where study participants are randomly allocated to different groups (e.g. a treatment or experimental and a non-treatment control group) to gain robust evaluation of efficacy. See *Control group* and *Experimental group*.

Reactivity The potential for participants' behaviour to be changed by the presence of a researcher and the act of taking part in a study.

Reflexivity Reflecting critically on and monitoring the effect of the self (i.e. the researcher's beliefs and assumptions) on the research conduct and outcomes.

Reliability The extent to which a study design will produce similar results if carried out by a different researcher and/or at a different time, using the same research methods.

Research diary Often used in qualitative research by researchers (and practitioners in action research) to keep track of and reflect on ideas as they develop during the research process; a useful instrument to prompt reflexivity.

Research question(s) A question or set of interrelated questions that formulate and delineate the phenomenon or phenomena that a study aims to address.

Semiosis Using signs, such as language, action and images, to make meaning.

Semiotic resources Used in social semiotics and other disciplines to refer to a material, social and cultural resource for meaning making. Defined by Van Leeuwen (2004: 285) as 'the actions, materials and artifacts we use for communicative purposes, whether produced physiologically – for example, with our vocal apparatus, the muscles we use to make facial expressions and gestures – or technologically – for example, with pen and ink, or computer hardware and software – together with the ways in which these resources can be organized.' See also *Inter-semiotic relations*.

Sensory ethnography An ethnographic approach encompassing sensory embodied experiences. See *Ethnography*.

Sensory methods Methods that focus on sensory bodily experience, recording data gained through multiple senses. In recent years, sensory methods have been used increasingly to investigate touch technologies.

Snowball sampling A non-probability sampling strategy where the first group of participants suggests the next participant cohort; this approach is particularly useful when researching 'hard-to-reach' populations.

Subjectivity The extent to which researchers' own feelings, biases and understandings influence what they notice and record (or not); subjectivity is socially constructed through discourse, language and practices.

Survey An approach used to discover broad, general or comparative information on a selected topic by surveying (often a large) number of participants. This may involve no personal contact between researcher and participant.

Systematic review A method for synthesizing findings from many studies on one theme using an explicit, transparent, replicable and accountable protocol. A systematic search strategy and application of inclusion/exclusion criteria and quality thresholds can be used to justify claims being made about the strength of evidence.

Thick description Used in ethnographic research to describe written accounts of observed behaviours that give sufficient detail for a study to be credible enough to test and/or build theory. Originally used by Gilbert Ryle (1971) and adopted by the anthropologist Clifford Geertz (1973; 2002).

Time series design One form of quasi-experiment design involving capturing data at multiple data points (not just before and after an intervention) that allows comparison with baseline levels and trends.

Transcription The act of deciding what data is described and how it is represented for the purpose of analysis; researchers should reflect critically on how information gathered 'in the field' is selected and transformed through the process of transcription.

Triangulation Using different methods so data can be compared from different sources, with a view to strengthening research findings and enabling more nuanced insights from research. For example, in early childhood education research, classroom behaviours might be observed alongside interviews with children, parents and staff, and analysis of school documentation.

Validity The degree to which the design of study produces credible and accurate data, which in turn informs the study findings and truth claims.

Video methods Methods that allow researchers to produce and analyse audiovisual data, including naturally occurring video data, video diaries and researcher-produced or -elicited video films. Subsequent data analysis may treat the video as a record of events or as an impression of events.

Video-stimulated recall/reflection/dialogue Using video clips of participants in action to stimulate their reflection and dialogue about the recorded event or interaction. This approach is used to probe what participants were thinking or feeling at the time. Control of the selection of units of analysis can be shared or handed over to participants.

Videography An ethnographic approach to video making that regards video as an aesthetic object and a reflexive mirror for researchers and participants to use in reorienting the power of researcher gaze.

Virtual ethnography An approach adapting ethnographic research methods for online research contexts. For example, netnography (Kozinets 2015) seeks to understand human interaction in online environments. See *Ethnography*.

Visual ethnography The use of analogue or digital technology to visually record ethnographic data and experiences, using video or still photography. See *Ethnography*.

ACKNOWLEDGEMENTS

We would like to thank our esteemed academic colleagues for their constructive and critical feedback on drafts of the chapters in this volume, particularly, Phil Jones; Alison Clark; Janet Maybin; Lesley Lancaster; Joseph Mintz; Jake Anders and Kelly Dickson. Many thanks also to the series editor Melanie Nind for inviting us to contribute to this innovative book series, and for providing critical feedback on the final manuscript.

Introduction

The early childhood years are specific and unique. We all know something about childhood because we have all experienced it, but every person's experience of childhood is different. According to Danby and Farrell (2004) 'childhood cannot be described as a universal experience, but one that is constructed within specific times, places and contexts' (p. 38). How children experience childhood depends on many factors – their family lives, social and economic circumstances; where they live; and their gender, ethnicity, religion, cultural background and health. Many children grow up in secure, stable and loving relationships, but many experience challenges and unsettling change that can be deeply distressing.

As early childhood education researchers, our understanding of children and childhood must allow for this diversity and complexity of experience. The different circumstances of children's everyday lives in economically developed and peaceful global regions may stand in stark contrast with childhoods in the developing world and in regions plagued by armed conflict and natural disaster. UNICEF publishes an annual report, *The State of the World's Children* (UNICEF 2017), which gives an overview of the circumstances that vulnerable children are born into. Despite the rapid proliferation of globalization, urbanization and digitalization, inequality continues to deepen. Many children are disadvantaged by myriad forms of adversity, such as poverty, exploitation, exclusion, conflict and other crises. In its 2017 issue, the UNICEF report estimates that nearly fifty million children are 'on the move' (p. 30), with twenty-eight million displaced by conflict, and millions more 'migrating to escape crushing poverty and the growing impact of climate change' (p. 30). Children continue to be profoundly affected by poverty and the wider economic conditions of the society in which they live. Even in rich, developed countries like the United Kingdom and the United States, children experience deprivation and their early experiences of life and education are profoundly different. To understand childhoods, it is therefore important that we examine the multidimensional factors that influence children's lives, and how these evolve and change over time.

Cross-cultural studies are particularly useful in highlighting the variations in childhoods around the globe. They enable researchers to explore how patterns of social behaviour, lifestyles and traditions are similar or different across communities and countries. In a study carried out in the early 1990s, Tobin, Wu and Davidson (1991) compared the early education of young children in three cultures – China, Japan and the United States. The study revealed the contrasting assumptions that practitioners and preschool professionals held of children and their disparate beliefs of how children should be cared for and educated. Researchers Correa-Chávez and Rogoff (2009) compared children's learning in Guatemalan Mayan and European American communities, and documented the significant cultural variations in which learning occurs through community activities and participation. On a larger scale, the interdisciplinary *Young Lives* project (see Oxford Department for International Development 2015) followed the lives of 12,000 children in Ethiopia, India (in the states of Andhra Pradesh and Telangana), Peru and Vietnam over 15 years. The study focused on two groups of children – one cohort born in between 1994 and 1995, and a younger cohort born in between 2001 and 2002 – noting changes in the same children's lives and communities over time, and comparing the life experiences of different children of the same age. These cross-cultural insights into children's lives shed light on the characteristics of childhoods that different race and ethnic groups have developed over generations, and on the drivers and impacts of child poverty. Studies such as these illustrate the ways that a particular time, place and society shapes how people think of childhood as a concept, and they generate robust evidence to help policymakers design health, welfare and education programmes aimed at improving the lives of children and their families who are living in challenging circumstances.

In this book, we share a broad conceptualization of early childhood education as including early care and education settings, and education at home and in the communities in which children live, and we reflect on the different insights that can be gained from diverse research methodologies and disciplinary frameworks. The perennial challenge for researchers in the field of early childhood education is how to capture the complexity, diversity and unpredictability of children's early experiences of life. We also recognize and value young children's role in contributing to the study of their own lives, and their capacity to describe clearly and accurately what they think and feel about issues that are relevant to them. The last two decades have seen a proliferation of funding for research that directly involves children and listening to their views. There are established and new methods to involve and consult with children in research through talking with them, using photography and diaries, drawings and videos. These creative approaches to involving children as well as young people as both participants and researchers consider children to be highly informed experts of their everyday lives. These participatory methods raise important questions about possible alternative approaches and theories to inform the study of childhoods.

In any research endeavour, it is important to reflect critically on the relationship between the chosen research methodology (the values and beliefs that guide a research study), the research methods (the particular techniques used to conduct research in practice) and the theoretical framework that underpins a study. In participatory research with children, the synergies in this relationship have wide-ranging implications for all aspects of the research process. Over recent decades, the theoretical tenets of poststructualism, postmodernism and post-foundationalism, for instance, have helped to create and sustain our critical reflections on children and childhood. The work of the French philosopher Michel Foucault (1975, 2007) has been profoundly influential in the interrogation of the relationship between knowledge, truth and power as a form of social control, and their effects on institutions and individuals. His theoretical ideas provide a critical lens to contest meanings of childhoods and what is commonly thought to be right or 'best' for children and their learning. Applying a poststructuralist stance and the work of Foucault, MacNaughton (2005) highlights the politics of knowledge that shape how we view early childhood education and practices, the 'effects of privileging one form of knowledge of children' and the 'shifting ways it advantages some groups and disadvantages other groups' (p. 2). A poststructuralist framework requires us to consider different truths and meanings to the world. For example, there is no universal or generic consensus of what constitutes 'good' early childhood education, and the notion of 'quality' takes on multiple meanings depending on particular cultural and social contexts. Building on a poststructural theoretical framework, Moss (2016) discusses the concept of post-foundationalism as an emergent paradigm in valuing complexity and context, 'encompassing a variety of perspectives – for example, postmodernisms, post-structuralisms, post-colonialisms and post-humanisms' (p. 8). Essentially, different theoretical frameworks challenge us to think about childhood and early years settings from multiple perspectives, as sites of ethical and political practice that influence what children learn and how they are supported in their learning.

Naturally, theoretical approaches to the study of early childhood have evolved, and these alternative frameworks require and reflect different methodological designs that enable childhood to be investigated as a constructed conceptual space. Childhood, as James and Prout (2015: 3) assert, has to be 'understood as a social construction. That is, the institution of childhood provides an interpretive frame for understanding the early years of human life.' Such approaches require social scientists to embrace the messy complexity and sometimes chaotic contexts of children's everyday lives, to design rigorous and robust methodological processes, and to reflect critically on their own subjective and culturally situated assumptions about childhood and about early childhood education.

We do not mean to imply that interpretive and 'post-' approaches (such as post-qualitative, post-human and post-truth[1] approaches) are radically new, and we recognize both the changes and continuities over time in research approaches (for further discussion, see Hammersley and Atkinson 2007). However, framing childhood as a social construct offers a fundamentally different alternative to experimental and survey research studies, which over the broad sweep of time have tended to be the dominant influences

---

[1]'Post-' approaches have emerged in research as a response to changing social behaviours. For example, contemporary society is increasingly referred to as a 'post-truth era', where decision-making in political discourse is swayed by evidence that is contradictory to research evidence, and political rhetoric is constructed around emotional responses to issues rather underpinned by research, including issues relating to inequality across the field of education.

on education policy development. We do not suggest that one approach has more value than another, but that it is important for researchers to construct a methodological framework that will enable them to address particular research questions. Whereas interpretive studies seek to embrace complexity, research conducted in a positivist framing tends to seek universal or statistical models to account for phenomena, and to establish findings that can be generalized across circumstances and can subsequently be 'tested' to prove their validity and refine their reliability. The primary methodological model is akin to research models used in the physical sciences, with variables that are measured quantitatively. Researchers working in this paradigm therefore seek to physically and/or statistically control variables, whereas early childhood researchers working in an interpretive paradigm seek to observe the world in its 'natural' state – to uncover, explore and understand the complexity of factors that bring to bear on the lives of children as *social* beings, and on how adults and children view their own and others' lives.

The book is presented in two parts. Part One has three chapters that introduce the cross-cutting themes of 'conceptualizing early education in a global context', 'ethics and early childhood research' and 'reviewing literature as a methodology'. In the opening chapter, we introduce the core concept of 'early childhood education' as an international phenomenon, and as a site where cultural expectations about child rearing meet the socio-historical and political world of education in a global flow of ideas about how young children should be cared for and educated, and how their lives and experiences should be researched. Chapter 2 reflects on why ethics matter in research with young children, how research ethics are regulated, and how researchers can make children's participation in the research process a positive and inclusive experience. The chapter presents practical examples of respectful processes for negotiating consent, sharing information and issues of privacy and confidentiality, particularly when reporting on visual data. Reviewing literature is a crucial aspect of research that requires particular skills, so we include it as a focus of attention in Chapter 3. We offer critical reflection on the processes of reviewing and synthesizing literature, and we discuss diverse approaches to reviewing literature across a continuum, from a 'traditional literature review' to a systematic review. The chapter argues that well-designed literature reviews make an invaluable contribution to the conceptualization and secondary analysis of knowledge, and significantly advance our understanding of early childhood.

In Part Two, we present six chapters that consider different methodological approaches in the context of early childhood education research. The opening chapter in this part, Chapter 4, draws on international research examples of participatory research with children, and discusses the different roles that young children play in research about their own lived experiences, as active researchers in studies designed and carried out *with* and *by* them rather than *on* them. Throughout this chapter, we reflect on the challenges and strengths of this shift in approach, and its impact on the role of the researcher. In Chapter 5 we discuss participatory research approaches with adults as key stakeholders in advocacy for early childhood care and education. This chapter offers examples of research that involve adult participants in researching and galvanizing transformative change, and considers the strengths and challenges in using participatory methodology to engender a policy-driven, social justice agenda for children. Chapter 6 traces the influential trajectory of ethnographic research in early childhood, from the early work of Margaret Mead in the 1920s through to recent studies. Drawing on vignettes of research from around the globe, the chapter clarifies how ethnographic accounts are based principally on fieldwork that investigates the lives, experiences and activity of young children in particular times, places and spaces.

Chapter 7 explores how multimodality offers a fundamentally different perspective on early learning in that it does not assume that language always plays a central role in meaning making. We present research examples to illustrate how a multimodal perspective offers radically new understandings of communication and learning processes – particularly in the current era where digital technologies have fundamentally changed the kinds of representational tools and modes that are used in research practice and in young children's meaning making. In Chapter 8, the focus turns to mixed methods research, where we consider the different insights that quantitative and qualitative methodologies offer to early education, and the different weight they can bear in influencing education change. Examples are presented of large- and small-scale studies from around the globe that have combined these approaches in mixed methods studies, and that have helped early childhood education researchers to arrive at broad and deep understandings of the phenomena investigated. In Chapter 9, we discuss issues and debates around the use of experimental research and randomized control trials (RCTs) in early childhood research. We reflect on the historical use of RCTs in the medical field and life sciences, and on ethical and methodological issues that arise when designing experimental and randomized trial studies for research about young children. Finally, in the concluding chapter we draw together core principles for research methods in early childhood education, and we consider cutting-edge approaches that may herald the beginning of a post-qualitative era in social science research.

Throughout this book, we emphasize the importance of recognizing how conceptions of childhood and conceptions of research evolve over time and space, and how all well-designed and robust research approaches contribute to the growing body of knowledge about young children's lives. Our aim is to offer insight into a range of research methodologies that are rooted in theory, with each chapter offering up-to-date discussion from diverse early childhood education research sources. We believe this book will be useful for a wide range of researchers, including new researchers, graduate students and experienced researchers who are interested in exploring unfamiliar methodologies. We hope this book will take you to exciting new adventures in your study of children and their early life experiences.

PART ONE

Cross-Cutting Themes

CHAPTER ONE

Conceptualizing Early Childhood Education in a Global Context

In this opening chapter, we introduce the core concept of 'early childhood education' as a global phenomenon and as a socially constructed site where cultural expectations about childcare practices and child development meet the socio-historical and political world of education. We highlight the tensions and disjunctions that prevail between the academic disciplines that have exerted most influence on how young children are educated, primarily developmental psychology, sociology and neuroscientific/biological traditions, and the epistemological and methodological questions that emerge in research about and with young children.

We start by tracing the lineage of child development research that underpinned much of early childhood education during the late nineteenth and early twentieth century, moving on to more recent research, which has shifted the focus from the child as an isolated individual to the social and cultural context of the child's ecological environment. This paradigmatic shift, we argue, is significant in shaping current conceptualizations of child development and understandings of early childhood care and education. It is also methodologically important in influencing the design of studies investigating children's learning in diverse contexts. In tandem with this historical background, we discuss how the concept of early childhood education is influenced by a global flow of ideas about young children's care and education, and how these different perspectives impact on research into children's lives and experiences. We raise questions about the role and status of children themselves within research and practice: whether they are viewed as objects and subjects in research or as active agents with legitimate rights to participate and engage actively in the research inquiry process. Our overall objective is to bring to the fore alternative perspectives of research, theory and practice in the global discourse of early childhood education.

Early childhood education: A global phenomenon

Early childhood education is a burgeoning global phenomenon, with early childhood care and education systems becoming more established throughout the world. For many countries in the global North as well as South,[1] that is, the parts of the world that are economically wealthy and those that are comparably socio-economically poorer, children's access to and participation in early childhood education is recognized as a vital resource and an essential 'public good'. This recognition is driven in part by supranational non-governmental organizations (NGOs) such as the World Bank, Organization for Economic Co-operation and Development (OECD), United Nations Educational, Scientific and Cultural Organization (UNESCO) and the United Nations (UN), and their advocacy for children's care and education. The World Bank's dominant rhetoric on investing in young children (World Bank 2011a) created an international platform for vigorous discussions among governments, researchers and other key stakeholders about

---

[1]The terms 'Global North' and 'Global South' are commonly used to denote the geographical and socio-economic orientation of countries which are generally considered low- to middle-income (the South) or rich and high-income status (the North). The terms do not always denote a neat polarization of countries and are sometimes used differently but they are nonetheless useful as operational definitions in describing the socio-economic disparities between countries around the world.

the role of early childhood in advancing social change. Similarly, the UNESCO 'Education for All Global Monitoring Report' (UNESCO 2015) placed early childhood education centre stage and highlighted early childhood and primary schooling as crucial determinants of social mobility and human development, and therefore an integral part of a global agenda. The UNESCO (2015) report reinforced a recurring theme endorsed by many NGOs that the role of education and educational interventions in supporting early learning is critical in laying the foundations for children's later success and achievement.

In many ways, international concern for early learning has helped to channel political will to making education a human development priority and a global policy target. This is evident most notably in the UN 2030 agenda for sustainable development, a suite of seventeen goals that recognize for the first time the crucial importance of early childhood education as a transformative social agenda, especially for the most vulnerable and disadvantaged children (United Nations 2015). Here, the drive for governments and the international community to commit to the global target of ensuring equitable education is clearly voiced (goal 4): 'Ensure inclusive and equitable education and promote life-long learning opportunities for all', as is the need for high-quality early childhood care and education (target 4.2): 'By 2030 ensure that all girls and boys have access to quality early childhood development, care and pre-primary education so that they are ready for primary education' (United Nations 2015: 21). The galvanization of early childhood was further emphasized by the former UN secretary general Ban Ki-moon in his remarks, 'The Sustainable Development Goals recognize that early childhood development can help drive the transformation we hope to achieve over the next 15 years' (United Nations 2015: 1). The prioritization of early childhood care and education as a global phenomenon is unequivocal. What is explicit is the role of education, particularly early childhood education, as leverage in attaining broader human development outcomes. As McGrath (2010) contends, 'Whether the call to action comes from international development agencies or from NGOs, the message above is a familiar one: education is central to development' (p. 1).

The international focus on early childhood education aligns with a stepped increase in research and knowledge generation.

The World Bank (2011) emphasizes the importance of a 'high-quality knowledge base on education reform' and 'evidence-informed policy making' in the advocacy for early childhood and education (p. 6). National and international studies about children, learning and education have expanded considerably in recent decades, and advanced our understanding of the multifaceted nature of children's early experiences. A wide range of research across academic disciplines has shown the importance of quality care and education provision, and its significance for young children's long-term well-being and outcomes, particularly when supported by strong national policies in achieving social objectives (e.g. Britto, Yoshikawa and Boller 2011; Sylva et al. 2010). It is widely recognized that children's early learning experiences can help build cognitive, social and emotional development during the early childhood years, with long-term benefits, especially for those from disadvantaged backgrounds (e.g. Siraj and Mayo 2014). There is also evidence to suggest that with a strong foundation in early childhood, children are more likely to achieve in schooling with better educational attainment in the longer term (UNESCO 2015). In addition, a body of longitudinal datasets undertaken in different countries have identified causal effects between children's mastery of particular early learning skills and their longer-term outcomes. These include the *British Cohort Study* and *National Child Development Survey* from the United Kingdom, the National Institute of Child Health and Human Development (NICHD)'s *Study of Early Child Care and Youth Development* in the United States (SECCYD), the *National Longitudinal Survey of Children and Youth* from Canada, and the *Effective Pre-school, Primary and Secondary Education 3-14 Project (EPPSE 3-14)* study in England. These large-scale, robust and rigorous studies all found that early development in key domains such as literacy, numeracy, executive function, social behaviour and self-regulation can have a predictive positive influence on children's later attainment.

Existing empirical studies have therefore made significant knowledge advances in our understanding of contemporary childhoods, and the international discourse on the importance of high-quality early childhood education offers us a sense of the magnitude of weight afforded to this global phenomenon. Yet it also challenges us to rethink our understanding of childhoods, learning and development, and to reflect on the paradigm shifts that have occurred over time in early education research. As the early childhood sector in many societies continues to experience sustained change, with evolving policy drivers and rising participation rates, there is an ongoing need for robust empirical data on the type and nature of early years provision that can best identify and enhance children's learning and overall well-being. The importance of further research, experimentation and evaluation to identify the knowledge gaps in early childhood education and to support children's learning is recognized internationally (e.g. World Bank 2011a), and there is much work to be done to build research and theory to help us to understand how different groups of children learn and develop within and across cultural and geopolitical contexts. This compels us to look at the historical contextualization of 'the child', to explore the plurality of children's experiences and the diverse social and cultural processes that influence their lives.

Origins: Early child development research

At its roots, research in early childhood education is underpinned by a long tradition of empirical studies about child development which featured the child as a focus of scientific research. Children were often studied as a genetic entity for their distinct nature that differentiated them from adult human beings. A central interest in early development research was the evolutionary, maturation process in human development or *Homo sapiens*. Developmental psychology in particular played a significant role in how children and childhood were theorized during the nineteenth and twentieth centuries. A preoccupation of psychologists at the time was to build systematic knowledge of how children develop, that is, the patterns or sequence of physical, cognitive and psychosocial changes that children underwent from conception to adulthood. As a result, the early observational studies that dominated much of early child development research were driven from a largely clinical, psychological perspective. These early understandings of children and childhoods, we argue (along with many others), largely adopted an approach to children as objects who were subjected to scrutiny and scientific study.

The first known rigorous and scientific study of childhood was attributed to Charles Darwin in his published work *Biographical Sketch of an Infant* (1877) which contained detailed naturalistic observations of early development, specifically that of his eldest child. Darwin's work provided one of the first systematic accounts of infant development and was perceived to have precipitated the early 'child study movement', an undertaking that emerged in part from his theory of human evolution. Darwin's scientific study of child development was followed by the work of other scientists such as the American psychologist Granville Stanley Hall, who was one of the first to recognize that a key factor influencing learning is what the learner already knows. Hall's (1893) research *The Contents of Children's Minds*, for instance, explored what young children know about their worlds, and charted children's knowledge according to a series of tests. Hall argued that 'by inspection of results, the mental ability of each child can be predicted' (p. 52). Hall's work had a profound influence on the philosopher John Dewey, who saw reciprocal interaction (i.e. give and take) between the teacher and learner as essential: 'Guidance [by the teacher] is not external imposition. *It is freeing the life-process for its own most adequate fulfilment*' (Dewey 1902: 17, italics in original).

One of the most famous and influential figures in child development research stemmed from the work of the psychologist Jean Piaget. His publications *The Child's Conception of the World* (Piaget 1929) and *The Origin of Intelligence in Children* (Piaget 1953) were seminal for their detailed observational account of children's cognitive development. The American psychologist Arnold Gesell's research into children's development from the early to mid-1900s contributed to the use of visual techniques such as photography and one-way mirrors to record developmental milestones from infancy to adolescence, and likewise paved the way for much early development research. Gesell's contribution was documented in a series of highly influential publications – *An Atlas of Infant Behavior* (Gesell 1934), *The Child from Five to Ten* (Gesell and Ilg 1946) and *Child development* (Gesell and Ilg 1949).

Research Example 1.1: Piaget and the methods that underpin his work

Working over several decades from the 1920s to the 1970s, the clinical psychologist Jean Piaget developed a model of intellectual development and a 'theory of mind', suggesting that children's cognitive development is organized in a series of logical operations which move from being simple to more complex. He based his theories on the findings of a series of experiments he had conducted in laboratory-like conditions, where he set tasks for children to complete, observed how they went about solving the tasks, and asked them about what they were doing.

Piaget's emphasis on the stage-like nature of cognitive development led to the notion that children can only learn if they are at the right age and 'stage' of cognitive development, that is, if they are 'ready'. Building on this perspective, Piaget argued that children up to the age of six or seven years are egocentric and tend to 'assimilate' knowledge, that is, they distort the meaning of what other people say to fit in with their previous knowledge. An amusing example which could be attributed to Piaget's concept of assimilation appears in Laurie Lee's novel *Cider with Rosie*, when Lee recalls his first day in school as a young boy:

> I spent that first day picking holes in paper, then went home in a smouldering temper.
> 'What's the matter, Love? Didn't he like it at school, then?'
> 'They never gave me the present.'
> 'Present? What present?'
> 'They said they'd give me a present.'
> 'Well, now, I'm sure they didn't.'
> 'They did! They said: "You're Laurie Lee, aren't you? Well just you sit there for the present." I sat there all day but I never got it. I ain't going back there again.'

(Lee 1965: 50)

As Margaret Donaldson (1978) discusses, this example touches us because the young Lee is not yet familiar with the multiple possible meanings of the word 'present', so in his hopeful naiveté he assimilates what is said to him in his existing field of knowledge – which involves receiving gifts called 'presents'. By contrast, Piaget argued that children in the later stages of development can 'accommodate' new ideas, that is, they can adapt and change their existing mental structures in response to novel concepts when they encounter disequilibrium between what they already know and different information they encounter through actions or talk (Bruner 1997).

Piaget's theories developed and changed during his long life, and were widely adopted in the world of education. His concept of 'readiness' led to the belief that children can only learn effectively if their educational experiences match their stage of understanding, and that due to their egocentrism and undeveloped logical operations, young children in the early stages of development learn best by discovering things for themselves rather than by being actively taught:

> Each time one prematurely teaches a child something he could have discovered himself, the child is kept from inventing it and consequently from understanding it completely. (Piaget 1970: 715)

From this perspective, the role of the early educator was not to teach, but to *facilitate* children's naturally active capacity to learn by exploring physical objects.

However, the methods that Piaget used to collect data and inform his theories of child development have been called into question. For example, in her seminal book *Children's Minds*, Donaldson (1978) argued that the tasks Piaget had set the children in his experimental studies were stripped of all 'human sense', and failed to take into account the importance of the social and cultural contexts of children's learning. Reproducing the same tasks with children in more familiar, everyday settings, Donaldson found that young children were indeed able to recognize others' viewpoints – long before Piaget's theories suggested they could. Similarly, Valerie Walkerdine (1984) argued that the operational structures and stages that Piaget had identified were not a universal feature of children's development, but they were constructed by the methodological design and instruments of analysis used in his approach to psychology, where the developing child is viewed as an object with certain capacities located within the psyche, rather than as a social being who learns through interaction. Despite these robust critiques of Piaget's experimental methods that call into question the very basis of his theories, the influence of Piaget's work has endured and continues to be used to validate approaches to teaching and learning that are based on individual children's ages and 'stages' of their development, and their 'readiness' to move on.

In this example, we do not mean to undermine the important and enduring contribution that Piaget's long lifetime of work has made to understandings of child development. Our aim is to clarify how the methods he chose to adopt, which were in keeping with his disciplinary background in clinical psychology, may have led him to underestimate young children's capabilities and the importance of social interaction in meaning making. As Walkerdine argues, the influence of Piaget's work is an example of how the particular history and ways of conducting research that prevailed in twentieth-century psychological research has led to the sedimentation of questionable ideas as 'taken-for-granted' practices that continue to be followed by contemporary educators in their daily lives (Walkerdine 1984: 164).

These early studies of child development that dominated early childhood research for many decades tended to depict the child or the infant as a biological organism separate from its wider familial, material and social environment. Although these ideas emerged in the global North, they served to regulate the ways in which research about the child represented a certain scientific notion of the 'universal child'. It could be argued that the child as a subject of research that emerged from these early positivist child studies became 'professionalized' in various related fields such as psychology, and the social and life sciences. In the realm of psychoanalytic theory, for instance, the theorist Sigmund Freud took to examining the psychosexual and biological drives of children as they progressed through a series of developmental stages and showed how this was crucial for healthy personality development

(Freud 1973, 1974). Similarly, the psychologist Erik Erikson further informed the psychoanalytic approach by building on Freud's work to develop a psychosocial theory that explored chronological stages from birth and across the lifespan in the development of identity and personality (Erikson 1950, 1968). These early observations of children were concerned primarily with the child as an 'individual' and separate from the adult, and the child as an object of study – an entity to be examined, tested and measured.

From these brief examples, we can see how child development research spans a long-standing and sprawling field of investigation, and has generated particular approaches to the child and to childhood which, although predominantly Western and from the global North, have had an enduring impact on education around the world. Their influence led to dominant theoretical perspectives that were built on the image of a 'normal' child whose growth and development was marked by inherent biological milestones. Although there were some divergences, a general perception was that through research it was possible to identify how children develop in a universal manner, and that 'normal' child development follows a series of fixed stages which unfold over time. Over the decades, these theories became embedded in the field of early childhood education and formally informed the Euro-American discourse that dominated the education discipline. It could therefore be argued that the science of developmental psychology fuelled universalist aspirations of 'the child' and constructed powerful normative models of child development.

However, the tenets of developmentalism have been fiercely critiqued for providing a pervasive model of childhood as seen through the lenses of Western discourses in the global North, and for carrying out the vast majority of studies within a narrow socio-economic context primarily in Europe and America. Nonetheless, the notion of the 'developmental child' has prevailed and continues to resonate in educational, political and psychological discourses. This is despite the fact that, as Penn (2005) noted, 'the situation of most of the world's children is very different from those we conventionally study in North America and Europe' (p. 102). When seeking to understand children in a global context, Penn argues that we are faced with differing cultural complexities that are wholly incongruent with the child conventionally studied in the developed world. As the next section will show, the basic assumptions of psychological research which contributed to the universalization of children and child development have been hotly contested by more recent theorists who have offered radically new perspectives of children and the diversity of childhoods that they experience.

Studying childhood in diverse worlds

During the nineteenth and early twentieth centuries, the scientific treatment of the child as a 'product of development' shaped knowledge about children in a number of professional realms including education, psychology and medicine, and dominated various disciplinary fields for centuries. However, a competing body of scholarship that looked beyond developmental psychology and the medical model offered a fundamentally different, much broader conceptualization of children and childhood, leading to more socially oriented methodological approaches to research. Significantly, studies that emanated from cultural psychology, anthropology and sociology provided an alternative disciplinary framework to understand the complexities of early development, and, some might argue, a more democratic view of children and childhood (Moss 2007).

While early development research was concerned largely with the construction of children as individuals, sociocultural and sociological research is preoccupied primarily with socialization and children's role as significant members of a larger whole – the family, community and society. The Russian psychologist Lev Vygotsky (1962, 1978) extended some of the early thinking of child development by emphasizing the social nature of children's learning and the importance of social interactions with adults in fostering children's cognitive development. The Vygotskian approach offered a more balanced view in addressing the social and cultural contexts of children's lives. Unlike Piaget, Vygotsky viewed development as a socially mediated process and was influential for his sociocultural theoretical perspective which has continued to inform ideas of children and childhood today. The emphasis on a social and sociological approach called into question the developmental model of childhood and 'the child' as an individual that was embedded in psychological research, and sociological theories of children and childhood have further served to critique the developmental construction of the child (James and Prout 1990/1997/2015; Rogoff 2003). As Burman argued in her seminal text *Deconstructing Developmental Psychology* (2007), 'Nowadays the status of developmental psychology is not clear' (p. 13).

In contrast to the traditions of psychological research, a starting point of sociological theory is the concept of childhood as socially constructed:

> Childhood is understood as a social construction ... as distinct from biological immaturity [it] is neither a natural nor universal feature of human groups but appears as a specific structural and cultural component of many societies. (Prout and James 1997: 7)

This approach draws attention to the importance of studying not only 'the child' but also the wider environment the child is situated in, that is, the social, cultural, historical and political conditions that influence how childhood is constructed. With this conceptual shift towards a sociology of childhood, it became clear that there were many gaps and imbalances in early development research concerning young children's learning, and these had to be addressed.

In 'Rethinking Childhood' (Alanen 1988) – one of the early sociological papers on childhood published during the 1980s – Alanen argued for a new research agenda within the social sciences that was concerned with the child in social life and the concept of childhood as constructed rather than inherent: 'Childhood is considered as a social construct and some demands for research on children and childhood are developed that may help to avoid the long-held and unnecessarily limiting views on these topics and make way for the emergence of a sociology of childhood' (p. 53). The idea of childhood within social theory influenced a paradigmatic shift away from the 'developmental child' to a focus on the child as a competent 'social agent' (Jenks 1982; Adler and Adler 1986). This conception of the child and childhood in turn precipitated a move towards new research methodologies that focused on children's participation in social life, and the active role they might play in research. Alanen (1988) pointed out:

Research methods do exist that give voice to groups that have normally been silent in research (particularly ethnography). By using these methods at least more 'democratic' and complete descriptions on the experience of socialization may come out (p. 59). ... Such methods may also help to produce evidence on the remarkable competence that children – even small children – have in constructing their everyday social relations. This may in turn contribute to children being seen in a new light, not just as objects primarily being acted on (even if this is largely true for children most of the time), but also as social actors in their own right. ... It is methodologically wrong then to victimize children in research, no matter how much they appear as victims in their various real life situations. (p. 60)

As described by Alanen (1988), the idea that 'childhood' is a social construction became the focus of much theoretical and empirical work, and heralded a fundamental shift in early childhood research methodologies (Jenks 1982; Prout and James 1997; Prout 2005). As ideas around childhood sociology expanded, pioneering work by Qvortrup et al. (1994), Prout and James (1997) and other sociologists (Mayall 2002; Corsaro 2005) became increasingly integral to the theorization of early childhood education. Children consequently became recognized for their active participation in development, and 'in the construction and determination of their own social lives, the lives of those around them and of the societies in which they live' (Prout and James 1997: 8).

Ethnographic and anthropological research as exemplified in the work of Prout and James (1997), Corsaro (2005), Levine and New (2008) showed that children are not passive recipients of knowledge. Rather, rich ethnographic accounts revealed children to be active participants in their social interactions and cultural learnings. Levine and New (2008) documented ethnographic evidence which showed that children as young as three are 'remarkably competent speakers of their native language', 'strikingly proficient in particular social and practical skills prevalent in their local communities' (p. 5) and as they get older, continue to shape and be shaped by the cultural and social mores of their environment. Cross-cultural studies offer further rich insights into the social and cultural contexts of children's lives and lived experiences. The research of cultural theorists such as Super and Harkness (1986), Moll et al. (1992) and Rogoff (2003) became significant for recognizing the way children mediate their learning through the complex and sophisticated belief systems and cultural practices that they inhabit. Moll et al.'s (1992) theoretical concept, 'funds of knowledge', has shown the importance of recognizing the value of children's varied and diverse competencies, and the need to value the wealth of knowledge children bring to their formal learning contexts from their everyday activities in their family and community environments. Rogoff's (2003) world-leading work with indigenous communities in Central America, Mexico and with US Mexican heritage communities has shown how children actively negotiate their learning through everyday activities with adults. These studies have been influential in problematizing some of the ethnocentric assertions that had been made in early developmental studies about the more individualistic subjectivity and needs of young children.

Research Example 1.2: Cultural variation in child-rearing practices

The developmental psychologist and anthropologist Barbara Rogoff has spent many years researching child-rearing practices in different communities and cultures, particularly how children learn through observation and participation more in some communities than in others. Here, we present one example of Rogoff's research, but encourage readers to engage more widely with her important body of work, particularly regarding *guided* and *intent participation* (Rogoff et al. 2003).

Through her own research and others' ethnographic work, Rogoff noted how children in Majority World (a similar term to the global South) cultures often have extensive opportunities to learn through observing and participating in adult work and community activities. By contrast, in many European/American communities, young children tend to be segregated from adult work, and to learn through adults involving them in specialized child-focused activities such as adult–child play and conversation with adults on child-related topics and 'lessons'. To explore the phenomenon of this cultural variation in child-rearing practices, Morelli, Rogoff and Angelillo (2003) conducted a systematic, comparative study, using time-sampled observations of two- and three-year-old children in four different communities. The study involved twelve children in each community, including two middle-class European American communities (West Newton, Massachusetts, and Sugarhouse, Utah); the nomadic, forest-dwelling Efe forager community in the Democratic Republic of Congo; and the indigenous Mayan community of San Pedro, Guatemala. This sample was carefully selected to observe potential similarities and differences across the two US communities and the non-industrial Efe and Mayan communities, where previous ethnographic research had indicated that by the age of five years, children begin to participate responsibly in the work of their community. There was no assumption that any of the four communities were representative of their respective countries. The Efe and San Pedro communities were distinct in that they had different means of subsistence (foraging versus agriculture and commerce), access to formal schooling and technologies. The Efe community was non-literate, whereas part-time schooling had become commonplace in the Mayan San Pedro community. The young age range for child participants was chosen with a view to investigating any cultural variations in children's early access to work and/or to child-focused activities, before they reached the age where they might begin to engage in their community's work and/or schooling.

The children's activities were time sampled by observing them wherever they went from the time they woke in the morning until they went to sleep at night, in three 4- to 5-hour sessions on two or three days within a seven-day period (total of 12 to 15 hours for each child). The findings showed that all the children were usually within earshot or sight of at least one adult (Efe=98 per cent; San Pedro=74 per cent; West Newton=84 per cent; and Sugarhouse=81 per cent). All the children had some access to work, but children in West Newton (30 per cent) and Sugarhouse (29 per cent) had less work access than those in Efe (73 per cent) and San Pedro (52 per cent). Children in Efe spent 26 per cent of their time observing adult work, as opposed to 19 per cent in San Pedro, and 13 per cent and 12 per cent in West Newton and Sugartown, respectively.

Unsurprisingly, although very few of these young children took part in work, there were differences in the extent to which they emulated work in their play: West Newton (4 per cent); Sugarhouse (3 per cent); Efe (12 per cent) and San Pedro (15 per cent). With regard to home-based 'lessons', all twelve Sugarhouse and West Newton children were observed in 'lessons' (e.g. skills training/ interpersonal behaviour), but only five Efe and three San Pedro children. About 17 per cent and 16 per cent of West Newton and Sugartown children played with adults, compared to 4 per cent and 3 per cent of Efe and San Pedro children, respectively. Among the Newton and Sugarhouse children, twenty-two out of twenty-four played scholastic themes, whereas only two Efe children and one San Pedro child did. All twenty-four West Newton and Sugarhouse children engaged in adult–child free-standing conversation on child-related topics, compared with nine Efe and seven San Pedro children.

Overall, the study findings suggest that in the middle-class US communities, where children spend stretches of time apart from adults and their involvement in work is limited, specialized, child-focused activities, informal lessons and talking with adults about child-related topics may help to prepare children for their later schooling and work, and adult involvement in children's play provides adults with a chance to teach children specific child-focused skills. By contrast, children in the Efe and San Pedro communities learnt by spending longer periods with adults and other children, often observing and participating in work-related activities. For these children, lessons and child-focused activities designed to facilitate their later entry into mature activities were superfluous as they were already integrated in the adult world of work. Although small scale, this study contributed important observations suggesting there are significant cultural and historical differences in how young children's induction into their communities is arranged, either through inclusion in the adult world or through higher levels of segregation and specialized child-focused activities.

In recent years, postcolonial cultural theories have influenced contemporary studies about the diversity of childhoods and early childhood education (Cannella and Viruru 2004; Cannella 1997; Gupta 2006). Postcolonial theory urges us to consider the multiple positioning of children and how views of childhood are multiple and ever-changing. Cannella and Viruru (2004) considered the impact of power discourses between unequal groups in their postcolonial critique of early childhood education, and emphasized the importance of recognizing the diverse cultural realities of young children's lives, in order that the field 'can move toward a thoughtful and more inclusive study of childhood' (p. 6). Informed by her observations of early childhood settings in India, Viruru (2001) questioned 'Western' frames of reference of child development, and described the transplantation of so-called universal standards of childhood as the 'continuing colonisation and marginalisation of diverse cultural perspectives and ways of living' (p. 13). As the influence of childhood studies has developed, it has been critiqued for its minority world conceptualization of childhood and for failing to include Majority World childhoods in its theory, methods and policy implications:

> These norms are being globalized, when in fact even in the Minority World they exclude large swathes of children and young people who work, who do not live with their biological parents, or who are otherwise excluded (e.g. by ethnicity or sexual orientation) or are out of place (e.g. on the street, traveller families, those applying for asylum or refugee status). (Tisdall and Punch 2012: 254)

Contemporary theories of childhood that have emerged in the new sociology of childhood paradigm and in developmental and postcolonial studies have therefore opened up space in early childhood research to reflect on the social and cultural variations that strongly influence how the concepts of care and education are perceived and enacted in different social and geopolitical environments, and offer alternative ways of examining categories of 'the child' and 'childhood'. Essentially, as Penn (2005) noted, 'development cannot be understood outside of a historical and cultural context' (p. 37), in the same way as our conceptualization of early years education cannot be seen in isolation from the rich mixture of the social, cultural and historical conditions that make up children's everyday lives.

In contesting the developmental model of childhood promoted by much psychological research, this cursory glance at approaches to childhood offered by the new sociology of childhood and postcolonial studies has shown new avenues in early childhood education research. These avenues have given rise to the pursuit of new knowledge and an acknowledgement of the relativity of children's early experiences in diverse worlds. This new knowledge has helped us to redirect our thinking towards a more complex understanding of childhoods in a global context, and shift our approach in investigating young children's lives to take into account their multiple experiences, views as well as their voices.

Researching children and early childhood education in the global context

What then does all this say for researching early childhood education in the global context? As new ways of understanding children constantly emerge, it is important to continue to question the assumptions of existing theories, and to extend and enhance empirical discovery. While some researchers have continued to turn to the field of psychology in understanding children's cognitive development, others have been drawn to theories that focus on the role of children's social and cultural contexts. Importantly, an increasingly vital area of research is the way inequalities between and within countries impact upon children's opportunities and outcomes in the global context of early childhood education (UNESCO 2015; World Bank 2015). A common theoretical thread is an ecological framework to conceptualize how macro-level factors such as socioe-conomic disparities and social inequality can impact on the micro-level environments of early childhood education, where children and families living in fragile conditions and deprived of basic resources become particularly vulnerable (Bronfenbrenner 1979; Ang 2013; Yale University and ACEV partnership 2012).

Inequality in its myriad guises – in terms of economic, health and social determinants – presents the greatest challenge that children face and is evident across all countries both rich and poor, in the global North and South. Cannella (1997) discusses early childhood education as a political discourse of social justice and revolution in the way that particular groups of children are more privileged than others, and recognizes the need to problematize dominant ideas of early care and education. In a similar vein, the educator and philosopher Paulo Freire challenged the governing institutional ideology. In his seminal work *Pedagogy of the Oppressed* (Freire 2000/1970) Freire drew the world's attention to the effects of oppression in drastically changing the lives of people and generations, and the role of education in bringing about social transformation. Freire's concerns remain pertinent in current times as the lives of children and families across the world are directly or indirectly shaped by powerful global divisions and the systemic organization of inequality.

It is important that research with and about children considers issues of wider inequalities and social justice, and offers opportunities to understand multiple and diverse childhoods. Research that involves longitudinal, international or micro-level studies that generate knowledge at an aggregate or individual level about children, their families and communities should address the broader discourses of social and economic capital, and take into account the ethical considerations of children living in the wealthy minority world and those in the less wealthy majority worlds. Although not all studies are large scale or have the scope to take diverse childhoods into consideration, even the smallest scale studies should consider the social, cultural and historical–political values that shape every child's life and ways of being. In this way, research has the potential to evoke strong responses on how early childhood education can serve to challenge or reproduce inequalities.

Concluding thoughts

Conceptualizing and researching early childhood education in a global context requires close examination of the rich legacy of empirical research, theories and methodologies that has come to shape the field of early childhood, and cannot be seen in isolation from global inequalities and wider socio-economic influences. It is also important to recognize that dominant ideas and methods of researching children and childhoods are not easily transferable and applied to all contexts, nor can they be universalized to all children across time, place and culture. The discourses discussed in this chapter have influenced the beliefs, knowledge and values that inform our understanding of how children develop and learn, and our understanding of the way 'childhood' and early childhood education are constructed in policy and practice. Ultimately, all researchers have to make vital choices in the investigative process they undertake. These choices relate to what the research is about, who it is for, which contexts to study, which children are included or excluded, how the research is designed, and how data is recorded, transcribed, analysed and interpreted and so on. These questions are part of the interpretive frame of beliefs and values that shape all social scientific research and pose inevitable complexities in the inquiry process when researching children's lives. As we focus on a range of research approaches and methods throughout this book, it is important for us to step back to consider the underlying image and positionality of the child, and how this informs our particular approach to early childhood research and practice.

Suggestions for further reading

The following readings have had an enduring influence on research with and about young children over the past decades:

Corsaro, W. A. (2005). *The Sociology of Childhood* (2nd edn). Thousand Oaks, CA: Pine Forge Press.
Freire, P. (2000). *Pedagogy of the Oppressed*. New York: Continuum.
Mayall, B. (2002). *Towards a Sociology for Childhood*. Buckingham: Open University Press.
Prout A. (2005). *The Future of Childhood: Towards the Interdisciplinary Study of Children*. Abingdon: Routledge Falmer.
Rogoff, B. (2003). *The Cultural Nature of Human Development*. New York: Oxford University Press.

CHAPTER TWO

Ethics and Early Childhood Research

Ethics is a central dimension of all research, regardless of the methodological approach, scale or scope of a project. In early childhood research, there is an expectation that all studies will reflect high ethical values, and will adhere to appropriate codes of practice, such as ethics guidelines for education research (e.g. BERA 2018). However, while universal ethics guidelines are helpful, applying ethics principles in practice is a complex and dynamic process that requires critical reflection throughout all stages of research – from the very inception of a project to the long-term dissemination of research findings. In this chapter, we consider the multiple influences that shape researchers' ethics decision-making and suggest that while ethics codes of practice may be helpful, researchers are likely to encounter situations, which require situated and dynamic responses. Our focus is on enabling early childhood researchers to develop their awareness of ethics issues so they are better able to respond to ethical challenges as they arise in the research field. We also promote the aim to make young children's participation in research a positive and inclusive experience, with respectful processes for negotiating consent, privacy and confidentiality. Our approach to ethics is guided by the core principle that the interests of those whose lives we are studying lie at the centre of all ethical decision-making:

> Our primary obligation is always to the people we study, not to our project or to a larger discipline. The lives and stories that

we hear and study are given to us under a promise, that promise being that we protect those who have shared them with us. (Denzin 1989: 83)

A framework for research ethics

We begin by presenting a framework that takes into account the multiple influences that shape ethics planning and decision-making. We briefly consider why and when formal ethics regulation came into being and the extent to which regulations can help early childhood researchers to plan for ethical challenges and inform their impromptu ethical decision-making when responding to the unexpected. Formal ethics guidance, such as the British Educational Research Association Ethical Guidelines for Educational Research (BERA 2018), the Concordat to Support Research Integrity (Universities UK 2012), the Social Research Association Ethical Guidelines (2003) and the Singapore Statement on Research Integrity (2010), are often referred to as principles for guiding ethical behaviour and for deciding on the 'right' thing to do in a given research situation. However, in arts and social science research, as in life more generally, making decisions is more complicated than a simple right/wrong dichotomy. Managing an ethical dilemma involves weighing up a range of possible benefits against the potential for harmful outcomes, rather than arriving swiftly at a clear-cut decision. Researchers invariably have recourse to the guiding ethics principles of the academic discipline(s) in which they are working, but individuals' judgements about how to apply those principles in practice are also guided by their personal, social and cultural views about rightness and wrongness, and by their previous experiences of research – hence the need for critical reflection at all stages of ethics decision-making.

Wiles (2013) succinctly summarizes the multiple factors that bring to bear on ethical decision-making as including professional and disciplinary regulations; legal regulations; personal moral values; and ethical frameworks. We will consider each of these aspects, moving clockwise around the framing proposed in Figure 2.1, and will then present illustrative examples of ethics

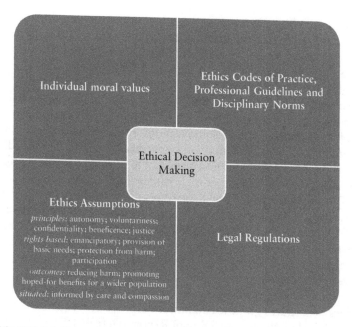

FIGURE 2.1 *Key influences on ethical decision-making (adapted from Wiles 2013: 12).*

dilemmas and decision-making from studies conducted in early childhood education research.

Ethics codes of practice, professional guidelines and disciplinary norms

Research ethics is complex and has evolved over time and across cultures as societal views have changed. Contemporary social research ethics derive principally from medical research, which is reputed to date back to ancient codes such as the Hippocratic Oath in the fifth century BC. Medical research ethics codes were subsequently formalized in the landmark Nuremberg Code (1947), which was developed in response to the horrors of human suffering that were revealed during the Nuremberg War Crime Trials, particularly during biomedical experimentation by Nazi physicians (Wiles 2013).

The Nuremberg Code[1] set out ten key principles to guide medical research, with consent and avoidance of harm to participants as central tenets to ethical conduct. This Code was soon followed in 1950[2] by the establishment of the European Convention on Human Rights and Fundamental Freedoms, which in turn informed the Declaration of Helsinki (1964). While the Nuremberg Code fell by the wayside, the Helsinki Declaration (WMA 2013) developed more highly formulated ethics standards for research involving human participants, focusing mainly on biomedical research, but including the right for children's informed consent to be sought where possible, in addition to the consent of their parents/legal guardians.

Despite these international measures that aimed to formalize and raise the standard of research ethics, it became clear in the 1960s and 1970s that poor research ethics standards were still being sanctioned, particularly in biomedical experiments where, for example, curative treatments were sometimes withheld from participants in order to investigate disease progression (Israel and Hay 2006). From such scandals, more rigorous and more tightly regulated medical research ethics procedures grew, which had widespread consequences for all academic disciplines. The Belmont Report (DHEW 1979) led to the nationwide establishment of Institutional Review Boards (IRBs) in the United States and Research Ethics Committees (RECs) in UK universities, which established formal ethics review processes at institutional level. Subsequently, major public funding bodies and charitable organizations also developed their own research ethics frameworks with the expectation that all members and funded projects would follow their ethics regulation procedures (e.g. BPS 2010; BPS 2013; ESRC 2016; National Children's Bureau 2011). These ethics guidelines are regularly updated in response to new ethics challenges, as indeed is the Declaration of Helsinki (currently

---

[1]Although the Nuremberg Code has been widely acknowledged as a turning point in the development of formalized contemporary research ethics, Ghooi (2011) argues that it was written hastily at the Trials, and drew six of its ten principles from the German Government's 1931 Guidelines for Human Experimentation. These guidelines in turn built on the Prussian Government's 1900 Berlin Code, which had already been incorporated in the legal framework of the German Republic, yet the defendants the Nuremberg Trials were tried for crimes against humanity rather than against the 1931 Guidelines.
[2]See http://www.echr.coe.int/Documents/Convention_ENG.pdf

in its 7th revision), reflecting the evolving nature of research ethics which are adapted to reflect societal changes. Consequently, researchers often need to devise project-specific ethical frameworks that may incorporate elements from two or more sets of guidelines.

One of the difficulties with global research ethics principles is that the ethical conduct of research is further influenced at the local level by social, political, cultural and economic differences and norms across nations and academic disciplines. For example, there is considerable variation in approaches to research between the British Educational Research Association (BERA 2018) guidelines and the Singapore Statement on Research Integrity (2010). The Singapore Statement is structured around the four principles of honesty, accountability, professional courtesy and fairness, and good stewardship of research on behalf of others. These principles are further informed by fourteen responsibilities for the ethical conduct of research, including integrity; adherence to regulations; using appropriate research methods; keeping clear and accurate records; sharing data and findings in accordance with permissions; acknowledging authorship; peer review; disclosing conflict of interest; reporting misconduct; responding to irresponsible research practices; fostering research environments that promote integrity; and recognizing social responsibilities. By contrast, the BERA (2018) ethical guidelines for educational research are built around the following five core principles:

1. Social science is fundamental to a democratic society, and should be inclusive of different interests, values, funders, methods and perspectives.

2. All social science should respect the privacy, autonomy, diversity, values and dignity of individuals, groups and communities.

3. All social science should be conducted with integrity throughout, employing the most appropriate methods for the research purpose.

4. All social scientists should act with regard to their social responsibilities in conducting and disseminating their research.

5. All social science should aim to maximize benefit and minimize harm.

Within this principles framework, BERA (2018) presents its guidelines under the following headings: responsibilities to participants, responsibilities to sponsors, clients and stakeholders in research; responsibilities to the community of educational researchers; responsibilities for publication and dissemination; and responsibilities for researchers' well-being and development. Changes in research with children across nations also reflect a broader shift in how children are conceptualized as knowledgeable agents who should be treated with full human dignity, as found in the (new) sociology of childhood (see Chapter 1, this volume; James and James 2004; Quennerstedt and Quennerstedt 2014; Rinaldi 2001, 2006) and increasing recognition of children's rights (see Freeman 1998; Quennerstedt 2010). A key influential force has been the 1989 UN Convention on the Rights of the Child (UNCRC), which established international principles for children's rights, including their right to express their own views freely in all matters affecting children.

Although the aim of universal ethics codes – whether international, disciplinary or organizational – is to ensure high-quality research while protecting participants' rights, the formalization of ethics regulation has been heavily critiqued. For example, in ethnographic studies, formal ethics codes have been considered incompatible with 'the emergent nature of ethnographic research focus and design, the nature and positioning of risk in ethnographic research, the power relationships between researchers and participants, and the public and semi-public nature of the settings normally studied' (Murphy and Dingwall 2007: 2223). Moreover, there are questions around the relevance for contemporary research of formalized ethics schemes that were established in a pre-digital age, and which enshrine structures, principles and metaphors that can be interpreted as meaning that all online research is de facto ethically problematic (Orton-Johnson, 2010). Consequently, as research methods have responded to changing technologies and social practices, method-specific ethics guidelines have emerged, such as guidance tailored to visual research (Wiles et al. 2012) and specialist guidelines for online research (BPS 2013). Similarly, substantial revisions have been made to disciplinary research guidelines, such as BERA (2018), which take into account the rise of social media, online communities and new legislative requirements.

Further critiques of ethics guidelines and protocols are that they are open to (mis)interpretation, that they are difficult to apply in practice and consequently fail to guarantee appropriate ethical conduct (e.g. see Goldacre 2009; Sharav 2003). Arguments have also been made that ethics regulation and governance position researchers as individually irresponsible, as needing close ethical surveillance (Sikes and Piper 2010), and that they focus on risk management rather than on enhancing the ethical conduct of research (Graham and Fitzgerald 2010). Hammersley (2010) further argues that the intensification of ethics regulation processes has led to a 'slow shift from universities being relatively independent of both government and commerce, and organized on a collegial basis, towards their being treated as part of the "national economy", and increasingly run in a managerial fashion that apes the private-for-profit sector' (para 1.7).

Despite these many misgivings about the ethics regulation at international, national, disciplinary and institutional levels, we suggest that the formality of ethics codes and review processes can be used productively as a valuable resource for researchers (Sargeant and Harcourt 2012). O'Neill (2010) argues that institutional ethics review boards offer the potential for a supportive and mutually educative process, where review board members share expertise and negotiate ethical principles with researchers, rather than impose authoritarian or restrictive ethical codes of conduct. In this more dialogic spirit, there has been a move in social science research towards sharing ethics decision-making not only between researchers but also in consultation with adult and child participants. This dialogic approach to research ethics creates space for an exchange of views between experienced and less experienced researchers, and between researchers and participants, encouraging multiple perspectives to be taken into account during ethics decision-making during the process of research.

Legal requirements

In the above section, we discussed ethical principles and guidelines that expect researchers to conform to disciplinary, organizational, national and international norms. We now consider how such ethics recommendations are further influenced by national *legal requirements* and by the different legal status of children across nations. For example, variation in national legal regulation across Europe has led to marked differences in guidelines regarding the need for researchers to gain parental consent for their children to participate in research. Comparative research conducted by the European Union Agency for Fundamental Rights (2016) found that parental consent for children aged up to eighteen years was required in Bulgaria, Cyprus, Republic of Ireland and Portugal; up to fifteen or sixteen years in Finland, Hungary, Latvia, Lithuania, Netherlands, Slovenia, Sweden and the UK; up to fourteen years in Croatia, the Czech Republic and Poland, while no clear regulation was in place for child age and parental consent in Austria, Denmark, Estonia, France, Italy, Romania, Slovakia or Spain. Within national requirements there are further complications, for example, UK guidance states that 'competent' children aged under sixteen should be consulted in their own right, with 'competence' defined as having sufficient understanding and intelligence to understand what is proposed. Yet it is up to researchers to gauge and interpret children's 'competence' to do so (see Alderson and Morrow 2004: 98–9).

There can also be tensions between research guidelines and researchers' legal obligations as responsible citizens. For instance, the researcher's duty to protect confidentiality can be compromised by the legal obligation to report potentially criminal activity, such as domestic violence, incest or other form of child abuse or mistreatment, or where a participant is at risk of causing harm to themselves or others. These issues may emerge during research observations in participants' homes or during interviews conducted in or distant from the home environment. In all such cases, we strongly recommend that researchers consult with their institutional ethics review committee to ensure that the appropriate course of legal action is taken.

For research conducted in the European Union, Regulation (EU) 2016/679 of the European Parliament (General Data Protection Regulation, or GDPR) has been enforceable since May 2018. This legal requirement is 'designed to harmonize data privacy laws across Europe, to protect and empower all EU citizens' data privacy and to reshape the way organizations across the region approach data privacy' (see https://www.eugdpr.org/). The GDPR aims to protect citizens' rights to know how and why their personal data is being stored, what it is being used for and who might have access to it. Researchers must have participants' explicit permission to disclose personal information to any third parties, and must ensure that such parties are permitted to have access to that information. Researchers are also required to independently confirm the identity of such persons to their own satisfaction, and must keep a record of any disclosures. Careful consideration needs to be given to the GDPR definition of personal data as 'any information relating to an identified or identifiable person', and the requirement to give sensitive personal data additional protection. It is therefore essential to keep accurate records of all data sharing, and to report any breaches as soon as possible to ensure that compliance with GDPR regulation can be proven. Organizations such as early education settings and schools may require a data protection policy and a named data protection officer.

Ethics assumptions about research

Intersecting with codes of ethics practice and legal requirements, ethics are influenced by fundamental assumptions about research. Here, we refer to the interrelationships between research aims and how research is theorized and designed, which all shape how ethics are understood and approached by individuals or teams of researchers, and the assumptions that underpin principles-based, rights-based, outcomes-based and situated approaches to research ethics. Many projects include aspects from each of these approaches, but when first formulating ideas for a new research venture it is useful for early childhood education researchers to reflect critically on how the conceptual framing of their study and underpinning assumptions may lead them towards a particular stance that will inevitably dominate their ethical decision-making.

Principles-based approaches would normally require some good to result from a project, and tend to prioritize the international ethics principles of autonomy, non-maleficence, beneficence and justice. The principle of autonomy includes voluntariness, informed consent, anonymity and confidentiality. However, this does not necessarily mean that participant identity cannot be disclosed or that some kind of monetary gain cannot be offered, merely that participant perspectives should be prioritized. These aspects are discussed through Research Examples 2.1 and 2.2 later in this chapter.

The principle of *non-maleficence* means avoiding harm to participants, but 'harm' can refer to a wide range of possible issues, and even if researchers agree it is wrong to cause harm for participants, they might still disagree about what might be 'harmful'. Researcher perspectives most likely will also be very different from the views and research experiences of child and adult participants. In research with children, Alderson and Morrow (2004) define harm as including physical, mental and emotional discomfort, in the short or long term, which may be 'invisible and elusive' (35). Harmful outcomes can include making a participant feel anxious, embarrassed, belittled or distressed. For example, if early childhood professionals are interviewed about their work, they may be reluctant to voice any concerns they have, and may not mention any views which could be interpreted as critical of the organization that employs them. Similarly, parents may be reluctant to share concerns about their child's care or education, for fear of possible detriment to their child, and children may be reticent to express their views for fear of 'getting into trouble' or being ridiculed by their peers. Avoiding harm can also include scheduling research at times that are convenient to participants, and ensuring that participation does not become a burden. In research with children and families, it is therefore essential from the outset of a project to establish trusting relationships with adult and child research participants. This may involve making multiple visits to the research site before commencing data collection, so participants feel more comfortable voicing their preferences and concerns, and are reassured that the researcher fully respects their right to remain silent on any issues they feel uncomfortable discussing, and their right to withdraw from or curtail the research at any time, with no need for them to explain why.

The principles of *beneficence* and *justice* refer to the positive benefits of research. This includes ensuring that a study is designed in such a way as to yield accurate and valid findings, so it can contribute original knowledge about a given topic. Even if a project does not cause harm, it is disrespectful to participants if research is so poorly designed it does not reach meaningful findings. The benefits of research might include bringing about change for the better to practice and/or policy locally, regionally, nationally or internationally. One such example was a study funded by the National Union of Teachers (NUT) and Association of Teachers and Lecturers (ATL) in England, which investigated practitioner responses to the government proposal to reintroduce baseline assessment for all children who enter Reception Class in England (Roberts-Holmes and Bradbury 2017). Using a mixed methods approach involving an online, nationwide survey completed by 1,131 people and 5 case studies of primary schools, the study found that the government plans lacked the support of teachers and school leaders, with under 8 per cent of survey respondents agreeing that baseline assessment was an 'accurate and fair way to assess children' and under 7 per cent agreeing it was 'a good way to assess how primary schools perform'. This study had a direct and nationwide impact upon government policy, and the plans were (temporarily) shelved. However, bringing about change for the better can also be small scale. For example, sharing research findings with participants by providing feedback in the form of a short report and/or presentation and/or discussion forum can be highly rewarding for adult and child participants at a local level, while academic publications arising from a study can contribute to the international stock of knowledge on a given topic.

Rights-based approaches tend to be more emancipatory in their aims than 'principles approaches', and often cite the UN Conventions on the Rights of the Child (United Nations 1989), where children's rights are grouped broadly into '3 Ps' (see Percy-Smith and Thomas 2010). These include the *provision* of basic needs with healthcare, education and other services supported by highest calibre research evidence; *protection* from harm, abuse, exploitation, neglect or discrimination; and *participation* rights, requiring children to be well informed about any research they are involved in, and for their views to be heard in the research process. However, Quennerstedt (2010) queries why the '3 Ps' are used for children rather than the established and highly theorized terms used for adult human *civil, political* and *social* rights. Quennerstedt (2010) suggests that *provision rights* position the child as the passive recipient of welfare, whereas the more adult-oriented term *social rights* points to the child's more agentive role and rights to *access* education, health care and other social benefits. Similarly, a child's right to *protection* is vague and diminishes the scope for self-determination and political influence. In sum, it can be argued that the '3 Ps' terminology constructs children's rights as substantially different to general human rights.

By contrast, in *outcomes approaches*, ethics decisions are likely to adhere closely to prescribed ethics codes. This approach is often adopted in covert research, on the premise that 'the ends justify the means'. By definition, covert research always involves some degree of deception that infringes participants' human rights to be informed about research that is relevant to their own lives. However, ethical decisions may be justified by the argument that the potential research outcomes warrant a covert course of action. There is considerable variation across disciplines regarding the acceptability of covert research. For example, in much medical and psychological research, 'experimental groups' and 'control groups' are frequently used, where even if participants know they are taking part in research, they have minimal information about the aim of the research, or they are purposefully kept unaware of which groups they are in (see Chapter 9).

Alternatively, research ethics can be framed as *situated and dialogic*, reflecting individual moral values rather than universal, normative ethics guidelines. A situated ethics approach challenges the relevance of universal ethics codes of practice, and instead argues that ethical choices may justifiably vary depending on the research situation and the researcher–participant relationship, which evolves over time as that relationship develops (Simons and Usher 2000). From this perspective, ethics are guided by care and compassion for particular research participants and the wider communities to which they belong. Held (2006: 3) proposes that an ethics of care develops 'on the basis of experience, reflection on it and discourse concerning it, an understanding of the most basic and most comprehensive values'. Christensen and Prout (2002: 477) advocate for researchers and research teams to 'develop a set of strategic values within which individual researchers can anchor the tactics required in their everyday practice in order to work reflexively'. The resulting 'ethical symmetry' between researchers can then be used to frame a set of orienting values which can be shared with research participants in the specific circumstances of any particular piece of research. This situated approach reflects the sharing and discursive nature of ethics decision-making, where establishing mutually respectful and trusting research relationships serves as an anchor for ethics decisions throughout the research process.

Individual moral values

However professional our research conduct aims to be, our understanding of the social realities we record always derives partially from our own experiences and expectations, which are shaped by our personal histories. This subjectivity presents an ethical challenge which is often denied or kept in research shadows. Particularly in interpretive research, and arguably in all research, information gathered in the research field is selected for close analysis through the filter of the researcher's personal knowledge of the contexts, participants and phenomena investigated. It therefore follows that the researcher's subjectivity in the choice of theory, collection and interpretation of data, and construction of knowledge should be problematized and laid bare. Peshkin (1988) argues for an open and critical exploration of one's own subjective beliefs and values, so the researcher can be aware of 'the thwarting biases that subjectivity engenders, while attaining the singular perspective its special persuasions promise' (p. 21). Through this process of subjective reflection, the potential impact of a researcher's emotional and intellectual vulnerabilities can be taken into account (Glassner and Herz 2003), and the researcher's reactions and interpretations can be recognized openly rather than resisted.

We now take a closer look at two research examples to see how early childhood education researchers have negotiated ethical pathways through their work. We focus on how the researchers foregrounded respect for participants of all ages, how they developed mutually trusting relationships and negotiated informed consent through dialogue with participants, and how they ensured participant confidentiality and anonymity, including when visual methods were used for data capture and representation.

Establishing trusting relationships

In qualitative research 'the strength of relationships established at the outset can have a profound impact on the progress and outcomes of the study' (Flewitt 2005a: 556). This is arguably the case in all research but is particularly so in ethnographic, anthropological and participatory research where researchers build close associations with participants and with their communities and cultures, usually over extended periods. Establishing reciprocal trust can take time, but even in studies of short duration, it is essential to establish trust. To achieve this, it is important at the outset of a project to create opportunities for participants to ask questions about any concerns they may have and receive satisfactory answers. This has more to do with creating 'quality time' in the early stages of research relationships than with 'how much time' is available. Researchers bear a responsibility to safeguard the physical, social and psychological well-being of child and adult participants, which means getting to know their interests and sensitivities, respecting their rights and protecting their privacy. The time invested in establishing these relationships will reap benefits for all parties, and help the researcher to minimize the disturbance that the research may cause to participants, and to the lives of others who are part of participants' home, work or community lives.

Protecting privacy can be particularly challenging when research is conducted in participants' homes, where researchers must conduct themselves particularly sensitively to avoid undue intrusion, and respond flexibly and respectfully to unforeseen events and interruptions. Researchers must also make clear the boundaries of their enquiry to reassure participants that they have no entitlement or intention to study phenomena other than those agreed.

All research intervenes in the lives of those whose lives are studied – however briefly – and covert research inevitably breaches ethical standards of trust and openness, as does overt research if participants are coerced into taking part. If there is a conflict of interests at any stage, researchers should always place participants' rights and interests before their own. For example, if participants indicate that the research is intruding into their private and personal domains, then the researcher must immediately remind participants that their involvement is entirely voluntary, and they can withdraw from the research at any time, or if they prefer, the boundaries of the research can be renegotiated.

Finding shared meanings and informing initial and ongoing consent

When conducting research with young children, all participants, regardless of their age, should be informed of the intended research processes, and of potential research outcomes *before* they agree to take part in a study, and consent should always be considered as *provisional* upon each participant's willingness to continue to be involved in a study (see Flewitt 2005a). When working with young children, researchers should seek their personal consent in addition to the consent of their parents or guardians, and allow a period of time to negotiate initial consent. This will help to give participants time to reflect upon the information the researcher shares with them, to ask questions, express doubts and to iron out any differences in researcher and researched perceptions of potential harm (Flewitt 2005a).

However, as Alderson (2002) argues, the central features of consent involve people inwardly digesting information, weighing it up in light of their personal values and previous experiences, wavering between consenting or not, and gradually reaching what might seem to them like a risky decision. These personal thoughts are conducted privately by each participant, but can be made visible and shared with the researcher through conversations, and revisited during the research process even after initial consent has been granted. Gaining informed consent can be particularly problematic when young children are involved, as they (like many adults) may have no clear idea of what 'research' is. It is therefore important to remember that interpretation is a constant thread in all research – not just in qualitative data analysis. The people who are approached to take part in a study *interpret* the information they are given, and base their decisions on their interpretation of what they are told. Researchers might therefore begin the process of gaining consent by exploring the concept of 'research' with children – asking them what the word means to them, showing them any recording equipment, encouraging them to handle it and try it out, and explaining what will happen during the research. Researchers might also build in a period of time during which they plan activities where children begin to try out research methods with each other, by taking photographs and talking about them, and/or using handheld digital media (such as a smartphone) to make short films (Flewitt et al. 2018).

Once an agreement is reached regarding initial consent, we suggest that early childhood education researchers should pay close attention to children's (and adults') willingness to continue as participants throughout the research process. Rather than assume participants' consent as ongoing, the ethical researcher is always responsive to any signs that a participant may prefer not to take part at times, constantly paying infinite attention to the other. By entering into dialogue with the participant, the researcher can then explore the possibility of renegotiating consent, or reassure the participant that it is fine to withdraw from the study altogether.

Some researchers refer to children's consent as 'informed assent', as it is not legally binding in the same manner as parental consent. However, it has been argued that making this distinction might be viewed as belittling children's right to make informed decisions about their own lives (Harcourt and Conroy 2005). MacNaughton, Rolfe and Siraj-Blatchford (2010) emphasize that participants must not be pressured in any way, and that all forms of consent must be documented and approved prior to any data gathering. At the very least, researchers have a responsibility to ensure that participants understand the nature of the research, what will be expected of them if they participate, any possible risks of the research, their right to withdraw at any time and what will happen to the information that is gathered about them.

To access young research participants, researchers are usually dependent on a 'gatekeeper'. That is, a parent or the manager or head of an early childhood education setting, who will metaphorically 'open the gate' to allow the researcher into a research site. Gatekeepers are likely to seek reassurance that the planned research will be conducted ethically, that it will not expose participants to risk, that it will not be disruptive or place undue burden on participating children and adults, and that it will be interesting for the setting and/ or for the children and their families. They may ask to see the identity documents of the researcher(s) (or in the UK, researchers' Disclosure and Barring Service check (DBS)) and permission from the institution that is supporting the research. Sometimes, further permissions may need to be sought, for example, from a school governing body or parent–teacher association. In an effort to be helpful, gatekeepers may suggest it is unnecessary to gain children's consent, or propose particular children to participate who may reflect well on the setting. However, as Shaw, Brady and Davey (2011) argue, it is important to tactfully resist such suggestions. There are further ethical concerns when accessing research participants through a gatekeeper as the researcher risks exploiting the relationship between the gatekeeper and the person they are introducing. For example, parents may feel a certain obligation to agree to participate in the research and fear that refusing to take part could damage either their relationship with the staff or the services their child receives. It is essential, therefore, to build in both formal and informal opportunities for all participants and guardians to say no in a safe environment.

Research Example 2.1: Young children and informed consent

A recurring challenge for researchers working with young children is how to create a research space where children are empowered to make informed decisions about their participation. Having researched with young children for many years in Australia and Singapore, Deborah Harcourt and Heather Conroy (2011) suggest that researchers' perceptions of children's competence determine the extent to which researchers are truly prepared to work in partnership with children. Working in partnership means foregrounding the belief that children have a voice worth listening to and entering into dialogue with them. It also means believing that children are sophisticated thinkers and communicators (Harcourt and Conroy 2005) and are able to think and act autonomously. Adopting Rinaldi's (2006) *pedagogy of listening*, and working in spaces familiar to children, Harcourt and Conroy (2011) created sustained opportunities for children to 'play' with the idea of participating, while they observed and listened to children's ideas about what taking part in research might mean.

In her doctoral study of 25 five- and six-year-old children's perceptions of the quality of their early education experiences in Singapore, Harcourt (2008) initially met with the children to discuss her research proposal, explored what they understood by the terms *research, investigate* and *project*, and discussed the kinds of things they might do together during the planned research. They also discussed what *quality* meant, related this word to their personal lives and agreed it was associated with 'good'. These dialogues helped to establish shared meanings and a common language that framed the project. They also talked about the different ways that children might want to express their views through talking, writing and drawing, and how Harcourt might ultimately present and disseminate the information the children shared with her.

In their earlier work with trainee and qualified teachers at the International Centre for Early Childhood (ICEC) in Singapore, Harcourt and Conroy (2005) ran a final semester assessment, where students were asked to present their findings on a community project entitled 'Children as Sophisticated Thinkers and Communicators through Play'. The students worked with children aged 1.8 to 8 years of age, and in time, this assessment project led to the students' developing a new image of the young child as capable and competent, and to use the term 'assent' rather than 'consent' to describe their agreement to participate. Harcourt and Conroy (2005) report how one student working with a three-year-old girl first thought that to gain the child's assent to participate, she would draw a smiley face and a sad face on a piece of paper and let the child choose which one to colour in, but changed her mind as she felt this would not tell her much about what the girl was actually thinking. Instead, she sat and talked with the girl, who agreed she would be happy to take part and asked the student teacher how to write 'happy'. The student was unsure if she should spell out the word, but a nearby member of staff resolved her dilemma by spelling the word, and the girl wrote two *p*'s and an *h*, along with other symbols on a piece of paper, and handed it to the student as a sign of her willingness to participate. Working with a boy aged 1.9 years, another student prepared two trays of paint, one red and one green, and talked with him about what he knew about red and green traffic lights. At the end of their conversation, the child chose green paint to print his hand, indicating his consent to 'go ahead' with a research observation.

Harcourt and Conroy (2005) point out that with very young children, the researcher can never be sure if they have understood what they have agreed to, so their assent must be seen as provisional, with researchers remaining alert for signs they may change their minds, to ensure their consent is genuine rather than a wish to comply with an adult figure of authority. This is particularly relevant in cultural contexts, such as in Singapore, where children are accustomed to didactic teaching and may find it difficult to exercise their right to say no.

This example shows how the young researchers worked hard to find ways to share meanings with their young participants, and to ensure high ethics standards. It could be argued that their approach to ethics reflected the disciplinary norms that they had learnt through their training, and that they foregrounded children's rights over their previously held personal views as they developed their approaches to ethics in early childhood research.

Negotiating anonymity and confidentiality

Issues of participants' right to privacy are central to anonymity and confidentiality, and this aspect pervades all stages of the research process. In any study, one of the first decisions to be explored with participants (and with those legally responsible for young participants) is the degree of anonymity required, which may vary depending on the research aims, framework and intended avenues for distribution of the research findings. In some instances, adult participants may prefer to retain their own or their child's name, and to have images of themselves included in the data presentations. Some participants may prefer complete anonymity, which requires changing all identifiable features. Sometimes, a parent may opt for a child's name to be changed, whereas the child may insist on their own name being used. Each of these scenarios presents an ethical challenge to be resolved, and the solutions found to issues of privacy will depend on the nature of the data collected, the institutional ethics requirements and the legal regulations of the country where the research is conducted.

Audio data is usually presented as transcribed extracts, where the identity of the speaker may only be apparent to fellow participants who know each other well, and is concealed from a wider readership. When working with visual data, concealing participant and place identities can be more challenging (Flewitt 2006). In some instances, participants or their legal guardians may prefer images to be obscured, or the researcher may feel there is no justification for using an identifiable image of a participant (see Thomson 2008). Digitally recorded visual data lend themselves obligingly to the technical equivalent of anonymizing written text. If fine detail of facial expression is not needed in data presentation, then Photoshop© is a widely available tool that researchers can use to obscure images permanently, by smudging or reducing the pixilation of photographs.

Research Example 2.2: Visual research, anonymity and confidentiality

The image in Figure 2.2 was part of a multimodal study of young children's communicative strategies in a preschool playgroup and at home (Flewitt 2003, 2005a), where ethnographic data were collected over one school year, including extensive use of video recordings. The main data corpus for this study was therefore video footage, and as the analysis focused on how children used combinations of words, body movements, manipulation of objects, gaze and facial expression to express meanings in the settings of home and preschool, the use of visual images was often imperative for the construction of a convincing argument that was securely grounded in evidence. This presented a potential ethical minefield in terms of anonymity and confidentiality. Although participants' names were changed in written accounts and erased from the audio track of the video recordings, the remaining visual images made them easily recognizable not only while in the public sphere of preschool but also in the privacy of their homes. This put the children at particular risk and rendered parents and practitioners vulnerable to possible criticism of their practice, and to self-doubt. Rosie Flewitt therefore made a selection of video exemplars to illustrate different analytic points, and shared these sample extracts with participants, deleting those where participants showed concern about their content. In practice, very few requests were made for examples to be cut, although several adult participants made requests, half in jest, for certain less flattering shots of themselves to be edited out. Needless to say, all requests were honoured.

Although the child participants and their parents had given permission for an agreed selection of video extracts and still images to be published, in some instances, images were needed only to clarify body positioning or gaze exchange, so a reduced pixel version was considered sufficient to clarify the analytic point being made, as shown in Figure 2.2.

The framework for ethics adopted in this study was informed primarily by a situated, dialogic approach, where the researcher prioritized child and adult perspectives over her own beliefs and values, and negotiated an ethical pathway that respected disciplinary norms while also respecting participant preferences.

FIGURE 2.2 *Pixel-reduced still image taken from video data (Flewitt 2003).*

In visual research, line drawings are sometimes used to protect participant identity in video or photographic images as an alternative to obscuring original visual data. Line drawings offer the advantage of participant anonymity while focusing the reader's attention on key analytic points (e.g. Goodwin 2007; Plowman and Stephen 2008; see also Flewitt et al. 2014). Nonetheless, however detailed the representation of visual data may be, it is still extracted from the richly situated context in which it occurred, and it is difficult for readers of research to 'read' an image unless the image is accompanied by relevant contextual details that situate each data extract in the complexity and particularity of its original occurrence.

The process of anonymizing visual data can be time consuming, expensive (for example, if line drawings are commissioned), and can compromise the quality and nature of the data. Moreover, editing software is now readily available to readers of research, which may enable them to reverse anonymized visual changes back to the original image format. There is therefore always the risk that the terms of anonymity that are agreed upon with participants may not be honoured over time, as digital software becomes increasingly sophisticated.

A further consideration is that researchers may occasionally feel it is necessary to pass on information about a child for issues of child protection, as mentioned earlier in the section on legal obligations. It is therefore advisable to include a clause to this effect in the information and consent sheets given to adult participants and to any older children. If unsure of the correct procedures for such reporting of child safety, then help is available for researchers from their institutional ethics committee, and confidential helplines, such as ChildLine (in the UK), can also be approached for reliable advice. Similarly, a researcher may find themselves wrestling with ethics decisions about whether to pass on information to a responsible adult, in the belief that doing so will help to resolve a problem in a child's life or reassure a parent. In such cases, it is best in the first instance to approach the person about whom you may wish to disclose information, and when the moment is right, gently suggest that they mention something themselves.

Ethics and data interpretation

Although ethics is recognized as an all-pervasive concern in research, less attention is paid to the ethics of data analysis, yet researchers are responsible for the ethical interpretation of data as their findings may have consequences for participants and wider populations. It is therefore advisable to build in collaborative interpretation, even if only on a relatively small data sample, where you share your interpretive process with others, such as a research supervisor or academic colleague. Researchers working in teams can use *inter-rater reliability* to check their interpretations of data, that is, where the same data is interpreted independently by different researchers and then shared, so each can bring their own unique analytic gaze to the process of interpretation. Researchers can also include *respondent validation* in the research process, that is, where participants are consulted about emerging findings, and encouraged to offer their own interpretations. These processes build checks and balances into data interpretation, and help to validate research findings. Ultimately, the science of interpretation is inseparable from ethical conduct – for every choice that is made, there is an alternative choice that could have been made. Sarangi and Candlin (2003) use the term 'motivated looking' to describe how the analytic gaze is inevitably directed towards certain features in data that correspond to the researcher's theoretical framing and research questions. To a large extent this is an essential part of conducting research – a professional skill that we learn as researchers – but we must be critically aware of this tendency to avoid misinterpretation or over-interpretation of data during analysis and interpretation.

Planning your approach to ethics

The formality of institutional ethics review processes requires researchers to develop a robust and credible plan for ethical conduct throughout a research project, and the time needed for this ethical planning process can be lengthy. For example, if a research committee meets only four to six times a year, and a first application is unsuccessful, then it may be a further two to three months before a second application can be re-submitted and approved. For the researcher, this means that the initial process of planning a robust and justifiable ethics approach is essential, but it could also be potentially problematic given that any ethics plan will need to be adapted to unknown possible future events. We suggest the following steps may be helpful for you in your ethics planning process.

Building your ethical stance: Consider the four quadrants of Figure 2.1, collate the ethics guidance and legal regulation relevant to your field of enquiry – including, for example, (inter)-disciplinary codes of practice; institutional guidance; ethics relevant to your chosen methods of enquiry; and ethics guidelines of your project funder (if applicable). Once you have read through and mapped the requirements implied by this documentation, reflect critically on the ethical framework of your particular study, in line with your study's main objectives and epistemology. Consider your own moral values regarding research rights and principles, your (honest) views of children's competence, and share your values with colleagues, particularly if you are working as part of a research team. You may find it helpful to write notes of key points, which you can reflect on and return to as you develop your ethics plans.

Reflecting on your research topic: Consider the topic of your research and your research questions, and reflect on the following questions:

- Are all your questions essential?

- What new insights will your research lead to?

- Does the phrasing of your topic and research questions position children as competent and agentive? For example, does the wording of your question(s) assume that children are vulnerable/strong, empowered/disempowered, subjects/objects, beings/becomings, marginalized/central? Does this positioning reflect the values enshrined in your work? Is your planned work of use to adult and child participants?

- What ethical issues have been identified and documented in previous research that is similar to your proposal in terms of topic and/or method?

- Have you consulted with adults and children about your research topic to gain their perspectives on your idea? This may not always be possible, but talking with young children about your research aims, in ways that have meaning for them and at an early stage in your plans, can lead to very interesting new questions or rephrasing.[3]

Research sample and gaining access: Once you have decided on your ideal research sample, consider how you will gain access to research participants, and what ethical expectations and values your gatekeepers might have. If you are researching in a school or early childhood education setting, you may need to explain to education professionals that different processes of consent are essential for adults' and children's participation in research, in addition to any parent/school agreements that are already in place regarding school-based observations, use of images and school records of individual pupils' performance and personal data. Further questions you might ask yourself include

- Is your sampling strategy random, purposively diverse or purposively focused and why?

- How does your sampling strategy correspond to your research aims?

- What criteria will you use to justify your research sample?

- How many participants are needed to produce sufficient evidence for a robust argument (i.e. have you included too many/too few participants)?

- How will you ensure that participants are informed about the aims of your project?

- What kind of information will you share with participants, in what format(s), and how will participant consent be documented? Consider ways to share information in meaningful ways with child participants, and in ways that they choose – as implied in Research Example 2.1.

Your approach to power relationships: During data collection, there are inevitable power imbalances between the researcher and the researched, and where there is a power imbalance, there is

---

[3]See Chapter 4, 'Participatory Research with Young Children', for ideas about how to gain children's perspectives.

always a risk of abuse of power, however unintentional this may be. Consider how you might conduct yourself with participants in ways that minimize the risk of you abusing your rights as a researcher, and participants abusing their rights as participants?

Assessing risks: When considering risk, the following questions can be helpful to prompt your planning and help ensure the smooth running of your project:

- Have you completed a risk assessment for the project, including risks for adult and child participants, and for researchers? For example, are there any potential psychological, emotional or physical risks to participants, and/or any risks that researchers might be found to be negligent during any phase of the research?

- Are there any particular risks associated with the research methods and data-collection processes you plan to follow? Will you be alone with children, and if so, what legal and disciplinary requirements do you need for this? For example, in the UK, all adults, including researchers, working with children are legally required to have a formal check of their police records through the DBS.[4]

- If you are using visual methods in a busy environment, how will you exclude children for whom you do not have permission to record?

Data storage, anonymity and confidentiality: Serious thought must be given to the safe storage of all data collected, and the following prompts will help to guide your planning:

- How will you store your data securely?

- Are you up-to-date with data protection laws in the country and institution where your study is being carried out and in the country where your research institution or university is based? It is becoming increasingly common to share research data via the World Wide Web, and to use password-

---

[4]https://www.gov.uk/government/organisations/disclosure-and-barring-service/about

protected virtual clouds for project sharing, yet all web-based information is susceptible to rogue use, so how much and what kind of data really needs to be stored or shared virtually?

• How will participant confidentiality be secured (see the section on 'Negotiating anonymity and confidentiality')? Will you negotiate anonymity and confidentiality openly with participants and if not, why? (This may be justifiable in some instances, but requires careful consideration.)

• How will your findings be shared safely with adult and child participants, in meaningful and helpful ways that will enable them to benefit from their involvement in the research process?

Concluding thoughts

In summary, research ethics decisions are influenced by multiple factors, including international and national guiding principles; formalized institutional recommendations; professional and disciplinary norms; requirements from ethics review boards; international and national legal regulations (which in international studies may differ between a researcher's country of origin, host institution's location and the multiple sites of a study); the choice of ethics framework; and researchers' own individual moral codes of conduct. Regardless of how stringent or dialogic the ethics review process may be, critical social science and arts researchers will almost inevitably have to negotiate ethical quandaries throughout the research process.

During the planning of research, there is a careful balance to be found between ethics regulation, legal requirements, established ethics frameworks and your own moral values, which you should reflect on critically. Depending on your research aims and the epistemological stance of your study, you may choose to foreground the disciplinary norms of your field of research as you plan, or you may develop your own ethical principles that respect legal regulations and disciplinary norms but are more reflective of your own values, and the values of the adult and child participants with whom you will be working. The key is to develop an ethical framework for your study that enables you to address all the above questions. If you can achieve this, then it is likely that the risk of harm to participants or researchers will be minimized, and you will have a robust and well-grounded ethical framework to help guide your decision-making in the face of the as-yet-unknown.

Suggestions for further reading

Alderson, P. and Morrow, V. (2004). *Ethics, Social Research and Consulting with Children and Young People.* Ilford: Barnado's.

Christensen, P. and Prout, A. (2002). Working with ethical symmetry in social research with children. *Childhood,* 9 (4): 477–97.

Flewitt, R. S. (2005). Conducting research with young children: Some ethical considerations, *Early Child Development and Care* 175 (6): 553–65.

Harcourt, D., Perry B. and Waller T. (Eds.) (2011). *Researching Young Children's Perspectives: Debating the Ethics and Dilemmas of Educational Research with Children.* London and New York: Sage.

Sargeant, J. and Harcourt, D. (2012). *Doing Ethical Research with Children.* Maidenhead, UK: Open University Press.

CHAPTER THREE

Reviewing Literature as a Methodology

This chapter discusses reviewing literature as a methodological approach which can support the critical examination of early childhood education and can inform policy decision-making and educational practice for the benefit of young children and families. The chapter examines the critical review of literature as a research process across a continuum from a traditional literature review, rapid evidence assessment and systematic review to a systematic meta-review, that is, the review of systematic reviews. Reflecting on the strengths and limitations of different research review designs, the chapter argues that reviewing literature offers an approach to early childhood and social science research that can contribute to new conceptualizations of knowledge and can advance our understanding of children and families. However, this is only the case if reviews are carefully designed, well executed and also recognize their own flaws and limitations.

The literature review

The first step to research is usually reviewing and synthesizing the relevant literature to understand what is already known about the subject matter. In the messy world of social science research, the ability to conduct a methodical review and to have the right tools to combine information effectively is vital. The art and science of identifying, collating and evaluating literature from multiple sources is a research method in its own right. It not only enables researchers to determine what evidence is available about the issue in question but can help to identify gaps in existing knowledge, and to advance conceptual and methodological developments that inform new research.

Reviews can vary considerably in their depth and breadth. Conducting a review of literature is the first and arguably the most complicated step in the research process, as researchers face complex choices about the most effective method of retrieving and assessing different types of knowledge to address a set of questions. This can be challenging when faced with a vast body of studies, which makes collating and selecting information a complex and laborious exercise. There is a spectrum of review methods, which we suggest is best illustrated through a continuum from a traditional literature review, to rapid evidence assessment, systematic review and meta-review.

The traditional literature review

Sometimes known as narrative review or desk-based research, traditional literature reviews are often conducted in a short space of time on a defined topic where researchers bring together a selection of studies that they regard as salient evidence. A broad thematic analysis or narrative synthesis of the literature is then undertaken and an argument is developed to address a particular research question or hypothesis. The purpose of reviewing literature is essentially twofold. Firstly, it is for researchers to acquaint themselves with a range of research that has been carried out in the subject area. Secondly, an effective literature review is useful for determining how the intended research adds to the existing knowledge base and makes an original and distinct contribution to the field.

In early childhood education research, literature reviews are routinely published on a wide range of topics related to children's care and education (e.g. Hobbs and Stovall 2015; Farrell, Kagan and Tisdall 2016). In a sector that is fuelled by increasing demands for more and better evidence to inform policy and practice, it is important for researchers to engage in critical debates about the use of different techniques to review and synthesize literature to advance the scientific rigour of the field. A well-constructed review will demonstrate the depth and breadth of the researcher's knowledge and understanding of the subject matter. Additionally, it will highlight the gaps and contradictions in existing research and potentially bring a fresh perspective to the topic area. However, researchers have argued that literature reviews in their simplest, most traditional form are limiting because they are not always carried out in a systematic way and are therefore not adequately reliable as a methodological tool. This is especially the case if the process of how the literature is retrieved, included and analysed is not explicitly delineated. Gough, Oliver and Thomas (2012) contend that traditional literature reviews tend to summarize what is known about a topic but do not necessarily explain the criteria used to select the literature or how they are evaluated, which can lead to selection bias: 'If the process of identifying and including studies is not explicit, it is not possible to assess the appropriateness of such decisions or whether they were applied in a consistent and rigorous manner' (p. 5). Thus, while traditional literature reviews are useful for providing information on a defined topic and are valuable in their own right in contributing to academic debates, they can have weaknesses, particularly in the assessment and interpretation of how the literature is selected and reviewed. We consider these weaknesses throughout the chapter, and particularly in the final section on critiques of this approach.

Rapid evidence assessment

The rapid evidence assessment (REA) approach, also known as a quick scoping review, was developed as a method of retrieving and synthesizing the available literature in a timely but rigorous way to meet the needs of policymakers and practitioners who are faced with increasing pressures to address important social concerns in short, rapid timescales (Collins et al. 2014; Thomas, Newman and Oliver 2013). The purpose of REAs is essentially to conduct a quick overview of a range of studies on a specific topic. REAs are considered to have an added advantage over traditional literature reviews by making more explicit the review protocol and assessment process when evaluating the quality and reliability of the studies included in the review. When conducting REAs, researchers usually set out a clear protocol of searches and assessment of the available evidence, often to address or solve a pressing policy issue. The benefits of working to a tight timescale mean that the REA is confined to a clearly delineated and defined scope, and has the advantage of mapping the available evidence to inform policy decision-making in a speedy fashion.

The UK Government Social Research Unit (GSRU) describes rapid reviews such as REAs as 'a tool for getting on top of the available research evidence on a policy issue, as comprehensively as possible, within the constraints of a given timetable' (GSRU 2018: 1). REAs are precipitated in part by the rapid demands of a 'knowledge economy', and by the increasing trend towards accessing new information and evidence to inform substantive areas of social science and public policy. However, reviewing research evidence thoroughly takes considerable time. The findings from REAs that are undertaken in a short time frame, while pertinent to informing policy decision-making, may run the risk of being inconclusive, and the stated research questions may have to be reformulated. While there are increasing calls for 'rapid reviews' to inform policy decision-making, researchers have also noted the inadequacies of this expedited review process which tends to result in less robust evidence. Thus, REAs offer the advantage of clearly defining their goals and search strategy, but are comparatively limiting compared to more comprehensive methods, such as systematic reviews (Gannan, Ciliska and Thomas 2010) as set out in the next section.

Systematic reviews

A systematic review is essentially desk-based research that employs a structured and standardized protocol to provide a rigorous assessment and synthesis of existing literature and evidence on a topic area. The key features of systematic reviews have been described as

transparency of methods used for searching for studies; exhaustive searches which look for unpublished as well as published studies;

clear criteria for assessing the quality of studies (both qualitative and quantitative); clear criteria for including or excluding studies based on the scope of the review and quality assessment; joint reviewing to reduce bias; a clear statement of the findings of the review. (Evans and Benefield 2001: 529)

Although the method has been described as the 'gold standard' in review design, in the way that it enables data to be systematically scrutinized and evaluated (Anderson and Shemilt 2010; Penn 2016), the place of systematic literature reviews in qualitative methodologies can be 'a polemical and divisive issue' (Dunne 2011: 111) (see the sections on 'Choices and challenges' and 'Further debates' later in this chapter).

The systematic review process entails a series of planned stages that involves the formulation of the research question(s), development of a review protocol and search strategy, application of inclusion and exclusion criteria, development of a conceptual framework and appraisal of the quality and relevance of the material (Oliver and Sutcliffe 2017). In systematic reviews, a thorough search for studies is typically conducted using a range of search strategies – for instance, through electronic and print databases, grey literature (unpublished/work in progress) as well as hand searching journals and textbooks, searching specialist websites, and using the researcher's personal contacts and networks to locate relevant literature. Each study or item found is then screened according to a standardized set of inclusion and exclusion criteria, with clear documentation of the reasons for including or excluding certain studies (Cochrane Library 2018). The systematic review technique can be applied to a wide range of questions using both statistical and narrative approaches including meta-analyses and/ or qualitative research, while drawing on a variety of study types such as effectiveness studies and impact evaluations. Quantitative reviews could include meta-analysis, a method that statistically evaluates the results of a number of studies. If more qualitative data are retrieved, then a qualitative synthesis can likewise be used to summarize the results of the review. Some reviews also do both, in that they integrate a meta-analysis of data from controlled trials with a synthesis of findings from qualitative studies (Gough and Elbourne 2002).

The origins of systematic reviews are rooted in the discipline of healthcare where it is commonplace for researchers to synthesize large bodies of knowledge to inform clinical practice and health related policies. The method was established in the UK by the Cochrane Collaboration; the first international network of reviewers which consisted of a group of researchers who came together with a shared vision '[t]o improve health by promoting the production, understanding and use of high quality research evidence by patients, healthcare professionals and those who organize and fund our healthcare services' (Cochrane Collaboration 2016). The impetus for the collaboration is to create a scientific methodology that brings together information from a wide range of sources as a guide for practitioners and students. The Cochrane Collaboration is thought to be the largest single producer of systematic reviews in health care, with more than 4,200 reviews published (Bastian, Glasziou and Chalmers 2010).

Importantly, systematic reviews are commonly known to offer aggregate summaries of available bodies of research on 'what works', and to address targeted questions or a phenomena of social importance (Cabinet Office 2014; Gough, Oliver and Thomas 2017). Beyond the public health sector, there has been a notable rise in the last decade in the use of systematic review techniques to enhance evidence-based policy development and advocacy (Lohr 2004; Oakley 2003) in a range of fields including education and the early years. The proliferation of the method has been precipitated as a result of growing demands by policymakers and practitioners to have access to the best available evidence for the purpose of decision-making (Harden and Thomas 2005). As opposed to the more traditional literature review or REA, a key strength of systematic reviews is arguably the highly detailed, transparent and auditable trail of the methodological process in documenting how a selection of literature is reviewed and analysed, including an assessment of the quality of the literature and potential bias.

Saracho (2016) argues that a systematic and methodical approach to reviewing and synthesizing literature is vital in the early childhood field where research is largely dominated by qualitative and descriptive studies (Saracho 2016). The method is increasingly undertaken to explore solutions to improve the quality of young children's childcare and education (Saracho 2016; Pring and

Thomas 2004; Pawson 2002, 2006). Notably, the work of the EPPI-Centre and International Initiative for Impact Evaluation (known as '3ie'), which is funded by the UK Department for International Development and other international partners, has led the way in building a repository of systematic reviews on evidence to inform future research and policy development focused on improving children's lives in developing countries. Examples of reviews that have been conducted include the effects of interventions and approaches used for enhancing poverty reduction and development benefits of 'within country migration' in South Asia (Babu et al. 2017); the benefits of early childhood interventions (Nores and Barnett 2010); the impact of day-care programmes on child health, nutrition and development in developing countries (Leroy, Gadsden and Guijarro 2012); and childhood vaccinations in developing countries (Shea, Andersson and Henry 2009). The corpus of published work indicates a growing trend towards systematic reviews being used in multidisciplinary research in the field of early childhood, and to inform policy development in the developing world (Snilstveit, Oliver and Vojtkova 2012). It also indicates the potential of systematic review as a method in opening up new areas of interdisciplinary research.

Systematic reviews of reviews

Systematic reviews are based on the premise that robust evidence for social change is derived not from single studies or a particular selection of literature, but from scientific analyses and syntheses of multiple studies to derive aggregate findings on the same topic. In this sense, reviews can also take the form of a systematic review of reviews where the research focuses on existing reviews, preferably systematic, rather than individual pieces of literature or primary studies. The *Cochrane Handbook for Systematic Reviews of Interventions* (Higgins and Green 2011) uses the phrase 'overview of reviews' to describe this approach to reviewing reviews of interventions rather than individual primary studies. Reviews of reviews (meta-reviews) are often conducted when considerable research has already been undertaken on a particular subject area, and this is a logical approach to allow the findings of disparate bodies of work to be compared and contrasted in a resource-effective way. Meta-review is particularly useful in the field of healthcare and the medical sciences where there is historically an extensive collection of empirical work on clinical and health interventions. The method is akin to conducting a systematic review of primary studies in that the process entails the searching and appraisal of published and unpublished literature – except that in this case, the review brings together a compilation of reviews in one place, so the researcher can assess the quality of the evidence and compare the strengths of the findings. The claims for the reliability of meta-reviews therefore depend on both the quality of the meta-review process and of the systematic reviews that are included in the analysis.

Experts in this approach contend that systematic reviews and meta-reviews are robust methods for reviewing evidence because they are set up to be as comprehensive and transparent as possible in the methodological process, in order to reduce the bias in the way studies are assessed (Gough, Oliver and Thomas 2012; Caird et al. 2015). Furthermore, the auditable and transparent methodological trail allows future studies to be added to the review over time to form a stronger cumulative body of evidence. Not surprisingly, however, the disadvantage of the method is that conducting a systematic review or a systematic meta-review is extremely resource intensive and time consuming. This approach is often only realistic when undertaken by a team of researchers either 'in-house' or contracted to carry out the work, within a given review scope, and provided that funding and other resources are available.

Research Example 3.1: A Systematic Review of the Effectiveness of Early Childhood Development Programmes (Anderson et al. 2003)

In this study, Laurie Anderson and colleagues conducted a systematic review of published scientific studies to examine the evidence base of the effectiveness of early childhood development programmes in the United States that demonstrated a positive impact on preventing developmental delay. Critical dimensions of early childhood development include self-regulation, establishing early relationships, knowledge acquisition and the development of specific cognitive, social and emotional skills. The review was undertaken by a team of researchers and was based on the premise that effective early childhood development programmes directly improve young children's cognitive and intellectual performance, which in turn leads to an increase in participants' motivation and performance in subsequent years, ultimately leading to higher educational attainment and a reduced drop-out rate. The research team defined early childhood programmes in this study as publicly funded comprehensive preschool programmes designed to increase social competence in children aged three to five years deemed at risk because of family poverty.

The research team designed a protocol-driven methodology, which involved the systematic searching and screening of published literature, undertaken alongside an iterative process of data searching, evaluation and analysis. Five electronic databases were searched: PsychINFO, Educational Resource Information Center (ERIC), Medline, Social Science Search and the Head Start Bureau research database. Strict inclusion criteria were employed to include only studies which

- documented an evaluation of an early childhood development programme in the United States;

- were published in English between 1965 and 2000;

- compared outcomes among groups of people exposed to the intervention with outcomes among groups of people not exposed or less exposed to the intervention; and

- measured outcomes defined by the analytic framework for the intervention.

Additionally, the search strategy included published annotated bibliographies of particular early childhood development research, reference lists of reviewed articles, internet resources, as well as referrals from specialists in the field. The research team recorded a step-by-step account of the screening process, and retrieved a total of 2,100 articles from their searches. These were screened by their titles and abstracts, and from this screening, 350 articles were assessed as compliant with the inclusion criteria. On closer reading of the full articles, most were excluded at this stage because they were descriptive reports and not intervention studies, with fifty-seven items identified for further screening. Of these, forty-one were subsequently excluded following an appraisal of their quality, which included a lack of a comparison group or clear outcomes. This rigorous screening process led to a final sixteen studies (featured in twenty-three reports) meeting the inclusion criteria for the final review. The findings of the systematic review were based on these sixteen studies.

In reviewing the evidence, an analytical framework or conceptual model was drawn together to illustrate key findings of the review of early childhood development programmes, which indicated demonstrable outcomes. The systematic review found that twelve studies (reported in seventeen papers) identified programmes that had led to positive cognitive outcomes, including increased child motivation and performance in school academic achievement and increased child readiness to learn in the school setting; nine studies (reported in thirteen papers) measured academic achievement through use of standardized academic achievement assessments and demonstrated increases in academic achievement for students who were enrolled in the childhood development programme; one study reported a negative effect and two studies did not provide data to calculate the effect size of the intervention. The systematic review also considered social, family and child health screening outcomes from the interventions, such as preschool children's social competence; supportive home environments and parental involvement in children's education; and increased use of preventive health screenings and medical care. Over 70 per cent of the reported effects related to children's cognitive development, with consistent improvements found in measures of intellectual ability (IQ measures); standardized tests of school readiness; promotion to next grade; and a reduction in referral to special educational classes.

Overall, the findings showed strong evidence of the effectiveness of early childhood development programmes in preventing delays in cognitive development and positive associations with children's increased readiness to learn. However, due to a lack of available studies, there was insufficient evidence to determine the effectiveness of early childhood programmes in improving child health screening and family outcomes. An important outcome of this systematic review was that it identified significant gaps in research evaluating the effectiveness of early childhood development programmes, other than in terms of cognitive gain. Furthermore, it identified significant methodological and design weaknesses in many studies, so their results could not be generalized across national programmes in the United States.

Choices and challenges when undertaking reviews

As illustrated by Research Example 3.1, there are complex choices to be made when undertaking a review of literature, with important considerations about the inherent strengths and challenges of any review design. These most commonly pertain to the complexity of searches and to the wide range of information sources, variability in the appraising of research quality and potential risk of bias.

Complex searches and diverse information sources

Reviews of literature require a clear search strategy and set of descriptors containing key concepts and terms that are used to identify relevant studies and to delineate the scope of a review. Searching and retrieving the relevant literature is challenging, yet crucial to the success of any review. By definition, the very nature of reviews entails the searching and synthesizing of studies that are usually found in a wide range of sources, conducted by different people and at different times. The complexity of conducting literature searches can be overwhelming, given the sheer volume of material to check through – especially as it is rare to find exact studies that replicate one another precisely. A comprehensive database search can capture a wide diversity of literature from a range of publication types and documents including books, conference papers, anthologies, journal articles, encyclopaedias, monographs and reference works; all of which add to the complexity of the search and the synthesis of a wide range of information.

This process can be all the more challenging when conducting an interdisciplinary review where the search for literature encompasses two or more academic fields and draws upon a diverse range of studies with different theoretical and empirical approaches. For example, in a cross-disciplinary subject area such as early childhood education and international development, searching the relevant literature involves the researcher applying methodological judgements across contrasting academic fields such as theology and geography. This inevitably raises predicaments about what essentially counts as valid knowledge and how this varies by discipline (Ang 2018). The complexities of searching, pooling and synthesizing discipline-specific knowledge are recognized by researchers even as they espouse the advantages of cross-disciplinary or transdisciplinary research approaches (Ang 2018; King et al. 2009). When searching vast databases across different fields, there are also lesser-known sources of valuable information or 'grey literature' such as government reports and more obscure research publications that are either unpublished or published in a language other than English. As such, it is possible that potentially relevant studies may not be included, and valuable information may be missed.

Yet, despite the challenges, the diversity or heterogeneity of reviews, as Gough, Oliver and Thomas (2012) contend, 'should be seen as a strength and an opportunity for analysis rather than as a problem and a barrier to producing clear findings' (p. 55). There are considerable merits in drawing on different transdisciplinary sources of knowledge when producing reviews, and combining concepts from across and beyond academic disciplines, not least because 'it can encourage respect for different ideologies and paradigms, and a better understanding and appreciation of disciplinary diversity'(Oliver et al. 2017: 5). Given the complexity of conducting literature reviews, it is imperative that the search strategies and research questions to be informed by the review are well developed. Ultimately, establishing a systematic and well-documented search is fundamental to successfully retrieving the appropriate information. Brunton, Stansfield and Thomas (2017) offer a set of useful guidelines for researchers to consider when conducting a search strategy and point to the need for researchers to be clear about

- the aim of searching, ensuring that the appropriate methods are used;

- what the most relevant sources of studies are likely to be;

- the benefits and drawbacks of searching each source;

- the resource available; and

- the benefits and costs of different combinations of sources within the available resources. (p. 116)

All searches are conducted within a defined timescale and scope. Brunton, Stansfield and Thomas (2012) argue it is a myth that an exhaustive review is possible because 'the total "universe" of potentially relevant literature is unknown' (p. 113). Addressing the challenge of completing complex searches effectively and managing a wide range of sources therefore requires the researcher to know precisely and clearly what the review is about, and to set out which key concepts are important, how they are defined, and then to plan and carry out a search strategy in a systematic and consistent manner.

Appraising research quality and variability in quality

The variability in research quality and appraising quality – that is, the process of determining *how* and *which* published material should be included in the review and assessing the strength of the evidence – is a key challenge in any review. The term 'critical appraisal' is sometimes used to describe the process of 'carefully and systematically examining research to judge its trustworthiness, and its value and relevance in a particular context' (Burls 2009: 1). Harden and Gough (2012: 154) contend, 'Assessing the quality and relevance of individual studies within a review is a crucial part of the review process and contributes to the quality and credibility of the review itself.' The purpose of appraising research quality is to enable the researcher to make informed decisions as to how closely an item of literature or study is related to the topic area, whether it should be included or removed from the review, and its significance in influencing the conclusions that will be drawn from the review.

The quality of a particular item is usually judged in relation to its relevance to the research question(s) posed in the review. However, as with any critical appraisal, there is a necessary element of judgement, not least because quality is essentially a value-laden concept and what constitutes quality is often dependent on the reviewer's or reviewer team's understanding of research. The process of selecting and appraising the quality of the literature inevitably involves an exercise of judgement when gauging the strength of the evidence and how it might address the research questions. As such, questions inevitably arise about how a reviewer can judge whether a piece of research is of high quality and warrants being given weight in the review process, or whether it falls short in terms of validity. There are also questions of whether there is consistency of judgement among reviewer teams, or even for one reviewer across the period of time it may take to conduct a thorough review of literature (which may be a slow process over a period of three to six years for doctoral study, for example). These factors all affect the findings and outcomes of any review.

To support the process of assessing the quality of the research and research reports included in any review, it can be extremely helpful to develop an appraisal tool. This could consist, for instance, of a list of questions, which prompt the reviewer to make informed judgement about the items being selected for review. For example, the following questions might be included 'Was the sampling strategy of the study appropriate to the research questions?'; 'Were steps taken by the author/researcher to minimize bias and increase rigour of the data?'; 'Were the data analysis methods systematic?'; and 'Were the findings adequately supported by the data?' An appraisal tool could also entail a scoring system with set criteria to evaluate each study. For instance, in a systematic review of early childhood development and cognitive development in developing countries (Rao et al. 2014), a rating scale was used to evaluate individual studies according to the rigour of the research design and the soundness of study. The design of each study was assessed according to the methods used in selecting the sample population and in terms of the differences between the identified control and intervention groups in experimental and quasi-experimental studies. A score of 1 to 6 was then assigned on a scale of (1) lowest level of rigour; (2) single group before and after; (3) retrospective controlled/secondary data analysis with constructed comparison groups; (4) other prospective quasi-experimental design; (5) quasi-experimental design with the use of an econometric model; and (6) randomized controlled trial (Rao et al. 2014: 11). Each study was then judged by an overall quality rating of low, medium or high. The same scoring system was applied to all selected studies and any studies that did not meet the quality criteria of the appraisal tool were excluded. The included studies subsequently formed the basis of the review, with conclusions drawn to address the research questions.

Although this approach may evidence the rigour of the selection of papers for inclusion in systematic and meta-reviews, the very adoption of such a numerical appraisal system speaks volumes about what the reviewers regard as valid knowledge and about their judgement of what counts as worthwhile research. As Oncea and Pring (2008) argue, approaches such as this are based on narrow assumptions about knowledge, which often run counter to core principles in education research:

> These are essentially about the nature of knowledge: what it means to know and to understand in the complex social world of interpersonal relations, partial knowledge, autonomous decision making, cultural influences upon individual preferences, the screening of facts through values held and frameworks taken-for-granted within particular communities. (p. 34)

It is therefore essential to make visible the methodological 'audit trail' of systematic reviews, which can include guidance on how discordant results from individual reviews have been reported, and also record decisions regarding the systematic set of inclusion and exclusion criteria, or coding frameworks to help readers of the research review make their own, more informed judgements about the review conclusions.

An alternative approach could be to adopt a standardized code set, as was the case in a systematic review conducted by Best et al. (2013), 'The Impact of National and International Assessment Programmes on Education Policy'. This review tool included the aims and rationale of each study; design; description of the sample; and data collection and data analysis methods. Methodologically, this meant that even though there was wide variability in the nature of the studies, the researcher was able to assess each item against the same criteria, and create a systematic basis for comparing the strengths and weakness of the reviewed items.

Reducing the risk of hidden bias

Importantly, the aim of any review is to ensure that the research process is thorough and transparent, and as free from bias as possible. Such 'quality' standards are embedded in existing review tools that early childhood education researchers might consult, adapt or adopt as appropriate to their own systematic reviews of literature and their own values of what counts as valid knowledge in early childhood education research. In health research, the Preferred Reporting Items for Systematic Reviews and Meta-Analyses (PRISMA) protocol was developed to evaluate randomized trials, and sets out a twenty-seven-item checklist for quality reporting of systematic reviews and meta-analyses in this field of research. The checklist includes using clear and transparent reporting standards for documenting the search, study selection, data collection and assessment of the risk of bias (Moher et al. 2009). Similarly, the instrument A Measurement Tool to Assess Systematic Reviews (AMSTAR 2) is often used to critically appraise systematic reviews of randomized controlled clinical trials. This instrument is based on a detailed assessment of the risk bias in individual studies to evaluate the best available evidence on a topic (Shea et al. 2017). However, it is important to remember that these guidelines were developed for the review of experimental and quasi-experimental research, and may be inappropriate for reviews of qualitative research.

As a methodology often associated with scientific rigour, the main aim of any systematic review is to minimize the risk of bias and error associated with single studies and non-systematic reviews, especially when examining a large body of evidence. However, the notion that research can be entirely impartial, unbiased and value free is a topic of recurring scientific debate. In reality, there will inevitably be a degree of bias even for the most comprehensive systematic reviews. For instance, a review may only include some evidence and not others (selection bias) or only include literature that is relatively easily accessible (publication bias). These factors run the risk of skewing the findings of any review. There is also the possibility of selective reporting bias where particular published studies do not report full details of their sample strategies, size and methodological quality. In some cases, bias can also occur when the researcher is over-reliant on particular sources that show results with positive outcomes. There is also a risk of bias that compromises the quality of reviews when researchers are inadvertently influenced by extraneous variables, such as the authorship of the article, institutional affiliations and journal prestige. The risks of bias are even higher in reviews where there is no explicit methodological trail for the review process, where inclusion and exclusion criteria are not stated, where details are lacking on how studies are appraised, and where the processes of arriving at particular conclusions are not articulated in a clear and transparent manner.

Ideally, to minimize the effects of reporting biases in a review, the search should be as wide as possible to maximize the likelihood of capturing all relevant data. The quality of a review also depends heavily on the focus and scope of the research question/s. When developing a search strategy, Brunton, Stansfield and Thomas (2012) suggest that, depending on the review question, it is important to be 'as broadly-based as possible in order not to be biased by your own preconceptions' (p. 118). Gough, Oliver and Thomas (2012) recommend a comprehensive electronic search as well as manual search of key journals and of the reference lists of reviews captured by the initial searches. Reviewers should also be alert to geographic bias and consider whether limiting a search by country or region can make the review more (or less) robust and manageable. Ultimately, whatever type of literature review is undertaken – whether traditional literature review, rapid evidence review, systematic review or review of systematic reviews – there needs to be careful consideration of the various dimensions that may influence the review conclusions and findings, and steps must be taken to ensure and make clear the credibility, transparency and principled approach of the review process.

Further debates about research reviews

Research review methods continue to fuel methodological debates, and will most likely always continue to do so. Despite the issues and challenges, researchers who favour the use of particular literature review methods have argued strongly that well-designed and well-executed reviews of literature are powerful tools for producing reliable and comprehensive syntheses of the most relevant evidence base and effectiveness of a given phenomenon (Gough, Oliver and Thomas 2012). Stewart (2014: 581) argues that 'systematic reviews of research evidence have the potential to "change the world" by providing accurate and comprehensive summaries of knowledge for decision-makers'. Literature reviews are also perceived by many researchers as an effective medium for enabling knowledge to be accumulated in a manageable way (Harden and Thomas 2005).

However, critics of the systematic review approach argue that the language used to describe and justify systematic review is 'a mix of old-style scientific positivism (systematicity, reliability, rigour, replicability) and the now-familiar rhetoric of the "audit culture" (transparency, quality assurance, standards)' (MacLure 2005: 395). The terms used in systematic reviews are not innocent and, as MacLure argues, derive from a concern for scientific objectivity – for clarity and certainty – that may lead to the exclusion of research from competing frameworks, such as small-scale qualitative studies about and with less powerful communities. Researchers have highlighted the difficulties encountered by social scientists and multidisciplinary research teams when conducting systematic reviews of literature. These include 'inconsistent definitions of social phenomena, differing use of key concepts across research fields and practical problems relating to database compatibility and computer processing power' (Curran et al. 2007: 289). We suggest that engaging with these debates, as we do here, is pertinent when considering the implications of review methods and their application.

Concluding thoughts

This chapter has offered some methodological reflections on reviewing and synthesizing literature as a method, and has reflected critically on a range of review techniques – from traditional literature reviews to more structured systematic review designs. While recognizing the methodological challenges, we argue that maintaining the principles of transparency and rigour are paramount in any approach to reviewing literature. As governments and commissioners of reviews place greater emphasis on gathering the most robust evidence to inform policy and practice that will improve the lives of young children, it is imperative that researchers understand the methodological tools available, the choices they need to make when employing particular literature review approaches, and the critiques and potential pitfalls of the systematic review process. Ultimately, literature reviews have to be fit for purpose. The crucial determinants of a quality review are its rigour, relevancy and explicitness about how the review was undertaken, and the extent to which it addresses the questions that it initially set out to achieve.

Critiques of systematic review processes highlight the need for researchers to reflect openly and critically about the choices they make throughout all stages of research reviews. If conducted to the highest standards of transparency and critical reflection, their content can be highly valuable even if the findings are inconclusive, as Penn and colleagues argue in their review of the impact of out-of-home integrated care and education settings on children aged between zero and six years and their parents:

> This review, its level of scrutiny and use of evidence, has been a wake-up call. We have been forced into thinking more carefully about the nature of research in early years and the uses it has been put to in justifying policy-making. Even if our own results were not as conclusive as we had hoped, clarifying the issues and highlighting the gaps has been an essential step. (Penn et al., 2004: 43)

Suggestions for further reading

Boland, A., Cherry, G., and Dickson, R. (2017). *Doing a Systematic Review: A Student's Guide*. London: SAGE Publications Ltd.

Collins, A., Miller, J., Coughlin, D. and Kirk, S. (2014). *The Production of Quick Scoping Reviews and Rapid Evidence Assessments: A How to Guide*. London: Joint Water Evidence Group.

Dunne, C. (2011). The place of the literature review in grounded theory research. *International Journal of Social Research Methodology* 14 (2): 111–24.

Gough, D. (2007). Weight of evidence: A framework for the appraisal of the quality and relevance of evidence. In J. Furlong and A. Oancea (Eds.), *Applied and Practice-based Research*. Special Edition of *Research Papers in Education* 22 (2): 213–28.

Gough, D., Oliver, S. and Thomas, J. (2012). *An Introduction to Systematic Reviews*. London: Sage Publications.

Petticrew, M. and Roberts, H. (2005). *Systematic Reviews in the Social Sciences: A Practical Guide*. Britain: John Wiley & Sons.

Thomas, J., Newman, M. and Oliver, S. (2013). Rapid evidence assessments of research to inform social policy: Taking stock and moving forward. *Evidence and Policy: A Journal of Research, Debate and Practice* 9 (1): 5–27.

PART TWO

Early Childhood Education Research Methods in Context

CHAPTER FOUR

Participatory Research with Young Children

One frequently asked question in early childhood research is, 'how old do children need to be for their involvement in research to be truly participatory?' We turn this question on its head and move away from the historical tendency in research for children to be regarded as 'too immature' for them to be able to express their own views competently or reliably. We consider how sociological approaches to early childhood studies have led to child competence being reconceptualized, underpinning a growing body of research that regards children of all ages as experts on their own lives (Clark 2017; Kellett 2014, 2005; Prout and James 1997; Rogoff 2003). We begin the chapter with a brief overview of how participatory research with children can be traced back to a wider call to action for profoundly democratic research that emerged with critical theory (e.g. Freire 2000/1970; Giroux 1989), which focused on constructing research *with* people rather than *on* them. We then reflect critically on children's involvement at different stages of the research process and how the roles that children play in participatory research are shaped by understandings of *child competence* and *child voice*. Throughout the chapter, we draw on national and international examples to illustrate how young children have been included in researching their own lives and interests, and in developing impact from their research.

Shifting from research *on* children to research *with* and *by* children

Participatory research is grounded in the profoundly democratic view that research can be conducted by ordinary people, rather than only by an elite group of specialists. The call to action in participatory research can be traced back to the works of critical theorists such as Freire (2000/1970) and Giroux (1983, 1989) who worked with oppressed, disempowered and underprivileged community group members to research their own lives, often to establish interventions that would bring about change to improve their lives collectively. In some respects, participatory research has much in common with action research, in that it aims to bring about change through participants' active engagement in the research process. However, participatory research as conceived by Freire in Latin America – and this legacy continues worldwide – is often more politically motivated than some action research, with the express intent of empowering groups of people whose voices are under-represented in research, including, for example, young children, elderly participants, people living with disability and people living with social or economic disadvantage. This agenda for change means that participatory research is often practical and dialogic, based on generating knowledge with participants, rather than extracting knowledge from them. Through dialogue, reflection and action, the intention is to transform lives for the better, by bringing about greater self-awareness through involvement in research that acts as a catalyst for change.

Participatory research lends itself particularly, but not exclusively, to qualitative enquiry, as it requires an epistemological and methodological framing that recognizes the significance, usefulness and relevance of involving research participants as equal partners in the production of knowledge, and foregrounds the unique insights they offer into their lives and communities. The defining characteristic of participatory research is therefore more about the degree and nature of participants' engagement in a study and its outcomes, rather than about using distinct research methods. The design of participatory research is pragmatic – each study is unique and is planned in dialogue with research partners.

People who are new to research need to feel comfortable with the methods chosen, and there is a tendency for participatory researchers to opt for creative approaches, such as arts-based, game-based and visual methods. Often, participatory research involves a process of mentoring, where experienced researchers work with new researchers to offer training in specific data-collection techniques and ethics, so that participants who are new to research can try out and discuss different approaches (Flewitt et al., 2018). During this time, researchers can get to know participants' interests and 'cultures of communication' (Christensen and James 2017). In early childhood research, for example, researchers pay attention to the ways in which children communicate their thoughts, views and intentions. This involves attending to children's language use, their silent ways of interacting and conveying meaning through actions, and gradually piecing together 'a picture of the social interactions and the connections between people. Through getting to know about different codes of conduct and communication [researchers can learn] how to behave and interact with and among children' (Christensen 1999: 77–8). By first attending to children's cultures of communication, researchers can begin to enter into meaningful dialogue with them, and the ensuing dialogue can be highly productive, potentially leading to the development of trusting researcher–participant relations and innovative methods for research with young children that are in tune with the participating children's ways of being.

Researching *with* children is a more recent development in the wider field of participatory research, reflecting a new phase in theorizing childhood and valuing children's perspectives that emerged in the new sociology of childhood and in global discourses of children's rights as encapsulated in the UNCRC (see Chapter 1, this volume), which recognizes children as having the 'equal and inalienable rights of all members of the human family' (UN 1989: 3). UNCRC and the new sociology of childhood have helped to establish children's right to represent their own views first-hand, rather than have their views represented by adult proxy, and this right is becoming more securely embedded in early childhood research.

Debates in the sociology of childhood have further emphasized the need to value children for who they are, as well as the adults they will one day become, and promote the importance of viewing children as both 'beings' and 'becomings' who have the right to shape both their present and future lives:

> The 'being and becoming' discourse extends the notion of agency offered by the 'being' discourse to consider the child as a social actor constructing his or her everyday life and the world around them, both in the present and the future. This perspective invites researchers and practitioners to consider what children say in relation to being and becoming agents in the world. (Uprichard 2008: 311)

UNCRC does not simply promote the need to respect children's views on all aspects of their lives (at home, in school, in policy-making, etc.) but is a legally binding obligation (Lundy 2007). Recently, children's rights to equality and empowerment have been more fully recognized in the UN 2030 agenda for sustainable development, which includes children as change agents in a transformative social agenda (United Nations 2015).

These universal principles and theorizations of children as active, agentic and knowledgeable have helped to recalibrate the role of young children in research. In participatory research, children are viewed as social actors who can offer unique and highly valuable insights into their own experiences and viewpoints on the diverse worlds in which they live (e.g. Carr 2000; Clark 2017; Corsaro 2017; Levine and New 2008; Scott 2008). Child researchers 'observe with different eyes, ask different questions – they ask questions that adults do not even think of' (Kellett 2005: 8), and make an original and highly valuable contribution to knowledge. Thomas (2017) notes the paradigm shift from research *on* children to research *with* children and the beginnings of a further shift to research *by* children, but argues that the future for children in research depends partly on how children are positioned politically in society more widely.

Participatory research with children has over recent years begun to reap rich insights into the diversity of children's experiences of childhood within and across societies and cultures, in cities (Christensen and O'Brien 2003; Derr, Corona and Gülgönen 2019) and rural areas (Powell, Taylor and Smith 2013; Riley 2009), and among children living in care (McEvoy and Smith

2011), children living with disability (Gray and Winter 2011; Wickenden and Kembhavi-Tam 2014), children living in the global South (Ansell et al. 2012; De Lange et al. 2012; Kumpulainen et al. 2016) and unaccompanied migrant children (Hopkins and Hill 2008). However, conducting research with young participants raises significant practical and methodological challenges, which champions of participatory work may sometimes gloss over (Arnott, Grogan and Duncan 2016).

Children's participation in different research stages

Morrow (2008) argues that children's participation in research has been plagued with misunderstanding, with researchers sometimes claiming to have conducted participatory research, when children's contributions have been tokenistic, and their involvement has been largely passive rather than active. Over past decades, various attempts have been made to clarify the gap between participatory research that is tokenistic and participatory research that promotes more empowered roles for children to fulfil. Hart's (1992) 'ladder of children's participation'[1] sets out eight levels of children's involvement, where the first three rungs on the ladder are described as non-participation and 'higher' rungs reflect increasing degrees of child involvement:

1. Manipulation (where children do what adults ask them to, and adults use some of their ideas without involving them in decisions);

2. Decoration (where children take part in a research event but are not aware of the issues);

3. Tokenism (children are asked their views on an issue but have no choice in how they express their views);

---

[1] Hart's 1992 model is adapted from Arnstein's (1969) 'Eight rungs on the ladder of citizen participation', designed to reflect the extent of adult citizens' power in urban planning processes.

4. Assigned but informed (where adults decide a topic and respect children's view and right to volunteer to take part);

5. Consulted and informed (where the project is designed and run by adults, with children consulted as part of the research process);

6. Adult-initiated shared decisions (adults choose the issue but children are involved at all planning stages and decision-making);

7. Child-initiated and directed (where children decide the topic and design a study, supported by adults);

8. Child-initiated shared decisions with adults (where children decide on the issue, set up a project, and *invite* adults to join them in decision-making).

Many researchers have found Hart's model helpful to evaluate the authenticity of children's participation when designing participatory research and to recognize the false impression of participation featured in, for example, items 1 to 3 above. However, others have critiqued Hart's ladder, suggesting that its hierarchical structure implies that 'best' practice is situated on the topmost rung (i.e. full participation as indicated on rung 8), whereas children's participation may justifiably vary depending on the research aims and the specific context and circumstances of a study. Adhering strictly to the belief that participatory research should always be child-initiated could lead to the unintended consequence that 'discourses of "participation" risk becoming tyrannous in research involving children' (Gallacher and Gallagher 2008: 501).

Shier (2001) offers an alternative five-stage model of 'pathways to participation', which focuses on adults' commitment to empowering children, rising from lesser to greater levels of child participation. Each level of Shier's model contains objectives that help researchers to evaluate the openings, opportunities and obligations offered by their study design:

1. Children are listened to.

2. Children are supported in expressing their views.

3. Children's views are taken into account.

4. Children are involved in decision-making processes.
5. Children share power and responsibility for decision-making.

(Shier 2001: 110)

As with Hart's model, some have found Shier's participation structure useful, whereas others have critiqued its failure to acknowledge that research decision-making is a dynamic process that inevitably involves some degree of power negotiation. Shier's model has also been critiqued for focusing on what happens *to* children in research rather than prioritizing children's active role and status in research, and for failing to adequately theorize children's participation (see Kirby and Gibbs 2006). To help guide participatory research design, Stephenson (2009) developed helpful 'checking questions' that are most useful to work with to ensure that children's perspectives are foregrounded:

- Have I begun with children's thoughts?
- How can the ideas of children be included at this stage?
- What are the assumptions?
- What questions might a child ask?
- How can children engage with this topic in a way that interests them?
- How can I avoid children giving me the answer they think I want?
- How can I ensure children's own agenda is minimally disrupted?
- What are the power dynamics in this data-generating situation?
- How open am I to following the children's lead?

(Stephenson 2009: 99)

In the early planning and research design phases, these questions and models can help researchers to think through the varying degrees of children's participation, with children taking the leading role in all research stages at one end of the spectrum and children informing research that is designed and carried out by adults at the other end. Most participatory research studies fall somewhere between these extremes, depending on the research aims, but the defining characteristic of participatory research is that children are recognized as experts in their own lives, that they are enabled to express their views in ways of their choosing, and their views are prioritized. This shift in approach necessitates a fundamental repositioning of research relationships, and calls into question the role of the academic researcher and participants in participatory research.

Role of the researcher and building trusting research relationships

A core aim in participatory research is to enable participants to be more active and powerful in research, to validate their knowledge about their own lives, and to bring about change for the better in their lives through their use of that knowledge. The role of the academic researcher is therefore fundamentally changed from being in control of the research process to being a facilitator, an enabler and a catalyst for change:

> The essence of participatory research, as its name suggests, is participation, the equal control of the research by both participants and researchers and the movement towards change through empowerment. (Cohen, Manion and Morrison 2011: 38)

Regardless of how inclusive the design of a participatory study is, researchers need to be thoughtful and critically reflexive in relation to issues of power, agency and voice. Researchers must also remember that adopting a participatory approach does not mean that the findings will necessarily be of better quality than those of non-participatory studies (Gallacher and Gallagher 2008), but that they will offer important and novel insights that could lead to innovatory change on the ground. Pascal and Bertram (2012) advise that participatory research requires researchers to develop a world view where reflection (phronesis, that is, drawing on the wisdom of experience) and collaborative action (praxis, that is, theorizing practice) are 'immersed within a much more astute awareness about power (politics) and a sharpened focus on values (ethics) in all of our thinking and actions' (p. 280). They return to Freire's (2000/1970) call for reflection on, and in, human action and argue for the need for a 'praxeological' world view for contemporary early childhood research:

> Praxeology leads not to the singularity and comparative hierarchy of 'best' practice models but promotes Goodman's (2001) notion of 'wise practice', that is, a selection of professional responses which are considered, flexible and chosen as appropriate to context. (Pascal and Bertram 2012: 481)

Refocusing the participatory research lens on praxis has two main objectives: to enable participants to produce knowledge and actions that are useful to them and to empower participants to seek social transformation by using the new knowledge constructed through their involvement in research. This involves 'outsiders' (researchers) and 'insiders' (children) working together to co-produce new knowledge (Tangen 2008: 160), with the quality of the knowledge produced often dependent on the levels of rapport, trust and confidence that are built between researchers and child participants, so that children's unique insights into their own lives can flourish in an ethical, democratic and dialogic research environment (Clark and Moss 2001; Flewitt et al. 2018).

Despite these laudable aims, breaking down the inevitable power imbalances between adults and children is not straightforward. Children who have become used to the expectations of school and early education environments may feel they have no choice other than to do what is expected of them, and may feel in some way obliged to give a 'right' answer to all questions that adults ask them, in what Gallacher and Gallagher (2008: 506) refer to as 'schooled docility'. Children may also feel compelled to participate in research through their parents' assent. Research Example 4.1 illustrates a novel approach where the researchers Rachel Levy and Philippa Thompson (2015) circumnavigated the impact of an adult researcher on how young children express their views by creating 'buddy partnerships' between younger and older children.

Research Example 4.1: Creating 'buddy partnerships' between younger and older children in participatory research

In response to a call from local government to investigate boys' underachievement in reading within parts of a city in the north of England, Rachel Levy and Philippa Thompson (2015) set out to investigate the attitude of boys between five and six years of age towards reading, including factors that promoted their engagement with reading and factors that put them off. The researchers chose to design their study methodology around 'reading buddy' partnerships, a technique which has been used extensively in schools to encourage children to enjoy shared reading. Twelve 11- to 12-year-old boys with 'core' reading ability were recruited from a local secondary school, along with twelve 5- to 6-year-old boys with 'core' reading ability from three local 'feeder' primary schools (four boys in each school). The boys were organized into pairs and where possible each eleven- to twelve-year-old boy was paired with a five- to six-year-old boy from his own primary school.

The researchers first met with the older boys and explained that they would each be paired with a younger 'buddy' in a research dyad, and that each dyad would develop material towards the creation of an information DVD to help teachers and parents understand what factors influenced the boys' reading engagement. The researchers subsequently met the five- to six-year-olds, and explained the project and the reading buddy partnerships to them. An event was then held for all the participants to get to know each other and learn more about the research project, and subsequently, each pair met on two occasions to interview each other about their experiences of reading, and to create material for the DVD.

This research design led to the younger and older children working together in order to create films for inclusion on the final DVD, in activities that were often directed by the eleven- to twelve-year-olds. The older boys bore the main responsibility for nurturing relationships with the younger boys, and both age groups carried out aspects of the research, including older and younger children interviewing each other about their experiences of learning to read.

This buddying technique meant that there was more common ground between the interviewer and the interviewee than there would have been if the adult researchers had interviewed the children.

The goal of making a DVD gave each dyad a strong focus: the older boys were taught how to use flip cameras, so they could use them independently and teach the younger boys if necessary. The children were encouraged to choose what they wanted to include in the DVD, but the researchers suggested some things they might consider, including extracts from their interviews about their experiences of learning to read; suggestions for printed and digital texts that other children might enjoy reading or have read to them; video clips of children sharing books they like; and information for teachers about what they enjoy and what puts them off reading. Once the children had completed two 'buddy' sessions together, the researchers edited the flip camera footage and collated the film into one information DVD. All participants, their parents and teachers were then invited to a celebration event at the end of the study, where the DVD was shown.

The researchers facilitated and observed each buddy meeting, and noted how the relationships the older boys built with the younger boys were central to the gathering of rich data. They identified three broad themes that sustained meaningful relationships: (1) *shared understanding* built on shared interests (such as sports, food and jokes) and shared understanding of what it is like to be a primary school child learning to read; (2) *creating comfortable environments*, with older boys often steering the younger boys away from desk-based reading and towards 'comfy corners' where the buddies could feel more relaxed – these comfortable environments prompted playfulness in both older and younger boys, and this playful attitude in turn led to rich data from the younger boys; and (3) using *communication strategies* effectively to prompt depth of dialogue with their partners. From video recordings of the buddies' interaction, Levy and Thompson noted the older boys used techniques such as leading questions, gesture and prompts in order to encourage the younger boys to talk in more depth about their perceptions of reading. Although the adult researchers carried ultimate responsibility for the design and implementation of this particular project, Levy and Thompson conclude that as adults they could not have replicated the kinds of relationship forged between the older and younger boys.

In summary, this study found that using buddy partnerships between older and younger peers was a highly effective method to elicit young and older children's views. However, the success of this technique was highly dependent on the children cultivating strong relationships throughout the duration of the project. As Waller and Bitou (2011) assert, it is not the tools themselves that enable participation when working with young children, but the research design and the relationships that lead to real participation and engagement.

Despite the shift in participatory research towards valuing the unique insights that child researchers can offer, there is still a persistent belief in many societies and academic disciplines that children, especially young children and infants, do not have the intellectual capacity to understand the concepts that frame research, the communicative capacity to convey their ideas, and/or they may not have the social skills and experiential knowledge needed to carry out systematic, sceptical and ethical research (Christensen and James 2017). This raises the fundamental issue of how children's competence is conceptualized in research, and in societies and cultures more widely.

Conceptualizing child competence

Danby and Farrell (2004) suggest that decades of psychology research have contributed to child competence being understood as a developmental learning process, where children are positioned on an age-related continuum, starting out as 'underdeveloped' and gradually progressing towards being 'more developed'. This perspective has led to child competence being valued for what it might become, rather than for what it is, and encourages a view of children as 'not grown up and thus *not something* rather than *something*' (Waksler 1991: 63, italics in original). The wording of UNCRC (1989) Article 12[2] reflects this age-related perspective of child competence by specifying that children's views should be 'given due weight in accordance with the age and maturity of the child'. Article 12 casts doubt on child competence by specifying that only children who are 'capable of forming his or her own views' have 'the right to express those views freely in all matters affecting the child'. This phrasing leaves a child's rights open to adult (mis)interpretation and can be used to justify the kinds of tokenistic child consultation discussed earlier, rather than to ensure children's right to autonomous and respectful inclusion in decisions about their lives (Horgan 2017). However, UNCRC (1989) must be viewed in its entirety, and aspects that may be missing or open to misinterpretation in Article 12 can be better understood in the light of other relevant provisions, for example, Article 2 (non-discrimination), Article 3 (best interests), Article 5 (right to guidance), Article 13 (right to seek, receive and impart information), and Article 19 (protection from abuse) (see Lundy 2007).

Perceptions of child (in)competence have generated debate about whether specific research methods are needed for participatory research with children, as distinct from participatory research with adults. Christensen and James (2017) argue that in any participatory research study, the methods chosen arise through dialogue between participants, usually facilitated by experienced researchers, so the term 'participant-centred' or 'person-centred' methods may be more appropriate than 'child-centred' methods (see also Waite, Boyask and Lawson 2010). This does not mean to imply that children should necessarily undertake the same methods as adults, but that researchers should be wary of underestimating child competence

---

[2]The full text of UNCRC (1989) Article 12 is:

1. States Parties shall assure to the child who is capable of forming his or her own views the right to express those views freely in all matters affecting the child, the views of the child being given due weight in accordance with the age and maturity of the child.

2. For this purpose, the child shall in particular be provided the opportunity to be heard in any judicial and administrative proceedings affecting the child, the views of the child being given due weight in accordance with the age and maturity of the child.

and plan research that respects children's strengths and preferred modes of communication. Whatever the participant age range, the essence of participatory research lies in getting to know participants' preferred ways of communicating through a process of dialogue and mentoring. As Kellett (2005: 10) suggests regarding the skills and attributes needed to undertake research:

> It soon becomes apparent that these attributes are not necessarily synonymous with being an adult, they are synonymous with being a researcher, and most researchers have undergone some form of training. Many, perhaps most, adults would not be able to undertake research without training. It would appear, therefore, that a barrier to empowering children as researchers is not their lack of adult status but their lack of research skills. So why not teach them?

Brooker (2011) further reminds us of the interdependent relationship between competence and interest, suggesting that in any endeavour, once children's interest is aroused in topics of their own choosing, adults can support them in acquiring the knowledge and skills to develop the necessary competence to pursue their interest – as exemplified in Research Example 4.1.

A particular challenge for participatory research with children is ensuring that research decisions are made *with* children and not *for* them, and this includes their choice of preferred research methods. This requires researchers to recognize and attempt to rebalance the inevitable power asymmetry between adults and children that prevails in almost all cultures. Children's lives are enmeshed in networks of power relations long before they take part in research, for example, in their peer relationships, family environments, in school and in care. Most research with children is conducted in institutional settings, such as in school, that is, in a place which Thomas (2017: 170) describes as 'in many ways the quintessential site for modern children's positioning and the systemic denial of their agency'. In school, children are obliged to be present; their movements are constrained; they are accustomed to being assessed; and their behaviours are strictly regulated and monitored. A central pivot for all participatory research is the extent to which the participants think that their own views matter and will be taken note of. A key challenge for researchers is therefore to ensure that participating children know that they have a voice that will be heard, respected and acted upon.

Problematizing child voice

The terms 'child voice' or 'pupil voice' will be familiar to readers, but these simple words mask the profound shifts that are needed to ensure that children's views are given due weight and have influence at local and societal level. Relationships of power are central to the performance of voice, but power relations are complex and dynamic (Arnot and Reay 2007) – the balance of power may constantly shift, and research participants can wield power by opting for silence, absence or dissent. Participatory research therefore requires a commitment to responsible ethical practice on the part of both researchers and participants. Lundy (2007) suggests participatory research requires a fundamental reframing of child–adult relations, where researchers should reflect on the spaces and opportunities children have to voice their views, which audiences listen, and what influence children's views have in terms of follow-up action.

The linguistic anthropologist Dell Hymes (1996) suggests that the concept of 'voice' encompasses both the *'freedom to develop a voice worth hearing'* and *'freedom to have one's voice heard'* (p. 64), and this applies to people of any age. However, as Maybin (2013: 383) points out, 'such freedoms are not as straightforward as they might at first sight appear'. With regard to child voice, these two aspects reflect how children are positioned in society, how their competence is perceived and how their views are valued depending not only on factors that define them as individuals (their age, gender, ethnicity, language competence, etc.) but also on the situation where their views are voiced (school, home, community, etc.), the relationships of power between adults and children that prevail in different social situations, and the nature and purpose of the interaction.

The notion of 'freedom to develop a voice worth hearing' suggests that a crucial phase in participatory research involves researchers attuning themselves to participants' 'ways of speaking' (Hymes 1996: 26) as well as listening, reading, writing, drawing and other modes of action. It is therefore essential to create a research 'space in which children are encouraged to express their views' (Lundy 2007: 933) – a space where children feel safe, included, valued and free to express their own views and perspectives – however unpalatable these may risk being. Gutiérrez (2008) refers to the liberatory capacity of creating 'third spaces', which can be literal – a physical research meeting place that is free of the constraints of a child's home or school, such as an after-school club for school-aged children. Or third spaces can be metaphorical spaces where meanings are always negotiated, and where knowledge, skills and dispositions are co-constructed.

When working with child participants, researchers need to allow time to get to know the cultures of communication and create dialogic spaces where they can gain children's trust, so children feel ready and able to express their views without fear of correction, ridicule or reprisal. Yet accomplishing this is far from straightforward, and many researchers working with infants and young children have encountered troubling dilemmas when trying to put this vision for participatory research into practice. In Research Example 4.2, we showcase the *Infants' Lives in Childcare* study, led by Jennifer Sumsion and colleagues in Australia between 2008 and 2011. In this study, the researchers adopted what they refer to as 'mosaic methodology' (Sumsion and Goodfellow 2012: 315), which they derived from the 'Mosaic approach' (Clark 2005; Clark and Moss 2001) to investigate zero- to eighteen-month-old infants' perspectives on their day-care environments in Australia (see Goodfellow et al. 2011; Sumsion et al. 2011; Sumsion and Goodfellow 2012).

Research Example 4.2: Working in participatory ways with infants

Increasing numbers of infants spend extended periods of time in day-care settings, at a time in their lives when they are highly sensitive to positive and negative experiences. Yet very few studies have investigated infants' perspectives on their daily lives in care, possibly due to the challenges of researching the lives of children who may not yet be able to express their views in words. In the *Infants' Lives in Childcare* project, Jennifer Sumsion and colleagues conducted a series of case studies of infants in diverse Australian day-care settings to investigate how infants participate as social actors in group environments. Citing Dewey (1938: 68) – 'Observation alone is not enough. We have to understand the significance of what we see, hear, and touch' – Sumsion and colleagues crafted a mosaic of methods (Clark 2005, 2017) and theoretical lenses to help them understand infants' perspectives on their daily lives in group childcare. Their methodological mosaic included multiple data sources – written documentation (unstructured observations, reflective field notes, time-use diaries, etc.); visual records (video recordings, 'baby cams', digital photographs, etc.); standardized measures (language and temperament assessment scales); parent questionnaire; and 'conversational interviews' with parents and educators (see Sumsion et al. 2008–11). Sumsion et al. (2011) argue that the metaphor of a mosaic enabled them to collate information from diverse theoretical, philosophical and disciplinary sources, and from researcher, educator, parental and child perspectives. Creating a dialogue between these often very different insights helped to unsettle and dislodge their own expert and adult views, and enabled them to be more receptive to infants' perspectives.

The long-term study has been written up in a series of papers (e.g. Goodfellow et al. 2011; Sumsion et al. 2011; Elwick and Sumsion 2013; Elwick, Bradley and Sumsion 2014). Here, we focus on one observational participatory approach the team used, which they describe as 'looking and listening-in' (Sumsion and Goodfellow 2012) and which was adopted to try to understand the experience of fourteen-month-old Charlie (pseudonym), during ten research visits made to his family day-care setting over an eight-week period. Close analysis of ten hours of video footage revealed that Charlie spent a lot of time 'looking and listening-in' to others' activities. The team decided to adopt Charlie's 'looking and listening-in' technique to their own analysis of his behaviours. They began by making a fifteen minute edited video featuring a carefully chosen selection of Charlie's 'looking and listening-in' episodes, viewed this with Charlie's carer and mother, and constructed co-narratives from the different interpretations of these episodes. They then selected short extracts for transcription and fine-grained analysis, and considered these in light of the mother's and carer's perspectives, their own interpretations and sociocultural theories of participation. Through this process, they came to realize that Charlie's 'looking and listening in' embodied the kind of focused attention to the activities of adults and other children that often precedes joining in others' activities. Through their own 'looking and listening in', they 'began to appreciate the fine-grained detail of fleeting, yet critical, moments that otherwise may have been impossible to see' (ibid: 324). Furthermore, their use of diverse theoretical frames sensitized them to possible meanings in his actions that may not have occurred to them had they limited themselves to a single perspective.

Although Sumsion and Goodfellow doubt that they will ever confidently be able to claim that their work accurately represents Charlie's experience of day care, they suggest that reproducing Charlie's 'looking and listening-in' strategy in their own analytic approach heightened their appreciation of the sophisticated cognitive and social capacities and intentional, strategic behaviours that infants bring to their day-care settings, and highlighted the possibility that these strategies may often pass unnoticed.

Some might argue that while this approach respects the child's 'voice', in that the research team valued the modes Charlie used to convey his interest in activities around him, and followed his lead in their research design, it does not fully meet the criteria for participatory research. The research team defend their approach by suggesting that 'looking and listening in' may be one of many ways to explore possibilities for participatory research with very young children. As readers, you might compare this approach to the questions posed by Stephenson 2009, mentioned above, and gauge your own views on this debate.

Hymes's (1996) concept of *'freedom to have one's voice heard'* relates to the sociocultural dynamics that shape the ideas children express and the different responses they experience. Research has traditionally been associated with gaining participants' perspectives through language, but as Research Example 4.2 evidences, there are multiple ways in which views can be expressed, and it is essential to listen actively and respectfully to children by recognizing 'the many ways in which children skilfully communicate their realities to us' (Pascal and Bertram 2009: 254).

Many researchers have found that children are enthused by practical research activities and have engaged with Malaguzzi's (see Edwards, Gandini and Forman 2011) notion of the 'hundred languages of children' to encourage young children to express their views, using child-led photography and drawings (e.g. Barker and Weller 2003; Dockett and Perry 2005; Einarsdóttir 2007), or by introducing a 'third party' into their fieldwork, such as glove puppets (e.g. Levy, 2011; Robinson and Nurmsoo, 2009) in attempts to mitigate the power imbalance in adult/child interaction. When working with school children with emerging writing skills, participatory methods have successfully included child diaries, oral and written stories and spider diagrams (e.g. Barker and Weller 2003; Punch 2002). As mentioned by Sumsion and colleagues in Research Example 4.2, a more expansive repertoire of approaches that can be developed with children in participatory research is suggested by the 'Mosaic approach' (Clark and Moss 2001; Clark 2005), which promotes 'a multi-method, polyvocal approach that brings together different perspectives in order to create *with* children an image of their worlds' (Clark 2017: 17). The Mosaic approach has been used in participatory research in the global North and South (e.g. Elwick et al. 2014; Waller 2014) with researchers and young participants tailoring methods to their own research aims and cultures of communication, using a wide range of data-collection techniques such as drawing and mapping exercises, child-led tours, role play exercises, photographs and book-making, alongside more traditional approaches such as observations and interviews.

Communication is a complex activity that is shaped by many personal, social and cultural factors; what a child expresses is influenced by the nature of the activity they are engaged in, the questions they are asked, and by their perception of what is expected of them in the research and what is usually expected of them in the physical location where the research is being conducted. It can therefore be helpful in the early stages of the research process to devise a series of activities to explore child participants' cultures of communication (Christensen 1999), and to observe how groups of children or individuals express their views through different modes, with a view to trying out research approaches with which they may feel more comfortable (Flewitt et al. 2018). Some children may be keen to learn about traditional research methods, such as questionnaires and interviews, but these require high levels of literacy and may not always be accessible for younger children, so a multi-method approach with combinations of creative, visual methodologies may be more appealing to some young participants. Rather than imposing particular methods on children, researchers can devise a series of exploratory activities where children can try out different methods, such as drawing, photography, video diaries and oral stories, and where they can contribute their own innovative ideas about possible methods. Having spent time exploring different approaches, participants can decide which methods they feel most comfortable with and would prefer to use, and consult with researchers regarding how to set about using them. Creative or visual methods not only tend to be effective with young participants but can also help to unlock the views of adult participants (see Reavey 2011). Devising an activity-based early phase of the research process can enable children of all ages to develop the self-belief and confidence to know they truly have a voice worth hearing, that they have choices in how they would prefer to express their voice, and that their voice will be heard.

Building influence into the impact of participatory research

Researchers committed to children's full participation in research have a responsibility to promote children's involvement in disseminating research findings and making choices about the impact of their work, yet children are often excluded from research write-ups and impact events and outputs. Porter et al. (2010) also caution that researchers must ensure that young researchers have realistic expectations about the potential impact of the research they are involved in, so they do not feel that their work is 'ignored ... spurned, ridiculed or accused of arrogance' (p. 225). There are many different audiences that researchers can engage with: the academic research community; local, national and international policymakers; education, health and care practitioners; charitable organizations that work with children; families and parents; and, last but by no means least, children. There is a growing body of exemplary research where children have been actively engaged in the dissemination of participatory research and have benefited from its impact. In Research Example 4.3, we present two brief and very different examples of participatory research conducted in Northern Ireland and sub-Saharan Africa, which had very different levels of impact.

Research Example 4.3: Participatory research and impact

Working with thirty-six preschool-aged children with and without a known disability in a participatory research project in Northern Ireland, Colette Gray and Eileen Winter (2011) enabled the children to choose their own research question: 'What do we like the most and what least about our school?' The participating children were involved at all stages of research decision-making including the dissemination stage, where the decision was arrived at to include the research in the end-of-summer-term celebration events. Working across four settings, children and teaching staff collated and presented the children's research photographs and drawings as a wall collage depicting the good things that they liked in their setting. Children in one setting also acted out various stages of the research process as a way to inform parents about their involvement. This enabled the children to show ownership of their work, and to see that their choices were valued and respected. It also helped to change adult perceptions of their competence and agency, and enabled the researchers to gain insights into the children's understanding of the research process. The children's work identifying things they did not like brought about practical changes, such as 'smelly bins' being replaced by new bins with tight-fitting lids, more outings for children and uninterrupted playtime.

Although the next participatory study example to illustrate impact that is of benefit to children was conducted with older children (aged around twelve years) on the topic of sex education, we include it here as the research design could inspire early childhood education researchers, particularly when working on sensitive topics and in contexts where children may not be used to their perspectives being given centre stage. The study reported here, conducted by Colleen

McLaughlin and colleagues (McLaughlin et al. 2015), was designed as participatory action research (Chambers 1994; Gaventa and Cornwall 2006), where researchers and participants collaborated to improve pedagogical approaches to sex, HIV and AIDS education in primary schools in Africa. The three-year study comprised two phases: in the first phase various interactive methodologies were trialled to access children's voices in eight schools in three sub-Saharan African countries (South Africa, Kenya and Tanzania) (McLaughlin et al. 2015). A key finding in this phase was children's preference to integrate their everyday knowledge – things they learnt from friends, popular culture and through observation of their communities – with knowledge they acquired in school. This was clearly a highly sensitive topic, so the researchers sought ways to include adults as advocates who could bring children's voices from the periphery to the centre. After consultation with teachers and head teachers, community stakeholders and parents, the research team identified the power of sustained intergenerational dialogue to address complex sociocultural problems. In phase two of the project, the researchers placed children at the centre of developing a novel curriculum in sixteen primary schools in the original three countries, plus Ghana, Swaziland and Botswana. The research team brought together 'curriculum development groups' comprising teachers, pupils, community members and representatives of NGOs and/or education departments. As a result of this study, which centred on promoting and facilitating dialogue between pupils, teachers and community stakeholders, the children's perspectives were included in curriculum planning about what should be taught and how, so their education on this highly sensitive topic resonated with their everyday experience while also addressing social, cultural and religious sensibilities.

Critiques of participatory research

Despite its laudable goals, participatory research has been critiqued for failing to achieve its objectives to bring about change, for underestimating the inevitable power imbalances between researchers and participants, for lacking a clear method of data collection and analysis and for being under-theorized (for further discussion, see Cohen, Manion and Morrison 2011).

In participatory research with young children, reservations have been expressed about the impact of participatory research on children's lives (Tisdall and Davis 2004), and concerns have been raised about the underrepresentation of some children in participatory studies, including those with disabilities (Gray and Winter 2011). Reason and Bradbury (2008) point to the paradox that participatory research, for all its democratic and egalitarian aims, still requires someone to take the initiative to begin a project and that someone will almost inevitably be a member of a privileged, educated group who has 'time, skill and commitment' (p. 324). There seems little doubt that participatory research with children is still in its infancy and may be racked with uncertainty, as Gallacher and Gallagher (2008: 513) attest:

> We do not believe that participatory techniques are inherently any better, or worse, than any other research method. They are not objectively 'right': an epistemological and ethical panacea. For us, what matters is not so much the methods used, but the ways and the spirit in which they are used: the methodological *attitude* taken. Good research practice cannot be reduced to ingenious techniques, planned in advance and carefully applied. Research is inherently unpredictable: the best laid plans are liable to go awry.

We therefore suggest that a key facet of participatory research involves tuning in to children's cultures of communication, creating opportunities for dialogue between children, and building trusting relationships with them. This in turn can have a positive impact on the relationships between children and adults in their communities. It is essential to follow children's lead, to be open and flexible, and to be able and willing to improvise throughout the research process in response to children's perspectives.

Concluding thoughts

Participatory research with children is a branch of research methodology that is still in its early stages of development. The term has been used to describe a broad expanse of approaches, ranging from dialogic methodologies to involving children in all stages of the research process, including identifying an issue, choosing a research question, selecting the research methods, gathering and analysing the data, disseminating the findings and children benefitting from research impact. Despite this diversity, participatory approaches are all united in their aim to listen to and to *hear* children's voices, in the belief that early childhood research 'should and could be more democratic, participatory, empowering and should also be deeply ethical and political in its orientation' (Pascal and Bertram 2012: 479).

As this field of research develops, there needs to be greater reflection on and synergy between theorization, methodology and research methods, with sustained problematization of the notion of 'voice' as a multifaceted and politically charged concept. Although it may not be possible to *fully* understand children's perspectives about their own lives and experiences, participatory research enables us confidently to evidence children's social, communicative, cognitive and ethical competences, and this evidence can in turn help to challenge and redress the power imbalance that prevails between adults and children not only in non-participatory research but in wider society more generally.

Suggestions for further reading

Christensen, P., and James, A. (2017). *Research with Children: Perspectives and Practices* (3rd edn). Abingdon and New York: Routledge.

Clark, A. (2017). *Listening to Young Children* (3rd expanded edn). London and Philadelphia: Jessica Kingsley Publishers.

Harcourt, D., Perry, B. and Waller, T. (Eds.) (2011). *Researching Young Children's Perspectives: Debating the Ethics and Dilemmas of Educational Research with Children*. London and New York: Sage.

Tangen, R. (2008). Listening to children's voices in educational research: Some theoretical and methodological problems. *European Journal of Special Needs Education* 23 (2): 157–66.

CHAPTER FIVE

Participatory Research Approaches with Adults

Building on Chapter 4 and participatory research with children, in this chapter, we discuss the use of participatory research approaches with *adults* as key stakeholders in early childhood education. We begin by considering the transformative potential of participatory research with adults, and we set out exemplars of participatory practices with adults in the inquiry process. Throughout the chapter, we focus on the potential of participatory research with adult participants for galvanizing transformative change at the level of practice, policy and wider society. The discussion illustrates the complex relationships that often underpin participation as negotiated by the researcher, participants and by organizations that commission and fund research. We also consider the potential strengths and challenges when employing a participatory methodology in engendering a policy-driven, social advocacy agenda to raise the profile of early childhood education for the benefit of young children.

Participatory research as transformative

Participatory research is a common methodology often adopted in education and the wider social sciences. It is based on the principle that participants in a study, usually key stakeholders in the field of enquiry, have direct knowledge and experience of a particular phenomenon or issue and should have greater authority in the inquiry process than others (see Chapter 4 for discussion of the origins of participatory research). The phrase 'participatory research' with adults has taken on varied forms and guises across different disciplines. Some familiar labels include participatory action research (PAR) (Guishard 2009), community-based participatory research (CBPR) (Pontes Ferreira and Gendron 2011), participatory rural appraisal (PRA) (Chambers 1994) and participatory activist research (Hunter, Emerald and Gregory 2013). A shared tenet to these approaches is essentially a method or way of working which results in participants having a voice in shaping the research concerning them, from defining the research questions to generating data, working through the analysis and, where appropriate, having influence over the way the results are used and disseminated.

Participatory methodology goes beyond traditional methods in recognizing participants' autonomy and influence over the research process. In an early article, Pratt and Loizos (1992) describe the methodology as a philosophical approach, in guiding how research is conducted in ways that prioritize the participants' close involvement with the researcher:

> The idea of participation is more an overall guiding philosophy of how to proceed than a selection of specific methods. So when people talk about participatory research, participatory monitoring and participatory evaluation, on the whole they are not discussing a self-contained set of methodologies, but a situation whereby the methods being used have included an element of strong involvement and consultation on the part of the subjects of the research. (Pratt and Loizos 1992: 9)

The idea of participation described here by Pratt and Loizos (1992) is underpinned by the belief that individuals who have first-hand experience of a given context have a right to be involved in analysing their own situation and working out how to tackle the issues they encounter. It is also informed by the notion that the perceptions and insights of individuals are key to achieving a more in-depth and meaningful understanding of the situation they are part of.

As discussed in Chapter 4, the extent and nature of participants' involvement during participatory research can vary, but the overarching drive is for the research to set in motion a social agenda and activate a desired change in a particular community or society. In this vein, participatory research has been described by some researchers as 'social research' (Bloor 2016), a 'transformative process' (Blackstock, Kelly and Horsey 2007: 726) where the inquiry can lead to significant shifts in the broader social conditions of a society 'through people coming to understand their own and others' interests, values, experiences, beliefs, and feelings, and through this understanding acting for the collective good' (p. 726).

The field of international development has a long-standing interest in participatory research with its focus on improving the lives of vulnerable populations in the global South, through a collective process of identifying problems and solutions (Holland and Blackburn 1998; Institute for Development Studies 1998; Blackburn, Chambers and Gaventa 2000). The practice of participatory research in development studies began in the 1970s, when the phrase participatory rural appraisal (PRA) was first coined to describe an approach that is primarily concerned with issues of social justice and equity, 'to enable local people to share, enhance and analyse their knowledge of life and conditions, to plan and to act' (Chambers 1994: 593). Chambers (1994) highlighted the characteristics of PRA in helping to empower individuals to free themselves from the constraints of societal impediments such as poverty and inequality, arguing that 'poor people are creative and capable, and can and should do much of their own investigation, analysis and planning; that outsiders have roles as conveners, catalysts and facilitators; that the weak and marginalized can and should be empowered' (p. 954).

Espousing a participatory approach in development research, Holland and Blackburn's (1998) early publication *Whose Voice? Participatory Research and Policy Change* was recognized as seminal for articulating a new way of presenting the realities of those who are vulnerable by advocating for their voices to be heard: 'Participation is about building partnership and ownership from the bottom up' (Blackburn, Chambers and Gaventa 2000: 1). They argue that individuals are more likely to contribute willingly to research if they have some control over how it is done, especially for those living in difficult, fragile conditions where their participation can offer a sense of empowerment in identifying their needs for themselves. Similarly, Chambers (1982) emphasizes the importance of taking a 'bottom-up' approach and the need to pay careful attention to local community knowledge and contexts when intervening in the developing world.

Importantly, the epistemology of participatory research has at its roots the work of social activists and philosophers such as Frantz Fanon (1952) and Paulo Freire (2000/1970), whose ideas are strongly associated with liberal social movements and anti-colonial crusades in the global South. Freire (2000/1970), for instance, writes powerfully about developing a critical consciousness in our interrogation of societal structures in order to disrupt the dominant social relations in which people are suppressed:

> The truth is, however, that the oppressed are not 'marginals', are not people living 'outside' society. They have always been 'inside' – inside the structure which made them 'beings for others'. The solution is not to 'integrate' them into the structure of oppression, but to transform that structure so that they can become 'beings for themselves'. (p. 74)

This drive to emancipate, revolutionize and liberate has been said to inspire much of participatory research.

Participatory action research (PAR)

A form of participatory methodology, PAR has an established history in social science inquiry. Applied to the context of education, PAR is closely aligned with but distinct from action research in that the latter has a more specific focus on addressing a problem or issue in a local educational setting in order to improve classroom practice and to enhance children's learning or the delivery of an educational service. Action research tends to have a more explicit practical focus than participatory action research, with a set of planned activities to collect data from the educator's own practice to reflect, evaluate and explore new practices. PAR, by contrast, is driven by a broader social agenda for advocacy, with an emancipatory intent to provoke new thoughts and new forms of education or schooling with a view to improving participants' overall well-being and quality of life.

PAR is underpinned by wider societal concerns and informed by the ideological premise of empowering individuals to directly influence the educational systems and communities that they operate in, to bring about new visions regarding how education might occur for the benefit of communities and society. Kemmis (2006) argues this is a necessary utopian stance towards envisioning new approaches to curricula, pedagogy and to learning and teaching, where schools become critical spaces in which students and teachers can engage in democratic citizenship within their communities and societies:

> Critical participatory action research will explore the constitution of practice in a deep, rich way, and bring to light and encourage communication about the variety of ways practices are understood, from a variety of standpoints and perspectives. It will explore themes of pressing contemporary interest, frequently in relation to contemporary social movements – themes that arise from shared perplexities, uncertainties, contradictions, conflicts and problems, and issues about contemporary educational practice, learning from and changing the (sometimes untoward) consequences of practice. (p. 471)

A hallmark of PAR is its explicit social and political focus in transforming educational communities. To this extent, PAR is often characterized as a social process (Kemmis 2006; Green et al. 2003; McIntyre 2008) where social interactions and power relationships among participants and significant others are foregrounded to better understand how new innovations about educational practice can be achieved. PAR is essentially driven by the democratic principles of collaboration and equal partnership between the researcher and participants. The focus on education as a medium of social transformation precipitates researchers to critically consider how individuals and communities can evolve and position themselves as the research allows them to reshape their environments in new or different ways. Individuals in a PAR study are not just seen as sources of information but they are respected as owners of their own knowledge, and as part of an inclusive research community. As Guishard (2009: 87) notes, 'PAR aspires to initiate transparent, democratic inquiry; that is collaboratively designed, conducted, analyzed, and disseminated in the context of equal partnerships *with* university scientists and members of disempowered groups' (italics in original).

Participatory practices with adults in early childhood research

In early childhood research, the term 'participation' is often associated with children's participation (Christensen and Prout 2002; Christensen 2004; Clark 2010; Salamon 2015). However, participatory practices involving adult stakeholders are increasingly employed as a form of advocacy to raise the status of early childhood and the crucial work of professionals in the field. It is well recognized that the 'discipline and practice of participatory, practice-led research has grown rapidly in recent years and it is now widely accepted as making an important and serious contribution to the knowledge base of early childhood' (Pascal and Bertram 2012: 479). Studies focusing on early years practitioners and teachers who are involved in participatory or praxeologic research is increasingly undertaken not only as a means of enabling participants to interrogate their practice in critical ways but to shape research as informed participants (Pascal and Bertram 2012; Formosinho and Formosinho 2012). A view strongly espoused by Pascal and Bertram (2012) and other researchers is the importance of embedding participatory methods in practice-focused early childhood research as a way of advancing and raising the visibility of the early years sector and early years professionals across the education sector.

In a study which explored the use of pedagogical documentation in an Italian early childhood education setting, adult participant stakeholders including families, professionals and the local community were invited to review and evaluate the quality and impact of different aspects of the setting's provision on the children's learning experience, and the extent to which organizational practices implemented by the early years staff helped to achieve social and educational goals. The study concluded that pedagogical documentation opened up an avenue of communication to promote the engagement and involvement of stakeholders in better supporting children's learning. Adopting a participatory approach in the study was perceived to have an important function in encouraging reflexivity among the setting's practitioners through sustained dialogues and knowledge exchange with other stakeholders in the local community. As the authors conclude:

> Indeed, documentation is not a mere collection of data and materials but also includes their analysis and interpretation by professionals. The analysis of documented activities and events stimulates professionals to identify the motivations and results of their practice and makes them aware of their own educational performance. All of this occurs within a framework of collegial discussion, where new knowledge about children's cognitive and socialization processes can be shared and new practices can be planned. (Picchio, Giandomenico and Musatti 2014: 134)

Increasingly, researchers are turning to visual and arts-based methods in research design to promote dialogic co-enquiry with both adult and child participants. Research Example 5.1 illustrates how visual participatory methods have been extended as tools for listening to early childhood education practitioners as well as to young children.

Research Example 5.1: Exploring visual, participatory methods with adults and children

Building on her participatory research with young children, Alison Clark (2011) extended the Mosaic approach to enter into dialogue with early childhood education practitioners as part of a three-year longitudinal study that involved adults and children in the design and review of two early childhood environments in England. One of these settings was a recently completed children's centre, which brought together a range of social, care and education services for children and young families. Citing Veale (2005), Clark emphasizes the importance of knowledge generation as a central tenet for participatory research with all age groups: a core principle of participatory research is the generation of knowledge (rather than its extraction) through a merging of academic with local knowledge to provide oppressed people with tools for analysing their life conditions (Veale 2005: 253).

Although the Mosaic approach was originally designed to gather and reflect on the perspectives of children aged less than five years, it is suitable for use with adults. Its firm grounding in participatory methods used in PRA means that dialogue and shared meaning making are integral to the research process. In this study, data generation was organized in three phases to enable different participant groups to bring their own unique perspectives to the research: Phase 1 focused on gathering the views of nursery practitioners; Phase 2 focused on the views of children, Sure Start practitioners and parents; Phase 3 involved workshops where children and adults shared their perspectives on the outdoor play space.

In the first phase, the nursery practitioners were invited to make a tour of the nursery environment and take photographs of things that were important to them – this could include things they felt negatively about as well as more positive aspects of provision. The practitioners then met with the researcher individually or in small groups of up to three practitioners to make a map of the environment based on their photographs. No specific guidance was given on how to design these maps, resulting in many different map designs – for example, one nursery practitioner sequenced the photographs she had taken into a long, rectangular map, another used colour coding to denote positive or negative aspects in her photographs. Whatever their format, the maps were then used as a basis for discussion in wider staff team meetings with an architect. As Clark (2011: 325) argues, these maps 'became important for knowledge mediation in which views and experiences of different participants were made visible to others'.

Clark found that working in this way helped to create a safe space where participants were comfortable sharing and exploring their own and each other's views. The visual nature of the research 'slowed down' (Prosser 2007) their professional lives so they were able to reflect deeply on the learning environment in which they worked, and adult participants found the visual modes of expression a welcome contrast to the dominant written practices of assessment and report writing that prevailed in their work.

This brief example illustrates how the Mosaic approach can be used as a person-centred methodology which foregrounds the generation of knowledge by participants of all ages, and can be used to create 'safe' research spaces that promote dialogue and 'intergenerational listening' (Clark 2011: 328).

By adopting participatory practices, researchers are fundamentally interested in how evidence and knowledge can be mobilized to bring about social and educational change. Recognizing stakeholders' autonomy and rights in contributing to the research agenda, the researcher becomes a learner and co-constructor of knowledge in the project, rather than a lead researcher; while participants become collaborators and advocates of their cause, capable of articulating their own agendas in the research (Denzin and Lincoln 2005). Researchers, and in some cases research funding organizations, see this as part of a more inclusive way of working to 'give something back' to society and achieve more direct and lasting change in the worlds of policy and practice for the benefit of young children and families. Research Example 5.2 offers a second case study of a participatory research design to help us understand this process at work.

Research Example 5.2: Participatory research with adult stakeholders in the advocacy for early childhood education

Lynn Ang undertook the project *Vital Voices for Vital Years* (Ang 2014) as part of a social advocacy endeavour to raise the profile of preschool education in Singapore and galvanize public support for the importance of early childhood education. The project was the first national study which examined the issues and challenges facing the preschool sector from the collective perspectives of leading early childhood professionals. The main motivation was to invoke systemic reforms at the level of policy and provision for young children and families. The study was driven by a research-led 'ground-up' approach in engaging the voices of key stakeholders. A participatory methodology was adopted with participants who played a central role in identifying the research agenda, shaping the research instruments and contributing to the overall inquiry process to maximize the impact of the research.

What made the research participatory?
Prior to the study, Ang elicited the views of potential participants through a scoping review with informal conversations and meetings on the relevance of the research, the appropriate design and areas of focus. An additional advisory group of early childhood professionals was set up to gain understandings of their views of the sector and key areas of concern. This provided participants and other adult stakeholders an opportunity to shape the research focus from the outset, and in turn the research questions and methodology. A mixed methods approach using individual interviews and an online questionnaire was employed. The participatory stance involved Ang working with participants to refine the research questions more effectively, which in turn maximized the relevancy of the research.

A purposive 'snowball sampling' strategy was used where participants suggested the names of others whom they regarded as important stakeholders in the sector. This resulted in a sample population that included a wide range of participant expertise and networks, which would otherwise not have been available to the study. The final list of participants comprised twenty-seven senior professionals who were leading practitioners in their field of work, including psychologists, child language therapists, child health and social services workers, preschool teachers, principals and directors of services from across the private, voluntary and public sector.

The design of the research tools was discussed at length with participant stakeholders regarding their potential accuracy and validity. Drafts of the interview schedule and questionnaire templates were drawn up through an iterative process of regular consultations, feedback and dialogue with the advisory group, participants as well as the study commissioners/funders. Participant interviews included open-ended questions such as 'what other issues do you feel should be explored as part of this research?'; 'what can be done to ensure that the research is relevant for the early childhood sector?'; and 'how else can we ensure that the study addresses the challenges that you have raised?' These open-ended questions provided opportunities for participants to extend the research agenda and to voice their personal views on the inquiry process. The researcher is responsible for building trustful relationships with participants and taking a political stand on behalf of the participant community. In the context of the study, this entailed empowering participants to take ownership of the research agenda and opening up avenues at strategic points during the research process to ensure that they had ample opportunities to raise any concerns they might have and that their voices would be heard.

How was advocacy achieved through participation?
The main aim in this project was to galvanize the views of key stakeholders in the preschool sector to engage with policymakers and the wider public in raising awareness of the importance of early childhood education. During the project's final stages, significant collaborative efforts were made between the researcher, commissioners of the research and a voluntary group of participants to generate public interest in the study through a platform of media and public engagement activities. A series of press releases were published in the local English and Mandarin newspapers to highlight the findings of the study, alongside televised reports. A cover article entitled 'A Long Road Ahead for Singapore's Early Childhood Education' was published in a special issue of a local education magazine (*Edunation* 2012) which highlighted 'the independent research has indeed awakened us from our slumber, and caused us to face reality' (p. 41). Additionally, a report in the local newspaper *Todayonline* (2012: 1) noted 'a raft of sweeping, urgent reforms to improve early childhood education' with strong advocacy to 'make preschool education free'.

In the wake of the study, questions were posed by a member of Singapore Parliament to the government regarding concerns raised by the study on the high turnover of the workforce and the need to build the capacity of preschool provision, especially in targeted local neighbourhoods where there is a higher proportion of young children and families (MCYS Parliamentary Questions 2012). The study generated a crucial response from the government, specifically the minister of state in his opening address at the 13th International Asia Pacific Early Childhood and Education Research Association (PECERA) conference where the study was described as timely and as providing useful input that would inform policy and programme development for the preschool sector. This subsequently led to the creation of a new government statutory board, the Early Childhood Development Agency (ECDA) in 2013, to oversee preschool services. The participatory nature of the study was realized not only through the project's methodological approach but in the collaborative efforts and ethos taken by the researcher to work with participants in mobilizing the research to influence public opinion and instigate advocacy for the vital role of early childhood education.

Problematizing participatory research with adults

Participatory research has several advantages in addressing social issues by recognizing the unique expertise of the people who have direct insights into the realities and phenomena that are being researched, and by prioritizing the importance of their involvement in the study as key stakeholders to ensure that their voices are heard and have influence to bring about change for the better. The goal of this collaboration with participants as the research end users and beneficiaries is to render the research more effective and enhance its impact. As Research Example 5.2 illustrates, adopting a participatory methodology can be a powerful tool for advocacy, even if it does not present a ready panacea for alleviating the challenges facing a particular community. Yet despite the methodological merits, it is important to problematize the notion of participatory research to explore the issues and dilemmas that arise from the approach.

It is well documented that participatory methodology raises professional, political and ethical challenges that go beyond the inquiry process and production of knowledge (Bloor 2016; Long et al. 2016). Questions about the researcher's professional role and relationship with participants, funders and other stakeholder groups can lead to misinterpretation of what the research is about or how the inquiry process should be shaped. For instance, it requires researchers to take on and negotiate their way around different roles as co-researcher, research trainer and advocate, to engage with participants as equal and consensual partners, and at times to work collaboratively with funding agencies. These roles all require nuanced mediation, confident research skills and high levels of trust and understanding between professional researchers, early childhood professionals, and often also parents and policymakers – all of whom usually have differently nuanced agendas.

Participatory research can therefore be challenging, especially for those who are comparatively new researchers. Ethical implications can also emerge from the potential imbalance of power between the researcher and participants who may feel that their participation in the study might result in them being penalized or that their professional authority might be compromised in some way. As such, it is important for researchers to acknowledge to themselves, as well as to participants, the inherent contradictions between their roles and presence as researchers of the study, on one hand, and the aim of participatory research to reduce power inequities, on the other. Bloor (2016) contends that the emancipatory intent of participatory research in advancing a social justice or policy agenda is possibly a 'chimera' – an illusion which may seem tantalizing for the researcher but which remains elusive. A central issue, he argues, is the value of neutrality in participatory research and the extent to which participants can realistically facilitate the emancipatory role of research:

> On one side, battle has been joined by those who argue that research should be explicitly politically participatory, embracing particular political aims, such as combating racism or patriarchy. On the other side are those who argue that no practice or policy prescriptions can be offered by researchers under any circumstances, since all knowledge is socially constructed and there are no grounds for the researcher to claim superior knowledge. (Bloor 2016: 22–6)

Integrating social activism and research with the aim of addressing social issues also raises issues of confidentiality and anonymity, especially when participation in a close collaborative relationship between the researcher and participants is enacted in a sensitive social and political environment. While it is important to achieve a common understanding about the desired benefits of the research and joint advocacy efforts, it is just as crucial to acknowledge the possibility that the research may not lead to a resolution or achieve full participation. In reality, there are varying models of participation, as discussed in Chapter 4, where different numbers of people may be involved in one or more stages of the research process, and to a greater or lesser degree in different aspects of the research process.

Critiques of participatory research have highlighted that unless it is conducted to a high standard, participatory research can be restrictive rather than transformative, particularly if the participatory nature of research activity is prioritized over the accountability and impact of the research on participants (Leal 2010). Cornwall and Jewkes (1995: 1668) contend that 'participation is rapidly becoming a catch-all concept, even a cliché'. This argument remains relevant, particularly if a prime reason for designing participatory research is to increase the chance of securing research funding, or if a participatory approach effectively co-opts local people into the researcher's or research funder's agenda. Amid such complexities and contentions, ethical issues become even more pronounced when engaging in participatory practices, and genuine efforts have to be made to establish an open and honest relationship between researchers and participants. In this regard, Long et al. (2016) offer useful advice:

> As a general principle, up-front agreements with local knowledge holders should be established to clarify how benefits will be shared and how community members will be able to participate in ways that protect confidential and sensitive information. (p. 256)

Concluding thoughts

Not all research is or should be participatory. However, participatory elements can be introduced into most research design frameworks in quantitative, qualitative or mixed method approaches. Where a participatory approach is adopted, the level of participation usually occurs on a continuum of less or more involvement, and involvement in different aspects of the research process (for example, see Shier 2001). Ultimately, the aim of participatory research is to create greater equality in the relationship between researchers and participants with a view to engendering social change and improving participants' lives and well-being. It is about empowering participants to influence both the research agenda and the research process. It is also about managing a delicate balance between appropriately guiding and eliciting participants' contributions without dictating or dominating the research process and agenda – and while this is far more easily said than done, it can be a highly rewarding and impactful methodological approach to research.

Suggestions for further reading

Ang, L. (2014). Vital voices for vital years in Singapore: One country's advocacy for change in the early years sector. *International Journal of Early Years Education* 22 (3): 329–41.

Chambers, R. (1994). The origins and practice of participatory rural appraisal. *World Development* 22 (7): 953–69.

Long, J. W., Ballard, H. L., Fisher, L. A. and Belsky, J. M. (2016). Questions that won't go away in participatory research, *Society & Natural Resources* 29 (2): 250–63.

McIntyre A. (2008). *Participatory Action Research*. Thousand Oaks, CA: Sage.

Nind, M. (2014). *What Is Inclusive Research?* London: Bloomsbury.

CHAPTER SIX

Ethnographic Research in Early Childhood Education

In this chapter we explore what it means to view young children's learning through an ethnographic lens. The core aim of the chapter is to familiarize readers with key concepts that underpin the design and implementation of ethnographic research as a process of reflective enquiry, and to share our understanding of what this approach offers to early education, to early education policy and to the mission to recognize and respect adults' and young children's views on their own lives. We begin by focusing on what ethnography is, the main characteristics of this approach and its roots in anthropology and sociology. We consider the rich insights ethnographic research can offer into the complex networks of interpersonal, social and cultural dimensions that shape young children's learning. We present a selection of ethnographic studies about young children's learning at home and in early education to illustrate how ethnography, guided by social and cultural theories, provides a strong basis for informed knowledge about early childhood that is grounded in the everyday unfolding of young children's lives.

What is ethnography?

Ethnography is a qualitative research approach that has been described as 'a way (or more accurately a set of ways) of exploring, knowing, and acting in and on the world' (Green and Bloome 2014:

181). This description may sound vague, but it is helpful to bear in mind that ethnography does not have a sharply defined meaning. This is largely because ethnography has developed over time and across disciplines, and has been taken up in many different ways to pursue a range of theoretical and philosophical perspectives.[1] Nineteenth-century anthropologists originally used the term 'ethnography' to describe fieldwork and descriptive accounts of different cultures or communities, which were often remote and non-Western. By living in a different culture for a long period of time, these early ethnographers sought to 'figure out' (Heath and Street 2008: 2) communities' values, beliefs and ways of being, from the points of view of the people being described.

One of the deepest influencers on the development of ethnography was Bronislav Malinowski, who spent the early part of his career documenting the lives of Australian Aboriginal tribes (Malinowski 1913) and the indigenous people of the Trobiand Islands in Melanesia (Malinowski 2007/1935). Malinowski highlighted the importance of ethnographers becoming immersed in the culture they are studying, of gathering data through observations and interviews and making meticulous notes to document ethnographic field work. He also drew attention to the crucial role of interpretation in ethnography.

Although the roots of ethnography lie in anthropology, this research approach was taken up by sociologists throughout the twentieth century to investigate communities closer to home. Between the 1920s and the 1950s sociologists at the University of Chicago conducted ethnographic studies of local, urban communities, including groundbreaking cross-cultural research into young children's lives (e.g. Mead and Wolfenstein 1955;

---

[1]For example: in anthropology to study human behaviours and cultures; in human geography to study people and their relations across space, place, in different communities, cultures and economies; in phenomenology to study human experience and consciousness; in structuralism to understand how human culture develops in relation to larger, overarching structures and systems; in poststructuralism to critique the socially conditioned nature of knowledge claims and value systems; and in post-humanism, to investigate how children's lives are shaped not just by humans but by the relationships between humans, places and objects, for example to understand young children's play with digitally connected 'smart' toys (Kuby and Rowsell 2017; Marsh 2017).

Whiting 1963). In these studies, the locus for research was 'any social network forming a complete entity in which social relations are regulated by custom' (Erickson 1984: 52). The 'Chicago School' approach to ethnography spread to Europe, and to the study of children's lives in urban and rural communities. Sociological ethnographic work subsequently informed the development of the 'sociology of childhood' tradition (e.g. Corsaro 2017; Prout and James 1997).

By the 1980s, ethnography had become an accepted, if not yet fully established, approach in education research, and seminal studies conducted at that time remain deeply influential to this day. For instance, Shirley Brice Heath spent nine years conducting an ethnographic comparison study of language practices between two small communities in the Piedmont region of the Carolinas, USA – one predominantly African American and the other white. Through immersion in these communities, making painstaking ethnographic observations and interviews, and taking meticulous notes, Heath documented how the child-rearing practices in each community prepared children very differently for school, with profound implications for their school outcomes.

Like many ethnographers, Heath used primarily audio technology and notes to record naturally occurring talk. The digitization of technologies has made visual recording devices more affordable and mobile, and has contributed to a visual turn in social science research, and to innovative approaches in 'visual ethnography'. Film and photography have a long legacy in anthropological work, and early ethnographers such as Mead (1930) and Malinowski (2007/1935) collected extensive moving and still images, but tended to use these primarily to illustrate their written descriptions. As Grimshaw (2001) asserts, anthropology (and ethnography) was 'not about making films, interrogating photographs, or experimenting with images and words. ... It was about writing texts' (p. 3). By contrast, visual ethnographers value the contribution that images make to knowledge in their own right (Pink 2013). For example, working with Korean children aged seven to fourteen years, Hwang and Charnley (2010) adopted visual ethnographic methods combined with participatory research to study the children's visual portrayals (drawn images, video diaries and home movies) of their experiences of living with an autistic sibling. Working with older children in what she refers to as a post-qualitative paradigm, Semenec (2018) has explored how engaging with contemporary art film and film-making invites new ways of thinking about children that inform and disrupt how we do research with children, and open up new possibilities for rethinking concepts of voice and agency. With the rise of web-based media, ethnographers have begun to study human behaviour online, and 'virtual ethnography' has become a buoyant field in contemporary early childhood research to understand how young children engage with digital technologies to play and communicate online (e.g. Erstad et al. 2019; Huh 2017).

For researchers, having the time and resources to spend extended periods of time in the research field is an infrequent luxury, and contemporary ethnographers are more likely to spend weeks or months rather than years in a research site. Green and Bloome (2014: 183) observe that as ethnography has evolved, there have been changes in what counts as ethnographic research. They propose that immersion in the field over long periods of time is one of three ethnographic approaches: 'doing ethnography' (a broad, in-depth, long-term study of a social/cultural group conducted, for example, within an anthropological framing); adopting an 'ethnographic perspective' (a more focused study of particular aspects of the everyday life and practices of a community); and 'using ethnographic tools' (using ethnographic methods and techniques during fieldwork in studies that might not be informed by cultural theories). We explore some of the implications of these different approaches in the research examples presented in this chapter.

What does ethnography offer to early childhood research?

In the field of early education, ethnographic research has offered rich and deep insights into how children make sense of the world, how they negotiate relationships, what interests them and motivates their learning, and how education can be made relevant to their interests. By spending long periods of time observing formal and informal educational practices and behaviours in schools, homes and communities, and by gaining insights into adults' and children's perspectives through interviews and documentation, ethnographers have been able to situate local ways of being within the broader scope of social, political and cultural influences, and to understand not only what happens in children's lives but also why adults and children act in the ways they do. An ethnographic lens helps us to understand how children's life spaces are organized, their materiality, the relationships and power plays between people, what is valued in those spaces, and how wider societal dynamics are played out in individual children's lives, such as gender, race and class. If we study young children ethnographically, we can therefore focus on who they are, rather than on who they might one day become (Wells 2009).

As discussed throughout this chapter, a substantial body of ethnographic research over many decades has offered holistic, deep and situated insights into the complexities of young children's learning and development, including, for example, children's early language and literacy learning (Flewitt 2005b, 2011; Gregory, Long and Volk 2004; Taylor and Dorsey-Gaines 1988; Worthington and van Oers 2017); young children's racial identity (Miller 2015); young children's maths learning at home and school (Baker, Street and Tomlin 2003); how young children learn in library and museum spaces (Smith, 2018; Hackett 2014); and how they play (Anderson 2018; Marsh 2017), including sensory ethnography of children's nature play (Nugent 2018). However, before presenting in-depth examples of ethnographic studies of early childhood education, we first outline some key characteristics of ethnographic research, to clarify how it is distinct from other forms of qualitative enquiry.

What makes ethnography ethnographic?

Despite variation in ethnographic approaches across disciplines, there are core principles that characterize ethnographic research. First, ethnography is a process of enquiry where there is a very close and interdependent relationship between methodology, theory and the researcher's epistemological stance with regard to what counts as valid knowledge. Ethnography in education is not simply a set of techniques with open-ended research design that includes observations and interviews, but theory drives the research design and underpins the research questions, and the relationship between the researcher and participants is key. The close link between theory and research design is essential if researchers claim they are doing ethnography or adopting an ethnographic perspective, rather than using ethnographic methods:

> Thus, theory, purpose, and practice within the research site ... implicate particular relationships between researcher and member of the social group being studied, and distinguish it from other forms of social research. (Green and Bloome 2014: 185)

Second, there are commonalities in what ethnographers do. Before entering the research site, ethnographers identify broad research questions based on their knowledge of particular phenomena in an area of enquiry, and their familiarity with relevant research literature. Broadly speaking, ethnographers then tend to spend significant periods of time in a research site (whether physical or virtual), observing what happens, listening to what people say, and learning. This process, aptly described as 'deep hanging out' (Wogan 2004; Powell and Somerville 2018), may lead to the initial research questions being refined. To explore the identified research issues, ethnographers make observations for a significant length of time and begin to ask questions in the research site – these might be spontaneous and part of everyday interaction, or they might be more structured in informal interviews. Ethnographers also collect documents and/or artefacts that are relevant to the research aims. An essential trait of ethnography is meticulous note taking and record keeping – by documenting and making accurate records of all the information generated throughout the research process, by writing notes, making audio and/or video recordings, taking photographs and so on. In short, ethnographers spend intensive periods of time gathering together and reflecting on lots of information from a range of sources that might seem relevant to the focus of enquiry.

The nature of ethnographic research is therefore often exploratory, flexible, open-ended and iterative. As ethnographers become sensitized to the study site, the research questions are often refined or transformed in response to issues that are teased out as being important to adult or child participants during the process of conducting research. This flexible and adaptive approach may seem disconcerting to researchers who are new to ethnography, or who are used to working in more tightly structured ways, yet ethnography can be defined by the following characteristics, which are discussed in more detail throughout the chapter:

1. The ethnographer usually brings a social and cultural theoretical framework and set of questions to the research field, but the questions may change over time during fieldwork, as the researcher develops a better understanding of local beliefs, practices and values.

2. Research data are collated from 'real world', everyday contexts, in ways that are appropriate to the research site. Ethnographic studies are *not* generated in experimental, intervention or structured conditions that have been designed by the researcher but are usually planned around a cycle of activity (Gray 2017). For example, if the topic of study is how children cope with the transition from home to preschool or nursery, then observations might be made over a period of months during the first term or year of attendance, in order to understand the *process* rather than focus on the *outcome*.

3. Information is gathered from a range of sources, usually through *observation* and *field notes*, along with *interviews*, the collection and/or photographing of *artefacts*, and scrutiny of relevant *documents*. This information is gathered as people interact using language, their bodies, artefacts, images, technologies and so on, so the sources of ethnographic information are varied.

4. Ethnographic researchers often position themselves in the research field as *participant observers*, that is, they become involved in the practices and behaviours they are observing. Alternatively, they might adopt a less interactive role as *observer participants* and 'hide in the shadows of contexts to document people, actions, movements, places and spaces, and the stuff or objects that represent the focus of research studies' (Dénommé-Welch and Rowsell 2017: 14). Throughout the process of observation, ethnographers need

to reflect on, and document, their own subjective beliefs in order to open their minds to others' perspectives.

5. Ethnographic analysis is detailed, iterative and cyclical, and the ethnographer often uses gaps between research visits to review the research material in a recursive process of reflection. Analysis begins by bringing some sort of order to complex data and by looking for patterns, categories, descriptive units and themes. These emerging themes are then revisited in light of new data and new issues that emerge when the ethnographer returns to the field.

6. Ethnographic accounts are usually highly descriptive and reflective, blending 'thick description' (Geertz 1973: 6) with theory and thematic analysis to build a rigorous, credible and authentic account. Although the term 'thick description' is often attributed to the renowned anthropologist Clifford Geertz, it was originally used by Gilbert Ryle (1971) to describe the process of writing descriptions of observed behaviours in such detail that they can be used to test theory.

7. Ethnographers do not claim to produce an objective 'truth', but to represent social reality as they experience it through the relationships they build with the participants whose lives they share. The aim is to balance an *emic* (insider or local) with an *etic* (outsider or analytic) perspective to describe the practices and behaviours of the community being studied. Ethnographers must therefore develop high levels of reflexivity and self-awareness, and recognize that how we make sense of others' actions and words is 'an expression of our own consciousness' (Cohen and Rapport 1995: 12).

To illustrate how these characteristics can be applied in ethnographic practice, Research Example 6.1 presents an ethnographic study with five-year-old children during their first year of primary school in Australia. In this study, the researchers' key aim was to understand the children's views of 'work' and 'play', and to 'encourage children to share their perspectives in open-ended ways where their views were taken seriously' (Breathnach, Danby and O'Gorman 2017: 439).

Research Example 6.1: An ethnographic study of young children's views of 'work' and 'play'

'Play' is notoriously problematic to define due to its dynamic nature, when and where it takes place, and who is doing it with whom (Grieshaber and McArdle 2010). Educators tend to have different understandings of what play is, and differing pedagogic beliefs and values around the role of play in supporting children's learning. Similarly, early childhood education policy can be ambivalent about the importance of play in the curriculum, and in many nations there has been a shift in early childhood education towards a focus on academic learning outcomes, rather than play-based learning experiences. In this study, Helen Breathnach, Susan Danby and Lyndal O'Gorman (2017) investigated the less well-known topic of young children's perspectives on play, focusing on five-year-old children's understandings of 'work' and 'play' during their first year in primary school in Queensland, Australia.

Their ethnographic study was framed by conceptualizations of children as competent and active constructors of their own social worlds, in keeping with the sociology of childhood (Prout and James 1997; Corsaro 2005). The study design involved regular visits to one classroom over a period of five months, throughout the last two terms of the primary school year. During these visits, the researcher built relationships by interacting with the children, their teacher and parents, and respected children's agency by only participating in their activities if invited to do so. This fairly long immersion in the research site resulted in a very rich data set, including sixty-five hours of video recordings of the children in class, along with researcher conversations with the children and teacher about what the children enjoyed doing and why, and which school activities they viewed as play or as work. Forty additional hours of audio recordings captured research conversations with children and parents outside the classroom, and audio recordings of children playing (when appropriate, audio was used in place of video to avoid capturing images of children who were not part of the study). The researcher also made handwritten field notes and collected artefacts such as children's drawings and writing. The authors describe how in this ethnographic study with children, the role of the researcher extended beyond listening as a technique, and involved co-constructing meaning through dialogue between the speaker and the listener. This process required the researchers to reflect critically on their own preconceptions, and to revise these in light of the children's perspectives.

The process of analysis was iterative and began by identifying concepts that the children, teacher and parents used to describe their experiences and perspectives on play and work, referred to as *emic themes*. In the second stage of analysis, data were organized according to *etic themes*, which included concepts from childhood studies theory and research literature.

The research dialogue with children over time led to new insights into children's nuanced interpretations of classroom activities. The study found that the children did not necessarily associate 'play' with the characteristics of an activity, the presence of an adult or the space in which an activity occurred, but with how activities were described by the teacher in the class timetable. That is, the children's interpretation of play followed the adult-constructed agenda. They associated many teacher-directed, structured activities as 'work', including writing, which they often reported they did not enjoy because 'it takes lots of hours, too much writing, and lots of groups' (Breathnach, Danby and O'Gorman 2017: 448). However, the children spontaneously engaged in writing activities during timetabled periods of free play, and enlisted the help of peers and adults to help them spell words which they needed to write for the purposes of their play. The authors conclude by proposing that educators should move away from dichotomous notions of 'play' and 'work' towards planning activities that offer opportunities for children's agentic participation and purposeful engagement in a range of learning activities, including learning to write.

Finding a position in children's worlds

Research Example 6.1 shows how ethnographers who are working with young children must be clear about how they position themselves in the research site as they try to find a place in children's worlds and gain their trust (Corsaro 2017). Given the length of time ethnographers spend in a research site, the success of an ethnographic study lies in the interpersonal relationships built with participants, based on mutual respect and shared understandings.

If you conduct ethnography in a child's home or classroom, you might initially feel that your role is unclear – potentially both to you and the participants – but if you assume the stance of a friendly and non-expert adult, children are usually keen to be helpful and inclusive. Once you have secured adult and child participants' consent to take part in your study (see Chapter 2, this volume), you might begin to build a rapport with children by sitting on the floor or low chair among them, on the same level as their activity, and explain that your work is to observe, to make careful notes of what is going on and (if applicable) sometimes to make video recordings. Children usually accept this, or if they are uncomfortable they may move away at first until they get to know and trust you. Sometimes, children will want to write or draw in your notebook, and such moments may offer new insights into the sense they make of your presence, and help to strengthen your sense of belonging in their social group.

It is also important for ethnographers conducting early childhood research to be respectful of adult authority in the classroom, and to position themselves as distant from it. Otherwise, children may come to think of the ethnographer as a teacher and curb their behaviours accordingly when the researcher is present. Some ethnographers prefer to avoid or minimize talking with teachers when children are present. It is therefore extremely important, before the research begins, to build a rapport not only with the children in your study but also with educator and parent participants by discussing your role and position in the research site, and by making sure they are comfortable with your presence and conduct. It can also be helpful to establish boundaries to your research and to agree breaks in the day when you will not be present – participants may prefer to have 'time out' from the researcher's gaze at certain moments during each visit. Dialogue and trust building are essential in ethnographic research, as the quality of the data generated is highly dependent on the rapport between participants and researcher.

One of the many challenges of being a participant observer is keeping a balance between 'insider' (*emic*) and 'outsider' (*etic*) status, and maintaining professional distance with participants who you get to know well over time and may begin to empathize with. Agar (1980) defined the ethnographer as a 'professional stranger' who enters an unfamiliar world but works towards an eventual understanding. Writing about ethnographic research with homeless children, Hall (2000) suggests that the best an ethnographer can do is negotiate a position of being 'one of us' without being totally immersed in others' lives. However, this can be 'a long and difficult process' (Hall 2000: 124) that requires reflexivity and consideration of the effects of the ethnographer's personal presence, beliefs and values throughout all stages of the research process. A further challenge arises at the end of an ethnographic study, when the time comes for the researcher to leave the field. Less is written about this aspect of ethnography, but Gray (2017) suggests it can be helpful at the start of a study to indicate when you will leave and plan some kind of event at the end of the research project to celebrate participants' involvement while also reminding them that your departure is imminent.

Ethnography, reflexivity and dialogue

To some extent, ethnography can be likened to the ways we all make sense of the worlds in which we live, and ethnographic accounts are sometimes referred to as narrative fictions that are 'inherently *partial* – committed and incomplete' (Clifford 1986: 7, original italics). However, unlike everyday interactions, conducting ethnographic enquiry is reflective, deliberate and systematic. Reflexivity – that is, the process of reflecting openly about one's own subjective beliefs, understandings, values and experiences – is a key characteristic of ethnographic work. Rather than presuming to represent an 'objective' and uncontested account of other people's lives, ethnographers openly reflect on how 'social researchers are part of the social world they study' (Hammersley and Atkinson 2007: 14), and recognize that their own identities, such as their race, ethnicity, gender, age, social status and life experiences, frame their interpretations of research contexts and shape how participants view and behave towards them. In early childhood research, we bring our own personal histories and beliefs about childhood and about learning to the research environment, and it is important to reflect on how these influence the choices we make throughout the research process – including the research aims, questions, theoretical framework, research design, analytic process, write up and presentations. As Bateson (1979) reminds us:

> We come to every situation with stories, patterns and sequences of childhood experiences that are built into us. Our learning happens within the experience of what important others did. (p. 13)

While ethnographic knowledge requires subjective reflection, it is produced through intersubjective relationships between researchers, participants and research sites, rather than by the researcher acting on her or his own – as we saw in Research Example 6.1, where Breathnach, Danby and O'Gorman (2017) co-constructed meanings through dialogue with the adult and child participants. Ethnographic texts are 'always dialogical – the site at which the voices of the other, alongside the voices of the author, come alive and interact with one another' (Denzin 1997: viii). This relationship between the familiar and the unfamiliar lies at the heart of ethnography: the ethnographer enters a community that has a different set of social and cultural practices, and slowly comes to understand them through the perspectives of participants in the field. By shifting between the familiar and the unfamiliar, the ethnographer moves along an axis of *emic* and *etic* perspectives, and this involves making the strange familiar, and the familiar strange – an *emic* perspective is offered through the perspectives of people within a particular social group, who may have understandings that are strange to the researcher, whereas an *etic* perspective is offered by the researcher, who may use terms that can be applied across cultures and theoretical concepts that may be strange to the participants (see Corwin and Clemens 2012). This dialogic process is far from straightforward, and is far more easily said than done. There are often tensions between trying to understand participants' perspectives while also attempting to view them and their behaviour more distantly through an analytical lens (Hammersley 2006). This is particularly the case if the researcher has a different linguistic, social or cultural background and different life experiences and expectations to those whose lives are being researched. Even if there seem to be similarities between researchers and researched, every individual's perception of any event is always different in some way. The argument of ethnography is that the tension between *emic* and *etic* perspectives leads to the exchange of ideas and perceptions through dialogue, and that the richest and most nuanced view of a community, society or culture can be gained when these two perspectives are balanced in *thick description* (Geertz 1973).

Research Example 6.2 summarizes some of the 'insider/outsider' dilemmas that ethnographic researchers Eve Gregory and Mahera Ruby (2011) encountered when working with young children and their families, and how these led them to extend theories about the dialogic nature of ethnographic reporting. This example is taken from a series of ethnographic projects conducted by Gregory and colleagues in East London, UK, where they investigated the home and community literacies in Bangladeshi British and Anglo communities.

Research Example 6.2: The 'insider/ outsider' dilemma of ethnography

Eve Gregory and Mahera Ruby (2011) drew on a broadly sociocultural theoretical framework to investigate the literacy lives and practices of young children growing up in Bangladeshi British and Anglo families living in the same district of London. They were particularly interested in how parents' and teachers' own past experiences and values shaped the ways that they supported children's literacy development through *finely tuned scaffolding* (Dunn 1989; Wood et al. 1976) and *guided participation* (Rogoff 1990, 2003). They were also interested in how younger and older siblings supported each other's learning through the synergies in their shared endeavours (Gregory, Long and Volk 2004). They approached their studies by viewing literacy and learning as ideological constructs and recognized that attitudes towards the value and purpose of literacy vary both across and within cultures (Scribner and Cole 1981; Street 1984). Given the focus of their work on children growing up in families with different heritage cultures, they were particularly interested in how the children became members of the different cultures, languages and activities that were dynamically intermingled in their day-to-day lives and became part of each child's cultural repertoire (Schieffelin and Ochs 1986).

Despite this very robust theoretical framing for their ethnographic study, they found that none of the theoretical constructs they were working with helped them understand how to interact with teachers and parents whose beliefs did not 'sit easily with our own' (Gregory and Ruby 2011: 165). As they researched the complexity of the families' literacy practices, they found themselves constantly questioning their own assumptions, and problematizing the future of ethnography in the study of increasingly fragmented, dispersed, pluralistic, disassembled and contradictory worlds. They adopted Geertz's (2002) description of the discipline as 'moving raggedly on' (8), and found this notion of 'raggedness' helpful when reflecting on the challenges and clashes they encountered in their work. Here, we present two examples of 'outsider' and 'insider' dilemmas described by Gregory and Ruby (2011) – a paper which we encourage budding ethnographers to read.

An 'outsider' dilemma: When planning this study of how Anglo and Bangladeshi British parents support their children's literacy at home, Gregory had anticipated encountering very different practices in Bangladeshi and Anglo homes. However, she was very surprised to learn from the British Bangladeshi researcher that the Bangladeshi British parents did not read *at all* with their children at home, and began to panic that they would not be able to gather the data they had planned. The researcher reassured her – although the parents did not read with their young children, the children's older siblings often did. The study therefore included older and younger siblings' co-reading practices, creating a unique and highly valuable data set, which subsequently led to a larger-scale, innovative study focusing on the role of siblings in young children's language and literacy learning. With the benefit of hindsight, Gregory realized that as an 'outsider' she had failed to understand the family's practices, which were completely understandable to an 'insider'. Of course it made sense for parents whose English was limited to leave literacy interaction to older siblings in the family, who were more able to 'tutor' the younger children in both English and Bengali.

An 'insider' dilemma: As a member of the Bangladeshi community, Mahera Ruby had assumed that she would be able to 'talk and walk' (ibid: 168) her way into Bangladeshi homes without any difficulty, with a view to observing grandparents interacting with their grandchildren in literacy activities. With a Bangladeshi researcher colleague, they decided the best way to attract participants was to send questionnaires home with children to find out if they had grandparents who might participate and then invite all respondent grandparents to a coffee morning, where they would present their research and offer attendees the chance to find out about the study before consenting to participate. The turnout was disappointing, and Ruby sensed an 'invisible wall' was put up when the attendees realized the research would take place in the privacy of their home. Nonetheless, a few grandparents consented, and Ruby made her first visit to one family's home. As an 'insider' of Bangladeshi culture, she had not expected to feel strange in the family home, but realized, as she sat laden with recording equipment in their living room, that as a researcher she had become an 'outsider' to the family. Once again, on reflection this was always going to be an obvious barrier, but this experience highlighted for the research team the intrusive nature of recording equipment, the complexity of overlapping cultural worlds, and the constant need to build trust and confidence gradually, which can never be taken for granted.

The authors conclude that as an outsider, it is simply not possible to represent an insider's perspective, but a more achievable aim is to create a dialogue between 'insiders' and 'outsiders'. This gives voice to people whose voices would otherwise not be heard, and the exchange of ideas leads the outsider to question their own assumptions, and opens their eyes afresh to the research context and to different ways of viewing the world. The dialogic nature of ethnographic understanding means being responsive to others and approaching the act of ethnographic writing as answerable and responsible. In this way, both participants and researchers are enriched through their ongoing exchanges of ideas 'joined in an inseparable dialogue' (ibid: 171).

Writing ethnography

Ethnographic research always involves painstaking processes of interpretative data collection and analysis, often over extended periods of time, with a view to gaining understanding of participants' perspectives and actions in their social and cultural worlds. How can an ethnographer capture the complexity, diversity and (often) enormity of ethnographic data sets in a research report? Even if an ethnographer has spent swathes of time in the field and manages through dialogue to balance *emic* and *etic* perspectives, is it ever really possible to describe the diversity of practices and entangled messiness of communities, societies and cultures with any semblance of authenticity? And then how can this complexity be represented for research purposes? Some ethnographers focus on everyday talk and transcriptions of speech, sometimes using Jefferson's transcription system (see Gumperz and Berenz 1993), while others create multimodal transcriptions (see Flewitt et al. 2014; Doak 2019). Digital media and research practices in more recent years have opened up new dimensions for ethnographic reporting, and have extended what we understand by text, which – if ethical consent is granted – can extend to hyperlinks, video clips and visual montages (see Boellstrorff et al. 2012; Dezuanni 2018). However, it is important to bear in mind Clifford and Marcus's (1986) remark that ethnographic writing often *makes* rather than *reflects* culture.

The task of the ethnographer is therefore to write with meticulous sensibility, to learn how to 'take the measure of a complex scene' (Shweder 2007: 200), faithfully to represent the dialogic nature of ethnographic investigation, and to write using what the anthropologists Ryle (1971) and Geertz (1973) refer to as 'thick description'. That is, rather than writing summaries or using overly simplistic labels to categorize the complex social worlds that the researcher has observed and experienced in the field (often referred to as 'thin description'), the ethnographer's task is to identify and describe patterns of behaviours and environments, and to link these with theory. The term 'thick description' has been interpreted variously in qualitative research (see Ponterotto 2006), and readers might find Holloway's (1997) definition helpful:

The notion of thick description is often misunderstood. It must be theoretical and analytical in that researchers concern themselves with the abstract and general patterns and traits of social life in a culture. This type of description aims to give readers a sense of the emotions, thoughts and perceptions that research participants experience. It deals not only with the meaning and interpretations of people in a culture but also with their intentions. Thick description builds up a clear picture of the individuals and groups in the context of their culture and the setting in which they live. ... Thick description can be contrasted with **thin description** [bold in original], which is a superficial account and does not explore the underlying meanings of cultural members. (p. 154)

When seeking coherence in complex social and cultural systems, the ethnographer must not be tempted to oversimplify complexity in order to assume an authoritative tone. Rather (a point made repeatedly in this chapter!) ethnographic texts are dialogical – they reflect the perspectives of participants as well as the researcher(s) and are anchored in human experience. Data may be scrutinized by the researcher and emerging themes identified, but these themes are then often (but not always) shared with participants and adapted to accommodate participants' views.

Critiques of ethnographic research

Ethnographers have often struggled with questions around the validity and replicability of their findings when compared with other social science methodologies, such as quasi-experimental or survey-based research. This is a particular issue for education researchers where many research funders often favour RCTs which can subsequently be 'scaled up' as nationwide interventions (see Chapter 9, this volume). Ethnographic research is by its nature interpretive, subjective, and any 'truths' are always partial. What matters in the validity of ethnographic findings is that the processes of decision-making must be made clear, and all decisions must be justifiable. When planning ethnographic research it is therefore helpful, if not essential, to be clear about the phenomenon being investigated; the aims of the research (a useful test here is to imagine how you would explain your research in a simple sentence if asked by a complete stranger what you are studying); who the participants will be and why this sample is chosen (the sample will be purposive and must correspond to the research purposes); the researcher's relationship to the participants and the site of research; how often data will be collected, over what time span and where; and how participants' identity will be protected. As the nature of ethnography is iterative, and the precise research questions may evolve, it is all the more important to document and justify all decisions that are taken during all phases of the research process.

In terms of empirical validity, ethnographers aim to produce a version of the truth that results from dialogue between the researcher and participants, rather than an 'objective' truth. Ethnographers must therefore ensure that data is presented in sufficient detail, through thick description, to 'come alive' (Heath and Street 2008: 45), to resonate with the reader and support the claims that are made. The multiple methods used in ethnographic research help in this regard to triangulate the findings, so, for example, an observation can be supported by evidence from interview and/or documentary data, and in this way a strong and convincing argument is built up. The findings must ring true to the reader, and in terms of comparability, validity lies in the extent to which the ethnographic account rings true with others who can identify similar issues in their own lives. In terms of theoretical validity, the ethnographic account and its theoretical framing must be robust enough to withstand critique.

Replicability in ethnographic research refers to the extent to which a study can be reproduced, so the research processes must be clear so other researchers can follow the same procedures and understand the rationale of each step in the research process. Although a different researcher in a different setting with different participants may well find different results, there are likely to be synergies in the ethnographic findings, and replication of the study will enhance its theoretical validity, potentially leading to the further development of theory.

Further critiques of ethnography lie in the overuse of the term to describe studies which, in essence, are not ethnographic. Reflecting on the increasing tendency for research projects to be relatively short term, Hammersley (2006) laments the potential loss of the rich insights that can be gained from the long, slow and immersed study of highly complex and fluid social systems. He cautions that ethnographers should not be lured into believing that what people do in the sites of study necessarily reflects what they do in other situations, or that what ethnographers observe just a few times in one setting constitutes a pattern of behaviour.

Concluding thoughts

Ethnography is an adaptive and highly valued methodological approach that captures the complexities of particular social phenomena and draws attention to the conventions of social life that are often taken for granted by the people and communities studied. Although the fieldwork carried out by many ethnographers today is more likely to last months rather than years, the easy availability, portability and affordability of audio- and video-recording devices has led to ethnographers producing large amounts of intensive and micro-focused data in shorter periods of time. The wealth and detail of the resultant data sets often lead to finely nuanced insights into the phenomena being studied, and these insights in turn can lead to theory development.

Ethnography is therefore *not* simply a method for collecting data but is a theory-driven approach that involves creating and representing knowledge (about individuals and the society and cultures in which they live) through dialogue between participants and the ethnographer. Ethnographic accounts therefore do not claim to be 'objective' portrayals of reality, but claim to offer a version of reality as experienced by the ethnographer through sensitive and reflective observations, while remaining as loyal as possible to the context of study and the relationships through which ethnographic knowledge is produced. Sharing the diverse perspectives of researchers and child and adult participants can lead to new ways of understanding the worlds in which children live, how they experience them and the relationships they form with others.

Suggestions for further reading

The following readings will serve as excellent points of reference for early childhood researchers interested in developing their understanding of ethnography:

Agar, M. H. (2008). *The Professional Stranger: An Informal Introduction to Ethnography* (2nd edn). Bingley, UK: Emerald Group Publishing Ltd.

Atkinson, P. and Hammersley, M. (2007). *Ethnography: Principles in Practice* (3rd edn). London and New York: Routledge.

Christensen, P. (2004). Children's participation in ethnographic research: Issues of power and representation. *Children & Society* 18 (2): 165–76.

Cohen, L., Manion, L. and Morison, K. (2011). *Research Methods in Education* (7th Edn). London and New York: Routledge (particularly Chapter 11, pp. 219–47).

Flewitt, R. S. (2011). Bringing ethnography to a multimodal investigation of early literacy in a digital age. *Qualitative Research* 11 (3): 293–310.

Gobo, G. and Molle, A. (2017). *Doing Ethnography* (2nd edn). London, Thousand Oaks, New Delhi: Sage.

Gregory, E. and Ruby, M. (2011). The 'insider/outsider' dilemma of ethnography: Working with young children and their families in cross-cultural contexts. *Journal of Early Childhood Research* 9 (2): 162–74.

Hammersley, M. (2006). Ethnography: Problems and prospects. *Ethnography and Education* 1: 3–14.

Heath, S. B. and Street, B. (2008). *Ethnography: Approaches to Language and Literacy Research*. New York: Teachers College Press.

Miller, E. T. (2015). Discourses of whiteness and blackness: An ethnographic study of three young children learning to be white. *Ethnography and Education* 10 (2): 137–53.

Nugent, C. L. (2018). Sensory-ethnographic observations at three nature kindergartens. *International Journal of Research & Method in Education* 41 (4): 468–79.

CHAPTER SEVEN

Multimodal Perspectives on Early Childhood Education

In this chapter, we take a look at multimodal approaches to researching young children's learning. Education research has historically tended to prioritize the role of language in learning, but multimodality offers a fundamentally different perspective on how children and adults use many different resources when they make meaning and interact. Multimodality does not assume that language is always present in meaning making or that it is always the most important mode for meaning making. Rather, speech and writing are viewed as part of a rich palette of communicative choices that sit alongside other expressive forms, where each form offers distinct potentials and limitations for meaning making (Flewitt 2012; Jewitt et al. 2016; Kress 2010).

Multimodality offers a robust methodological framework for researchers to study how meanings are constructed through the relationships between different resources (through language as well as through physical movement, gestures, gaze exchange and facial expressions during interaction) and through different sign systems in texts (written language, images, design, use of colour, etc.). Over recent years, scholars from diverse disciplines have turned to multimodality to investigate much-debated issues around children's learning with screen-based texts, touch-responsive devices and interactive digital media, where making meaning often involves interpreting combinations of still and moving images, icons, spoken or written language, screen layout, colours and sounds. While digital technologies have generated a new environment for communication and meaning making, we are still reliant on our bodies and symbolic resources as we negotiate our way through our physical and virtual lives. In this chapter, we share our understanding of what multimodality offers to knowledge about young children's meaning making in the contemporary world by presenting examples from early childhood research in mainstream and special education settings, and in museums. We begin by clarifying what multimodality is, what it can offer to early childhood education research, the theoretical assumptions that underpin multimodality, and the implications of these core concepts for multimodal research design.

What is multimodality?

Multimodality is an interdisciplinary approach that was developed in the 1990s, mainly through the work of Gunther Kress and Theo van Leeuwen (1996, 2001), who were interested in how different modes are used in communication. It has also been influenced by the work of scholars in the traditions of conversation analysis and ethnomethodology, such as Charles Goodwin (2000, 2003a, b), and by scholars of discourse analysis, such as Sigrid Norris (2004), who have moved beyond a focus on verbal texts to consider the relationships between language, cognition and action. Researchers in many different disciplines have adopted multimodality as a new framework that can offer telling insights into social practices, and this has resulted in some diversity in how multimodality is applied. However, a common core that unites this diversity is the intertwining of three interconnected assumptions that characterize multimodality, as set out below.

First, multimodality assumes that *communication and meaning making always involve a multiplicity of semiotic (sign-making) resources*, which might or might not involve language, but all of which contribute to the making of meaning. Although some linguistic studies also pay close attention to 'para-linguistic' or 'non-verbal' features of communication, these features have often been viewed as ancillary to language, or have been singled out and studied with a degree of isolation from other expressive modes (e.g. McNeill 1992; Streeck 1993; Kendon 2004). Multimodality offers a fundamentally different approach, by studying how multiple modes work together to create meanings in a 'multimodal ensemble' (Kress et al. 2001). This broader conceptualization of meaning making enables researchers to study how different modes play a central role at different times during interactive sequences. For example, in a nursery context a child might fix their gaze on another child who is playing at the water tray, the playing child might respond by moving to make a space for the approaching child, and in so doing, invite the child to join in. The two children might then play together, and begin to exchange a few words or they might continue to play silently together and negotiate their play successfully through action rather than through language. Multimodality provides a robust theoretical and methodological framework to analyse such interaction, and refutes the assumption that language is *always* central in interaction (Norris 2004; Flewitt 2012).

Second, multimodality assumes that *there are often patterns in how modes are used*. By observing, describing and analysing the full repertoire of modes that children and adults use to make meaning in different interpersonal, social and cultural contexts, multimodality researchers seek to identify the organized principles that underpin meaning making and to understand the influences that shape people's choices of different modes and modal combinations. The more a set of modal resources is used in the social life of a particular community, the more fully and finely articulated it becomes. In order for something to 'be a mode' there needs to be a shared cultural sense within a community of how modes can be organized to realize meaning, and newcomers to a community may struggle to understand these organizing principles. For example, if a practitioner in a nursery holds up their arm with an outward facing palm, this action may mean 'Calm down' or 'Please be quiet', but this message may not be clear to a child who has only just joined the nursery. Over time, by observing others' behaviours, newcomers come to understand and learn the communicative expectations in different social environments, including learning about when and where speech is an appropriate mode to use, when it is not and what other modes and modal combinations might be more acceptable and/or more effective.

This connects with the third assumption underpinning multimodality that people *orchestrate meaning by choosing to configure modes in particular ways*, and the choices that individuals make about which modes to use are significant. These choices might be conscious and intentional, or they might be habitual. Either way, all communicational acts are shaped by social and cultural norms and by the rules operating at the moment of sign making, but the act of communicating is also influenced by people's motivations and interests in specific social contexts. Unravelling the modal choices that individuals make – which modes to choose, why, and in what combinations – is therefore a central aspect of interaction and meaning. As Kress (2010: 9–10) suggests:

> Humans *make* signs in which form and meaning stand in a 'motivated' relation. These signs are made with very many different means, in very many different modes. They are the expression of the *interest* of socially formed individuals who, with these signs, *realize* – give outward expression to – their meaning, using culturally available semiotic resources, which have been shaped by the practices of members of social groups and their cultures.

Multimodality therefore not only takes into account the cultural, social and interpersonal contexts that people are communicating in, and how those contexts shape the ways that modes are used, but also considers individuals' modal choices and their personal motivations for making those choices. Multimodality has been found useful to offer new perspectives on well-known areas of research, such as young children's interactions and communicative capabilities, to understand the principles of multimodal meaning making across diverse contexts, and to investigate comparatively new fields of research, such as digital and online environments (see Flewitt 2005b; Jewitt 2014).

What does multimodality offer to early childhood education research?

Many early childhood researchers have turned to multimodality to explore how young children and adults use combinations of action, artefacts and language when they interact. Whereas a linguistic approach might struggle to make sense of what is going on when children are playing together or responding to adults without speaking, multimodality enables the researcher to pay close and equal attention to all forms of meaning making. Multimodal research has offered many exciting and new insights into children's uses of gesture, movement and gaze (Goodwin 2000; Lancaster 2001; Flewitt 2005b, 2006; Taylor 2006); children's early literacy and writing (Dyson 2001; Siegel 2006; Lancaster 2007); how children express meaning through talk and artefacts (Pahl 2006); how children use actions and talk as they interact with objects and with each other (Wohlwend 2009, 2017); how they interact with digital media (Rowe and Miller 2016; Neumann and Neumann 2017; Wohlwend and Rowsell 2017); and how children's play moves fluidly across offline and online media (Marsh 2014).

Researchers have found that multimodality offers a rigorous framework to observe and analyse how material resources, and how cultural and social norms shape interaction. For example, in early education and home settings, multimodality researchers have considered how children's interactions with other children and adults are influenced by the design of the learning environment; how the arrangement of spaces and artefacts configure social relations; how these configurations reflect particular social and cultural beliefs about childhood and children's capabilities; and about the purpose and aims of early education, including in special education (Flewitt, Nind and Payler 2009; Doak 2019). Considerations such as how chairs and tables are arranged in classroom settings, how accessible the learning materials are to children and teachers, and what kinds of relationships the classroom design makes possible can all be accommodated in a multimodality framework to unravel how the arrangement of material and human resources both enables and constrains children's activity and interaction. In this way, multimodal analysis can lead to detailed insights into how social values are instantiated in material configurations, as illustrated through research examples later in this chapter.

Multimodality and theory

As mentioned, multimodality is an innovative field of enquiry that has been adopted by researchers across disciplines but has its roots in social semiotic theory (Halliday 1978). Michael Halliday was interested in how language is shaped by different social situations and pointed out through rigorous and fine-grained analysis of language use in practice that 'language is as it is because of its function in the social structure' (1973: 65). According to Halliday, to understand any utterance or piece of writing, it is necessary to reflect on why particular words, phrases and grammatical and rhetorical structures are chosen. From a social semiotic perspective, researchers ask themselves questions such as 'out of the range of possible utterances, why did the speaker/writer choose that particular grammatical structure and those particular words in that particular social context?' Understanding the choices that people make (whether consciously or not) when they interact is also central to multimodality. However, rather than focusing exclusively on language, early childhood education researchers working with multimodality might ask themselves, 'Why did that young boy use language to say "Hello", gestures to indicate what he wanted to do, and body movement to attract attention to his choice of preferred activity? What does the way he uses different modes tell us about the communicative practices, social relationships, social setting and power relations within the setting?'

These questions can be addressed by considering four key concepts that underpin multimodal research: semiotic resource, mode, modal affordance and inter-semiotic relations. It is important to be clear about what these core terms mean, so here we offer brief definitions. For more detailed information on these terms, see the research examples in this chapter, Jewitt (2014) and Jewitt, Bezemer and O'Halloran (2016).

Semiotic resource: This term is used in multimodality to refer to the meaning potential of material resources that are used to make signs (semiosis). The semiotic resources of a mode can be thought of as the connection between representational resources and what people do with them. Semiotic resources might be produced by our bodies – such as vocal apparatus and the muscles we use when we make facial expressions – or by technology – such as a pen or digital medium. Semiotic resources therefore have certain meaning potentials and constraints, depending on their material features and the organized social principles for their use. Kress (2010) has drawn attention to how semiotic resources are transformed over time, by individuals and by societies, for example, the gradual transition of writing from the page to the screen.

Mode: In multimodality, a mode is understood as a semiotic resource for making meaning. To count as a mode, semiotic resources must follow organized principles in their use that are recognized and shared in a community. Modes are therefore an outcome of the cultural shaping of a semiotic resource through its use in the daily social interaction of people. How modes are used might be culture-specific (recognized in a particular community or culture), or it may not be universal. For example, nodding your head in many cultures indicates agreement, and shaking your head from side to side indicates disagreement. Yet in other cultures the opposite is true (nodding means 'no' and moving the head from side to side means 'yes', see Andova and Taylor 2012).

Modal affordance: The term modal affordance refers to the material and the cultural aspects of modes – what it is possible to express and represent easily with a mode. It is a concept connected to both the material and the cultural and social historical use of a mode. Modal affordance raises the question of which mode or modal combinations are 'best' for what. The concept of affordances derives from the work of the psychologist James Gibson (1986), who used the term to refer to the 'action possibilities' that are latent in the environment, and which human beings may or may not perceive or be able to use. In multimodal research, the term 'affordance' is used to describe how different modes offer different potentials for meaning making, depending on the materiality of the mode, the perceptions and abilities of social actors and the social context in which they are used (Flewitt 2005b). The material properties of different semiotic resources and their established social use offer different possibilities and constraints for communication and learning (Hull and Nelson 2005). Modal affordances are therefore shaped both by the materiality of semiotic resources and by the values attributed to them in a given community or culture. Studying the affordances of individual modes enables the researcher to understand what they can or cannot accomplish well in a given context. However, when several modes are used simultaneously – as is usually the case in communication – then multimodality scholars analyse the relationships between modes and semiotic resources.

Inter-semiotic relations: This term is used to describe how different modes are used together to construct or 'orchestrate' meaning. Just as the different instruments in an orchestra all contribute to a particular musical piece, so different modes contribute to a communicational act, with each mode carrying only a part of the whole message. At times, one mode (or instrument, to continue the orchestra analogy) may be salient, and then fade into the background of the communicational act, as a different mode becomes central, and so the flow of communication and meaning making continues. Sometimes, different communicative modes might all align to emphasize and draw attention to a particular point, for example, through spoken words, gaze direction, pointing and shared gaze attention. Such an alignment of modes might form a pattern of consistent behaviour that suggests high-quality interaction between educators and learners. Or there may be contradictions across different modes, for example, an early childhood educator might say one thing to a child, but their facial expression, body posture and action might simultaneously convey a completely different meaning, and this can be confusing for the child. Making sense of a communicative act always involves deciding what to attend to and usually involves attending to more than one mode.

These four concepts provide the starting point for multimodal analysis. They can be used to unpick the complexity of meaning making for young children (and for adults) and to gain deep and rich insights into the norms and rules that exist in different places and spaces about how people talk, move, position themselves in and arrange the material world.

Multimodality in early childhood education research practice

Research Examples 7.1, 7.2 and 7.3 present three different studies to illustrate how early education researchers have turned to multimodality to gain highly original insights into young children's meaning making and movement (7.1), the communication strategies of a minimally verbal child with autism (7.2) and developing early childhood education pedagogy to support young children's multimodal learning with tablet technology (7.3). Research Example 7.1 features a study by Abigail Hackett (2014), about young children's learning in museums. In many early childhood education settings, children can spend a lot of their time moving freely around the environment, making choices about whom they interact with, and what they do. However, many classrooms for young learners are organized in ways that constrain children's movement and choices, while teachers are free to move around. These different 'rules' or norms of practice for teachers and children implicitly convey meanings about the power relations between teachers and children in education, or between adults and children in informal learning spaces. In her study, Hackett reflects on the importance of free movement for children's learning in museum spaces.

Research Example 7.1: Young children's meaning making and movement in museums

Many museums have transformed their appeal as learning spaces by developing interactive displays and visitor experiences. Rather than gazing at precious artefacts in hermetically sealed glass cases, children and adults can often touch and interact with museum exhibits, and museums have been reaching out to enhance very young children's interest in their displays. How can we understand and improve young children's interest, engagement and learning in museum spaces? This dilemma was puzzling researcher and museum educator Abigail Hackett (2014), who studied how children aged twenty-four to twenty-six months co-construct meanings through multiple modes and through sensory, place-based experiences as they explore museum exhibits.

The theoretical framing for Hackett's study built on neo-Vygotskian and multimodal ideas (Finnegan 2002; Kress 1997, 2010) that gesturing, moving and interacting with objects are all significant aspects of meaning making, and that learning is not necessarily reliant on spoken and written language. Hackett was also interested in Christensen's (2003) argument that children attribute meanings and memories to familiar places in their lives and that their meaning making 'emerges from embodied movement through place' (p. 16). The conceptualization of walking as 'place making' (Ingold 2007) became fundamental to Hackett's analysis, as it provided a framework to think about how the children she was observing often chose to walk (or run) along similar routes each time they visited the museum. These pathways then became familiar places for their own learning.

To understand children's movement and choices in the museum, Hackett designed a small-scale ethnographic study, with observations of eight families' monthly visits to the same museum over the course of one year. Data collection included field notes and video-recorded observations, sometimes made by Hackett and sometimes by the children's mothers, who were asked to film anything they felt was significant for ten continuous minutes during each visit. For ethical reasons, the mothers were asked not to film any other museum visitors. This collaborative approach to data collection resulted in a very rich resource of video observations of the children exploring and revisiting the same museum space on multiple occasions. During data analysis, Hackett paid close attention to children's modal choices and to their sensory experiences in the museum.

Scrutinizing the data through a multimodal and space-based lens, Hackett found that individual children's sensory experiences of the museum spaces were imbued with meaning and significance. By making 'walking maps' of individual children's pathways through the museum, Hackett was able to show how the museum as a 'place' was neither static nor fixed but represented something different for each child, with the children's choice of pathways through the exhibits reflecting each child's subjectivity and agency. For example, two-year-old Millie was attracted to a plasma screen in a display area about 'The power of nature' and her mum picked her up so she could touch the screen. This created a lightning effect on the screen, with shards of light emanating from where Millie's hand touched the screen. Millie looked around, and said 'zigging and zooming' as she continued to move her hand around the screen. When her mum put her on the floor again, Millie began to run across and up and down the display area, calling out 'zigging and zooming all over the place' to a friend who was visiting the same space. She subsequently returned many times to the plasma screen, often retracing the same pathways as though trying to remember and share this experience with others.

This is just one example of many similar observed episodes that enabled Hackett to identify how the children moved through the museum both as a way of coming to know the spaces and as a way to communicate and share their interest with others. This suggests that to understand how very young children make meaning in learning spaces such as those offered in museums, we need to understand the relationships between the children's lines of walking, gesture and speech:

> By taking seriously where and how young children go, we can recognize the full range of modes via which young children can express their ideas and responses, and thus acknowledge the agency of young children to both construct meaning and communicate about their developing experiences of the world. (Hackett 2014: 20)

Representing multimodal data

Hackett's study aimed to capture the complexity of children's learning through embodied action, and was enabled by the affordability and portability of digital recording devices that were less commonly available to researchers ten or twenty years ago. However, rich video data presents new challenges for researchers in terms of transcription and representation, and raises many questions regarding how to write about visual research in ways that capture at least some of the complexity of the data (Bezemer and Mavers 2011; Cowan 2014; Flewitt et al. 2014). This was a challenge faced by Lauren Doak, who investigated the multimodal classroom communication of five children who were on the autism spectrum, as described in Research Example 7.2. In this example, we focus on how Doak developed a series of transcription styles that enabled her to capture how the children's actions, gaze, body postures and vocalizations were fluidly co-ordinated during interaction with their peers and with adults.

Research Example 7.2: The classroom communication strategies of a minimally verbal child

In this study, Lauran Doak explored the multimodal classroom communication of 5 children aged from five to seven years on the autism spectrum, who attended a special school in the English Midlands. The study acknowledged clinical differences in neurodevelopmental in non-typically developing children but combined this recognition with critical reflection on how dis/ability is enabled or constrained through social and discursive practices. The focus in this extract is on the communication and multimodal choices made by one boy 'Luke', aged six, during snack time. In the special school where Doak conducted her study, minimally verbal children learnt how to use picture exchange communication system (PECS) – one of several augmentative and alternative communication (AAC) systems that are taught as a communication tool to supplement or replace speech if a person's oral language skills do not fully meet their communicative needs.

During snack time, the children in this setting were offered a tray of snacks, with each food type in a different section of the tray (e.g. apple slices, raisins, carrots, etc.). Children were encouraged to request food by using PECS to choose the image of the food they wanted to select and show the image to the member of staff who would then offer the chosen snack. The repetition of this established ritual during snack time and other structured activities aimed to embed the principles of the AAC systems in children's communicative repertoire and to give a purpose to their use.

Through her study, Doak learnt that at home, Luke tended not to use PECS but to communicate with his family through embodied action, such as pointing to the cupboard where the snacks were kept, supplemented by (often) single words (such as 'there' or 'here') – and this generally worked well in terms of achieving the purpose of his communication. However, the special setting had a different teaching and learning agenda, and on several occasions, Doak observed that Luke actively challenged adult decisions about how he should communicate. For instance, during one snack time, he wanted to choose more raisins after all the raisins had been eaten. However, the way the PECS system was used in the classroom did not allow children to ask for items that were unavailable – the assumption was that children would show a different image to select a different snack. However, Luke wanted more raisins, so rather than make an alternative choice, he placed his left hand on the empty space on the tray where the raisins had been and asked 'Uh?' The adult signalled 'All gone' using Makaton signs of upturned palms, which Luke imitated several times. This exchange was repeated, with Luke persistently refusing to show an alternative PECS card. In doing so, he enacted his own agency by orchestrating a different meaning ('I'd rather have more raisins') through the use of the 'multimodal ensemble' of eye gaze, vocalization, gesture and artefact manipulation.

Representing visual data in multimodal research can be problematic (see Flewitt 2006; Plowman and Stephen 2008), and for Doak, the rich video data generated by this study presented many challenges. Doak deployed three multimodal transcription methods to visualize the data from the different theoretical perspectives offered by conversation analysis and multimodal interactional analysis. The methods chosen included narrative vignettes, multimodal matrices and annotated video stills, as shown below.

All gone ... finished!

4:42.4

'finished'

8. Jane nods head and raises eyebrows. She Makaton signs 'finished' along with speech.

FIGURE 7.1 *Luke making food choices at snack time. Courtesy of Dr Lauran Doak.*

Through her fine-grained analysis, Doak argues convincingly that AAC is not inherently enabling. Rather, when AAC is used in communities where competence and power are asymmetrical – as is the case in most schools where adults wield considerably more power than children. Rather than truly enabling children's communication, how AAC systems are used reflects rather than challenges unequal power relations. This further highlights challenging issues around the imbalance of power in interaction between disabled and non-disabled people. Doak's multimodal methodological approach offers unique and innovative insights into the children's communicative competence since it (re)values their embodied modes of expression through action, posture, haptics, eye gaze and gesture, and does not assume that these modes are *a priori* more or less significant than speech or similar language systems (such as AAC) in the multimodal orchestration of meaning.

Researching young children's digital lives

Developments in information and communication technology have transformed everyday literacy practices in contemporary society. Handheld and mobile devices with touch-sensitive screens offer varied potentials and an array of modes with which we can make meaning, such as sound, moving and still images, emojis, stickers, written and spoken language and video links. These can all be combined in the construction of modally complex ensembles. For young children, digital platforms offer new tools for learning and communication, and can help to equip young twenty-first-century learners with the skills and knowledge they need to be creative and critical producers and consumers of information (Kalantzis and Cope 2012). Digital technology offers diverse modes of communication, such as voice and video recording, and telling moments in children's learning can be captured to document and assess their development over time (Flewitt and Cowan 2019). The more teachers and children interact with digital technologies, the more comfortable and proficient they become, yet many early childhood educators lack the confidence, knowledge and training needed to embed digital media in their pedagogy (Flewitt, Messer and Kucirkova 2015). Research Example 7.3 reports on how researchers worked with early childhood educators in a longitudinal study in Australia, with a view to creating 'contexts for multimodal learning in the 21st-century childhoods' (Yelland 2018: 847).

Research Example 7.3: Young children and multimodal learning with tablets

In this study, Nichola Yelland worked with early childhood educators and children between four and eight years of age from schools in areas of socio-economic disadvantage in one Australian state. The specific aims of the study were to provide empirical evidence about the potential of new technologies for literacy learning and to enable teachers to transform their pedagogy in ways that reflect the digital nature of literacy practices in the contemporary world. The research design followed the principles of participant observation, with the researchers' observations documented in narrative form. The study was informed by the theoretical constructs of multi-literacies pedagogy (New London Group 1996), which offers a much broader view of literacy than traditional, language-based approaches. A multi-literacies perspective recognizes the diversity of media, culture and languages that characterize communication in the world today and considers that the ability to negotiate the array of modes and media available is central to the learning, work and private lives of children and adults. This view of literacy is in line with the broad definition of literacy promoted by UNESCO (2004):

> Literacy is the ability to identify, understand, interpret, create, communicate and compute, using printed and written materials associated with varying contexts. Literacy involves a continuum of learning in enabling individuals to achieve their goals, to develop their knowledge and potential, and to participate fully in their community and wider society. (p. 13)

The researchers looked into the learning potential of different types of apps, beginning with what they term 'entry-level' apps, that is, apps that aim to help children learn particular literacy skills, such as letter and sound recognition, and vocabulary learning (e.g. *Alpha Tots* and *Monkey Lunch Box*). Apps such as these involve a series of hierarchically organized, sequential tasks, which must be completed before a learner can move to the 'next level'. The tasks tend to be 'drill and practice' in nature, and their content is usually closed, that is, it is not possible to change or add to the app content. Although limited in their scope, these apps were useful as a starting point for adults to start conversations with children about particular skills and concepts, and to integrate these skills in other learning activities and resources as part of planned learning.

The teachers also introduced 'open content' apps, such as Book Creator, where children can create narratives about their own lives and experiences, using literacy for a purpose and creating highly original multimodal texts. For example, Yelland reports how one setting included digital media in a classroom project about a trip the teacher and children had made to a local, Indigenous cultural centre, where they had taken photographs and made recordings while they were there. Back in class, they created an eBook as a dynamic record of the trip, with photographs, video, written text, oral recordings, illustrations, and maps they had found on the internet. This new digital resource could be revisited whenever the children or teachers wanted to remember the day, and a (less interactive) printed version was also made. Using different apps (e.g. Sock Puppets and Play School Art Maker) the children created artwork and plays, wrote a 'play' with different scenes and characters, and then made a one minute animated video of the play that they had co-created.

Yelland discusses how incorporating digital media in early learning requires much more than purchasing recommended apps. Practitioners need to consider how different digital resources can be incorporated in planned learning activities that complement and extend established pedagogy and practices through playful and creative exploration, with carefully planned scaffolding that extends children's knowledge and expression through multiple modalities. The paper illustrates the ways in which multimodal learning can be fostered by using digital technologies to complement rather than replace more traditional learning resources and suggests that being a contemporary educator is not just about using tablets and apps, but incorporating them into planning and pedagogy for a dynamic learning programme.

Critiques of multimodality

Multimodality has struck a chord with academics from a range of disciplines and the term has been adopted in policy documents, classroom practice, teacher education and professional development. However, as a comparatively recent field of investigation, multimodality is not without its critics. For example, Bazalgette and Buckingham (2013) suggest that the social semiotic theoretical framing for multimodality is complex and is consequently often misunderstood or misrepresented:

> Inevitably, the theory has been simplified in order to make it usable by classroom teachers and attract the attention of policy-makers with neither the time nor the inclination to read academic tomes. (p. 96)

Bazalgette and Buckingham (2013) argue that 'multimodal texts' are mistakenly often thought of as equivalent to 'digital texts' and that 'modes' are thought of as simply 'methods of communication'. As discussed throughout this chapter, neither of these simplifications is correct. As Research Example 7.3 illustrates, it can be helpful for researchers to work with practitioners to work out how a multimodal approach to meaning making can be built into teachers' planning and practice, with a shared goal to enhance opportunities for young children's learning. Bazalgette and Buckingham further critique multimodality for seeking rational decision-making processes in individuals' choices of modes in interaction and text creation, and for ignoring 'the haphazard and improvised nature of much human communication, as well as its emotional dimensions' (p. 98).

Similarly, Lemke (2014) has noted the importance of aligning multimodality with more established traditions, such as media studies, and argues the case for developing 'a political economy of transmedia signs' (p. 150) which pays close attention to the institutional contexts of media production, and issues of power, accessibility, convenience and suitability. Such critiques are extremely useful to attend to in one's own work, and point to the need for greater clarity and agreement in the growing field of multimodal research.

What makes a study multimodal?

We suggest that if you are interested in how young children communicate, how they make meaning, or how they interact with people or artefacts in different social situations, then multimodality offers a robust methodological framing to support your work. If you are thinking about using a multimodal approach in your research, then here are some pointers that might help you design your study. Examples of research questions in multimodal research include, for example:

- How are some children constructed as more socially confident and better communicators than others? (see Flewitt 2005b)

- How do young children with learning disabilities cope with moving between the three different communicative and social environments of home, a special early childhood setting and a mainstream/inclusive early childhood setting? (see Flewitt, Nind and Payler 2009; Nind, Flewitt and Payler 2010)

- How do young children develop literacy knowledge as they engage with printed and electronic media? (see Wolfe and Flewitt 2010)

Jewitt, Bezemer and O'Halloran (2016: 5) suggest that researchers tend to either 'do multimodality', that is, multimodality is central to a study's research aims, methodological framing and theory, or 'adopt methodological concepts', that is, multimodality concepts (such as mode, semiotic resources and modal assemblage) are used selectively, in tandem with other methodological and theoretical framings. However, it can be problematic to mix concepts that originate in different theoretical or disciplinary traditions as they may not be 'epistemologically compatible' (Flewitt 2011). It is important to remember that the theoretical underpinning for a study must be closely aligned with the methodological design, in order to produce the kind of evidence needed to address the research questions. In essence, if you mix and match too much, you can end up with a confusion of ideas and methods that can pull a study in different directions. It is therefore essential to be clear about the place of multimodality in your study.

Concluding thoughts

In summary, multimodality offers a fundamentally different perspective on human interaction and meaning making in the social world. Rather than examining modes in isolation, multimodality researchers consider how multiple modes work together to create meanings in a 'multimodal ensemble' (Kress et al. 2001). While acknowledging the central role that language can play in interaction, multimodality recognizes that language is just one part of a complex *ensemble of resources* for making meaning and communicating. This significant shift in perspective offers radically new insights into understandings of communicative and learning processes.

Multimodality offers a theoretically grounded methodological framework to explore social interaction and learning in classrooms, at home, in more informal learning spaces (such as museums and libraries) and in texts (whether visual or written, printed or digital). Multimodality has been critiqued for being overly complex, yet it is underpinned by three clear and distinct assumptions: (1) *humans orchestrate meaning by selecting and configuring modes in particular ways*; (2) *there are often patterns in how modes are used, and these patterns are shared in particular communities and cultures*; (3) *people make motivated choices to orchestrate meaning by selecting and configuring modes in particular ways.*

As the research examples have shown, the more a set of resources is used in the social life of a particular community, the more fully and finely articulated it becomes. However, as seen in Doak's research, there is often a hierarchy of modes in education settings, with language (and standardized communication systems such as PECs) at the 'top' of this hierarchy, and other modes, such as gaze and action, less highly valued. A multimodality perspective argues that there needs to be a shared cultural sense within a community of how multiple modes can be organized to realize meaning, and how children's subtle signs of learning can be observed, documented and valued in early childhood education (Cowan and Flewitt 2019; Flewitt and Cowan 2019).

If you are new to multimodality you might consider how this approach could be useful to help you to

- collect, document and systematically catalogue the semiotic resources that people use to make meaning, bringing new kinds of data into the analytic frame by making a range of modes available for analysis;

- understand, through detailed analysis, how different modes are used in specific contexts, and what factors drive their use, including how social norms and ways of being shape how resources are deployed in particular sites of practice; how the social histories of these resources are materialized in their use; how modal choices reflect power dynamics in any given social situation; how meanings are carried differently across modes; and how modal ensembles are orchestrated for particular effect;

- investigate how new semiotic resources are used, such as emerging technologies, sensory learning with touch-responsive technologies, children's online and offline learning, and the development of effective pedagogy to support learning with digital and touchscreen technologies; and

- study young children's multimodal learning during face-to-face social interaction with their peers, siblings and adults.

Multimodality therefore offers a robust set of concepts that can be applied across different kinds of data and across different digital and non-digital research contexts: to study printed or written texts, artefacts and social interaction, and to think about how different spaces and places shape the ways in which people behave and interact. This is particularly useful in environments where there is complexity in the data, such as in the home environment or in nursery or primary school education, where there are many different artefacts and texts being used and different kinds of interaction, and where language often plays only a partial, if significant, role in young children's meaning making.

Suggestions for further reading

The following readings will serve as useful points of reference for early childhood researchers interested in working with multimodality:

Flewitt, R. S. (2005b). Is every child's voice heard? Researching the different ways 3-year-old children communicate and make meaning at home and in a preschool playgroup, *Early Years: International Journal of Research and Development* 25 (3): 207–22.

Flewitt, R. S. (2012). Multimodal perspectives on early childhood literacies. In J. Larson and J. Marsh (Eds.), *The SAGE Handbook of Early Childhood Literacy* (2nd edn, pp. 295–309). London: Sage.

Halliday, M. A. K. (1978). *Language as Social Semiotic: The Social Interpretation of Language and Meaning*. London: Edward Arnold.

Jewitt, C. (Eds.) (2014). *Routledge Handbook of Multimodal Analysis*. Abingdon: Routledge.

Jewitt, C., Bezemer, J. and O'Halloran, K. L. (2016). *Introducing Multimodality*. London and New York: Routledge.

Kress, G. (1997). *Before Writing: Rethinking Paths to Literacy*. London: Routledge.

Kress, G. (2010). *Multimodality: Exploring Contemporary Methods of Communication*. London: Routledge.

CHAPTER EIGHT

Mixed Methods in Early Childhood Education Research

In this chapter we reflect on mixed method design, that is, research that includes both quantitative and qualitative methods. We begin by considering the methodologies associated with quantitative and qualitative research, the different insights they offer into early childhood education, and the different weight they can bear in influencing education change. We present examples of small- and large-scale studies from around the globe that have combined these approaches in mixed methods research, and we consider how these studies can help us to arrive at a fuller understanding of the world.

Mixed methods research: Bridging the qualitative and quantitative divide

The term 'mixed methods' refers to research which involves the mixing or integration of both quantitative and qualitative methods and/or data within a single study or design. Mixed methods inquiry is a relatively new field, and its growth in popularity has been attributed to the social sciences, including education and sociology (Pearce 2012). Mixed methods have subsequently expanded into the health and medical sciences, and academic fields such as nursing, family medicine, mental health, pharmacy, and other related life-sciences disciplines.

As a methodological approach, mixed methods research has been defined in several different ways. It has been described as

the type of research in which a researcher or team of researchers combines elements of qualitative and quantitative research approaches (e.g., use of qualitative and quantitative viewpoints, data collection, analysis, inference techniques) for the broad purposes of breadth and depth of understanding and corroboration. (Johnson, Onwuegbuzie, and Turner 2007: 123)

Other definitions emphasize the extent to which qualitative and quantitative approaches are integrated, for example, Cresswell (2008) suggests the term implies not only the collection or analysis of both quantitative and qualitative data in a single study, where the data are collected concurrently or sequentially, but also the integration of data at one or more stages in the process of research. Tashakkori and Teddlie (2010) identify mixed methods research as the combination of quantitative and qualitative data-collection procedures such as surveys and focus group interviews to address a set of research questions, as opposed to a multi-method research, which adopts two or more quantitative or qualitative data-collection instruments. For some, mixed method research is referred to as a third paradigm, with positivist/quantitative research being the first and interpretive/qualitative research being the second (see Creswell 2008; Gray 2017).

Historically, qualitative and quantitative methods were perceived to present two mutually exclusive epistemological paradigms that are underpinned by contrasting philosophical viewpoints of the world (Kuhn 1962; Rossman and Wilson, 1994). Quantitative methods were considered positivist in their underlying assumption that there is an objective social reality which is observable and measurable ('facts'), while qualitative research takes on a social constructivist or interpretivist approach which assumes there is no objective reality and human beings actively construct knowledge as they interact with the world around them ('meanings'). Researchers have also described the process of conducting qualitative research as being inductive (moving from specific cases and observations to theory development) and quantitative research as being deductive (moving from theory or hypotheses to representative cases) (Johnson and Gray 2010). There are also significant differences in the relationship between the researcher and the research participants – in quantitative research the researcher is often positioned as distant, as an 'outsider', whereas in qualitative research, the researcher usually aims to form close relationships with participants, and to move towards being more of an 'insider'. Perhaps the most salient difference lies in the nature of the data that is scrutinized – in quantitative research data are usually numeric, whereas in qualitative research data tend to be textual (language-based texts, visual texts or performance as texts, and so on).

Understanding the profound implications of these different paradigmatic stances and their philosophical and theoretical assumptions is important when considering the foundations that inform mixed methods research. Within these contrasting paradigms, it was often deemed problematic to combine two research approaches which were underpinned by such clearly distinct and irreconcilable philosophical assumptions. Polemic debates about the 'qualitative versus quantitative' divide were encapsulated in what was referred to as the 'paradigm wars' (Bryman 1984; Johnson and Gray 2010) which prompted discussions around the incompatibility of the contrasting philosophies that permeate the ways in which knowledge is produced and interpreted.

Advances in research in the last two decades have precipitated the bridging of the gap between the contrasting paradigms and the 'qualitative versus quantitative divide'. To this end, researchers have explored the benefits and versatility of research that is carried out from a range of philosophical stances beyond a simplistic dualistic standpoint as positive or constructivist; qualitative or quantitative. The attraction and possibility of bringing together distinct paradigmatic approaches has been evident in the steady growth of studies combining qualitative and quantitative research, particularly over the past two decades (Smith 2006; Ridenour and Newman 2008; Tashakkori and Teddlie 2010), where the methodology has been refined to suit a wide variety of research questions across disciplines (Creswell and Plano Clark 2011). Some researchers argue that the combination of methods produces studies that are richer and more robust than studies that follow a single methodological approach. Creswell and Plano Clark (2011) highlight the generative value of mixed methods research in engendering new intellectual possibilities: 'Today, we see cross-cultural international interest, interdisciplinary interest, publication possibilities, and public and private funding opportunities for mixed methods research' (p. 18). However, others argue that mixed methods research has become 'methods centric' (Hesse-Biber 2010: 456) and that by focusing on established mixed methods methodology there is a tendency for theory to be misplaced or misaligned, and for the quantitative aspects of a study to be prioritized over qualitative findings (for further critique of this approach, see the section on 'Choices and challenges' in this chapter).

Nonetheless, researchers have highlighted the merits of taking a creative approach in mixing methods to capture a novel degree of complexity and diversity of a specific subject area (Cook and Reichardt 1979; Greene, Caracelli and Graham 1989; Brannen 1992), and of implementing a qualitative approach to mixed methods practice, with 'the goals of understanding, promoting social change, uncovering subjugated knowledge, and providing a unique venue for qualitative researchers to generalize and test out their ideas' (Hesse-Biber 2010: 467). The benefits of using mixed methods have been attributed to advancements in research rigour and the development of new research questions and designs. Researchers who favour mixed methods argue that the integration of quantitative and qualitative approaches offers a more comprehensive and synergistic use of data compared to the deployment of distinct methods and datasets. It has also been argued that the methodology has the advantage of enhancing the validity of more internally consistent data sets, offering greater triangulation (Johnson, Onwuegbuzie, and Turner 2007) and thereby allowing for what Fielding (2012) describes as greater 'analytic density' (p. 124).

Early mixed methods researchers Rossman and Wilson (1994) remarked on the capacity of mixed methods to investigate complex phenomena in ways where 'the divergent, the unexpected and the problematic are sought out, attended to, and incorporated in the emerging understanding' (p. 324), while contemporary researchers Sligo, Nairn and McGee (2018) advocate conjoining qualitative and quantitative components to address complex research questions in health and social sciences to achieve better research outcomes. Indeed, by combining both qualitative and quantitative methods, researchers often aim to elicit broad and rich data compared to single study approaches where the findings may be narrower and more simplistic (Tashakkori and Teddlie 2010). Mixed method research also offers the potential to cultivate new lines of thinking, and can increase the chances that a study will elicit new ways of looking at the issues and new research questions, as well as maximize the possibility of new discoveries and unexpected findings. Arguably, a mixed method inquiry can illuminate the paradoxical and contradictory dimensions that compel researchers to look for explanations, which in turn may lead to the reframing of research questions, or reconceptualizing of researchers' assumptions. In summary, after great debate over many years about the incompatibility and impossibility of undertaking quantitative and qualitative approaches within the same study, the approach is now securely recognized as a methodology in its own right: 'Mixed methods research has evolved to the point where it is a separate methodological orientation with its own worldview, vocabulary, and techniques' (Tashakkori and Teddlie 2003: x).

Designing mixed methods research

In order to address complex social questions effectively, a mixed methods study must be exceptionally well designed. An important consideration is the extent and nature of the integration of methods, and the analysis of the resulting data. The *Handbook of Mixed Methods in the Social and Behavioural Sciences* (Tashakkori and Teddlie 2010) recognizes that mixed methods research encompasses a wide range of approaches, designs and interpretations of how the methods work in synergy. Integrating qualitative and quantitative approaches involves a creative process of sequencing and implementing each method at different phases or in different strands of the research, while engaging with different types of activities and data (Creswell 2003). Creswell (2008), for example, describes two basic types of mixed methods designs: concurrent or sequential. A sequential design occurs when qualitative and quantitative information are collected in two phases, with one form of data collection followed by the other. A concurrent or parallel mixed methods design acts to elicit quantitative and qualitative data simultaneously. Here, we outline four established approaches to mixed methods design.

Design 1 is a sequential design where an exploratory qualitative phase helps to identify themes and concepts in relation to the phenomenon being investigated, and these themes are then used as the basis for a larger-scale survey that will render data for quantitative analysis.

Design 2 is a sequential design where a mixed methods study might begin with a questionnaire which reveals issues that can then be explored in more depth through qualitative enquiry, often with a smaller study sample chosen purposively to explore the issues unmasked by the initial quantitative phase.

Design 3 also follows a sequential pattern of investigation but includes multiple phases in a broader research study, in what Miles and Huberman (2014) refer to as 'an alternating style' (p. 44). Following this approach, an initial questionnaire might highlight important phenomena, which are then investigated through a qualitative phase aimed at building a strong conceptual understanding of the phenomenon, followed by an experiment to test a phenomenon, or competing phenomena and statistical analysis.

Design 4 involves the concurrent and integrated use of quantitative and qualitative approaches, as deemed necessary to investigate particular phenomena. For example, a large-scale survey might begin by asking for demographic information (such as parental gender, age, income bracket, place of residence, child age and gender), followed by a series of statements and ratings (such as *strongly disagree* = 4, *disagree* = 3, *agree* = 2, *strongly agree* = 1). The survey might then end with more open-ended questions, which prompt the production of qualitative data. In the subsequent analysis, descriptive statistics can be used to analyse the demographic data, the ratings responses can be analysed statistically, and the open responses can be coded and key themes can then be identified through qualitative analysis. This approach therefore enables the researcher to interpret the different data in relation to each other.

Sequential mixed methods design is widely used in the social sciences, where quantitative data is first collected and analysed, followed by a second phase of qualitative enquiry, designed to lend deeper insights into the phenomena suggested by the quantitative phase. Or conversely, a first phase of qualitative investigation might be deployed to explore a topic, followed by a quantitative phase. A two-phase study which investigated the parenting practices of Italian mothers and child misbehaviour offers a useful exemplar of a sequential design which incorporated a highly structured, quantitative questionnaire and semi-structured interviews to gain both broad and deep insights (Bombi et al. 2015). The study was designed with qualitative and quantitative measures, including standardized questionnaires with children and parents, followed by one-to-one interviews with parents to address the main research question: 'What practices do mothers use when trying to correct their children's misbehaviour?' The study was based on a subset of a larger longitudinal study of parent behaviour where participants were recruited from schools in Rome, Italy. The overall sample included 103 mothers and 103 children aged eight years. The results showed a range of different parenting practices along a continuum of reasoning and punitive authoritarian styles. Notably, the qualitative findings cohered with findings from the quantitative analysis and helped the researchers to interpret them. The researchers found the qualitative data and analysis particularly beneficial for informing a better understanding of the contexts and narratives of differing parenting styles and disciplinary practices: 'Qualitative data deepen understanding of parenting because they shed light on what parents think about themselves; their self-descriptions, in turn, help to identify ways of parenting that may have long-lasting consequences for children's adjustment' (p. 207).

Research Example 8.1 presents a small-scale study with exploratory, sequential mixed method design conducted in China to explore parents', teachers' and principals' perceptions of three-year-old children's readiness for early childhood education.

Research Example 8.1: Perspectives on three-year-olds' readiness for preschool in China

China has an ambitious policy goal to provide universal early childhood education for all three-year-olds by 2020. In this study, Sha Xie and Hui Li designed a sequential mixed methods investigation to explore how Chinese parents, teachers and principals perceive children's preschool readiness. Xie and Li conducted semi-structured interviews with 24 parents (2 of whom were fathers), 11 teachers, and 4 preschool principals, in four preschool settings, followed by a questionnaire completed by 231 parents to validate the findings from the interviews.

During the initial phase of interviews, the researchers began by using group interviews in two preschools, but they found that partly due to the collectivist culture in Chinese culture, participants tended to agree with each other rather than offer their own opinions. Interviews in the remaining two preschools were therefore conducted one-to-one. Once responses from all thirty-nine interviews had been conducted and analysed, the key findings were used to design a questionnaire to probe the issues raised with a wider population. A total of 327 questionnaires were distributed, of which 231 were completed and returned. This good return rate rendered sufficient data for statistical analysis.

Overall, the study results suggested that preschool readiness was conceived by stakeholders as a three-construct concept: child readiness, family readiness and preschool readiness. Child readiness included social–emotional readiness as well as academic competency and pre-literacy skills. Three concerns were expressed regarding preschool readiness, namely, lack of adequate 'educare'; the need for childcare prior to preschool; and identifying an appropriate age for preschool entry. Overall, the findings imply the need for increased collaboration between home, schools and communities, in order to develop contextually and culturally relevant practices that promote preschool readiness among young children.

Mixed method design has also been used in evaluation research, where combining RCTs with qualitative methods has reaped considerable benefits in studies which seek to assess the effectiveness of complex interventions in education. For example, a significant and original study by Spillane et al. (2010) at Northwestern University, USA, followed a mixed method research approach using RCT and qualitative methods to evaluate the impact of a professional development programme for head teachers in urban K-12 schools (from Kindergarten to age twelve). Sequential quantitative and qualitative approaches were used during data collection and analysis to gain insights into participants' perspectives of the outcomes and key challenges of the intervention. An RCT design was employed where one group of head teachers (the treatment group) was randomly assigned to participate in the treatment at the beginning of the study, and the remaining principals were randomly chosen to begin the treatment one year after the first group (delayed-treatment group). The treatment or intervention was a development programme aimed at improving student achievement by enhancing head teachers' leadership knowledge and skills. The programme consisted of workshops, study groups, case studies and action research projects led by the teachers, as well as distance learning for professional development delivered over fourteen sessions. The topic areas covered by the programme included strategic thinking for principals, instructional leadership, effective student learning experiences and the development of a professional learning community. Quantitative measures included whole-school staff questionnaires, head teacher questionnaires, structured observations and student achievement data. Qualitative approaches included observations of the professional development workshops, follow-up interviews, and observations of a sub-sample of school principals' practice over the course of one working day, followed by sixty-three in-depth interviews with twenty head teachers and the school district office staff. The research team found that combining qualitative and quantitative methods allowed them to triangulate the findings generated by different data sources about participants' knowledge and leadership practice. Overall, the study findings offered rich understandings of the local context and more importantly, demonstrated the extent to which different variables in the study context interacted with the treatment to shape the delivery of the professional development programme.

In research about young children's health, mixed methods that include RCTs are routinely used to test the effectiveness of interventions (Lewin, Glenton and Oxman 2009). However, the effects of randomization are not always clearly discernible where local, cultural and other variables interact with the intervention, so the reasons for variation within each treatment group or arm of the RCT are not always explicable. It is crucial to understand why an intervention is or is not effective, so that patterns from the findings can be derived and the results can be usefully rolled out to wider populations. Furthermore, identifying factors that influence the success, or not, of interventions is essential to enable other researchers to develop similar types of interventions that can build on the proven effectiveness and weaknesses of previous intervention designs and are therefore more likely to be effective. In this regard, qualitative research methods can help to lend deeper insights into why interventions do not work in some circumstances, by exploring whether interventions have been delivered as planned or whether they have encountered barriers to successful implementation. Using qualitative methods, researchers can further explore reasons for the findings of the trial and explain possible variations in effectiveness within the sample. This can in turn generate new questions or hypotheses. This is especially pertinent in the context of increased demands for empirical evidence of government-driven 'what works' agenda, particularly in the United Kingdom and the United States, where the Department of Education has tried to accumulate findings from research to enable educators to make 'evidence-based decisions' via the US 'What Works Clearinghouse' (WWC) (see https://ies.ed.gov/ncee/wwc/).

The above studies feature sequential mixed methods design, but as mentioned, a concurrent approach is also sometimes used to elicit both qualitative and quantitative data simultaneously from a single instrument. A study of early childhood educators' perspectives of parental involvement in Finnish day care was conducted through a five-part survey questionnaire administered to early childhood educators working in Helsinki, Finland (Hakyemez-Paul, Pihlaja and Silvennoinen 2018). A questionnaire was completed by a representative sample of 287 educators in two phases to collect quantitative and qualitative responses. The quantitative dimensions incorporated a standardized Likert rating scale to explore respondents' general attitudes towards parental involvement, while open-ended questions allowed the opportunity for participants to further explain their responses. The open-ended answers generated qualitative data and participant insights to supplement the quantitative material. Mixed method analytic procedures included factor analysis for the quantitative data and content analysis for the qualitative responses, thus offering a combination of measurements and interpretations of the composite data. As a result, the research teams were able to show that Finnish early childhood educators in general have a positive attitude towards parental involvement, particularly for children's learning at home. Probing more deeply into the qualitative data suggested that poor parental motivation and a lack of time on the part of both educators and parents contributed to difficulties in parents' close involvement in their children's learning.

The studies discussed here show some of the variations that are possible in mixed methods research, and possible combinations of qualitative and quantitative methods that have been employed to investigate particular phenomena. The studies demonstrate how researchers can employ variations flexibly in mixed methods research by designing individual studies to suit their particular research questions and aims. However, as with any other design, researchers must first understand and carefully consider the various dimensions of a mixed methods design. Combining the merits of quantitative and qualitative methods will then allow the opportunity for new theoretical and paradigmatic reflections.

The following section illustrates an example of a seminal, large-scale longitudinal mixed methods study into effective provision for young children's education that continues to have significant impact on early childhood education in the UK and to influence early childhood education research and practice on a global scale.

Research Example 8.2: Mixed Methods in a large-scale investigation of the effects of preschool provision (EPPE)

Over the past two decades, a growing body of research has shown a wide range of benefits from early childhood education and care that act as a foundation for lifelong learning, including, among others, better child well-being; better and more equitable child outcomes; increased intergenerational social mobility; and better social and economic development for society at large (Melhuish et al. 2015; OECD 2012; Siraj and Mayo 2014). However, research has also shown that the benefits of early childhood education and care are largely dependent upon its quality (Sylva et al. 2004, 2011).

The first systematic longitudinal research study that identified clear links between the quality of early childhood education and positive outcomes for children and families was the Effective Provision of

Pre-school Education (EPPE) project (Sammons et al. 2005) in the United Kingdom, which was extended to the Effective Pre-school, Primary and Secondary Education Project (EPPSE), and ran from 1997 to 2014. Funded by the UK Department for Education and Skills (DfES), this longitudinal study investigated the influence of preschool education on children's academic and social–behavioural outcomes, and also studied the role of the home learning environment (HLE), the family, neighbourhood and other school experiences on children's learning, progress and learning dispositions.

The robust mixed method research design enabled the study to achieve these outcomes. EPPSE followed the lives of 2,800 children from 6 English Local Authorities, beginning with their attendance at 141 private, voluntary and maintained preschool settings (Sylva et al. 2004). A further 380 'home educated' children were recruited when the preschool cohort of children started primary school (at age five). Qualitative and quantitative methods were employed in this unique large-scale study, including standardized child assessments carried out over time, case study child profiles and interviews with parents and preschool staff, as well as classroom observations and evaluations of the settings' quality through the use of standardized rating scales.

Quantitative analysis was applied in the first phase of the study to isolate the independent variables that explained variations in the progress and social–behavioural development of young children during their time in preschool. Multilevel analyses were also used to explore variations in the effectiveness of preschool institutions in terms of different child outcomes. To complement the quantitative data, qualitative case study observations and interviews were undertaken in the Researching Effective Pedagogy in the Early Years (REPEY) arm of the study (Siraj-Blatchford et al. 2002) which included detailed observations of pedagogy in a range of settings, as well as systematic target child observations to document individual children's learning. Qualitative data were also collected through interviews with parents, and with staff and managers in the settings.

The findings were derived by taking an iterative approach to data analysis. Statistical analyses including multilevel modelling were used to synthesize the multiple sources of data and to examine the effects of preschool on a range of child factors, taking account of a range of child, parent and home background factors. The qualitative data collection and analysis provided in-depth descriptions of the structure and characteristics associated with effective settings (Siraj-Blatchford et al. 2008) and traced the different developmental pathways of children who 'succeeded against the odds' (Siraj-Blatchford, 2010; Siraj-Blatchford et al. 2011).

The findings of this exceptional mixed methods study offered a rich depth of analysis and rigour from the quantitative and qualitative data sets. The study showed the positive effects of high-quality preschool provision on children's intellectual and social development, and also showed that the duration of attendance was an important indicator for children's overall development. Furthermore, the study found that well-trained qualified teachers and a quality HLE can significantly extend children's learning.

Overall, the researchers attributed the success of the project to its mixed methods design, stating that it 'enabled a study of pre-school influence that is more meaningful, and provides a wider evidence base for both policymakers and practitioners than reliance on only one form of data gathering and approach to analysis' (Sammons et al. 2005: 221). Although the EPPSE research ended in 2014, its methodology has been adopted in other large-scale, longitudinal studies in England and elsewhere, including the Millennium Cohort Study (Hansen and Joshi 2007).

Choices and challenges

The growth in educational research that combines qualitative and quantitative research methods is testament to the inevitable conclusion 'that numbers and words are *both* needed if we are to understand the world' (italics in original, Miles and Huberman 2014: 42). Many researchers have espoused the benefits of mixed methods research (Brannen, 1992; Creswell and Plano Clark 2011; Johnson and Onwuegbuzie 2004; Yin 2006), yet effectively managing the interplay between qualitative and quantitative methods comes with notable challenges. Researchers often face difficult choices when deciding whether to adopt the methodology, depending on the complementarity and complexity of the methods, and the type of knowledge they wish to convey about the research topic. Successful mixed methods research is more than just simply combining qualitative and quantitative data, methods or paradigms in a research study or set of studies. The process and degree of integration, that is, the mixing and assimilation of data, is a major challenge facing researchers when adopting a mixed methods approach. The methodological challenge is such that some researchers have questioned whether integration is truly possible, arguing that 'while integration is a desired goal, it is not always successfully achieved in practice' (Uprichard and Dawney 2016: 1). This is due to the complex and at times conflicting nature of social research when data sets are generated using methods that are not compatible:

> We outline a fundamental paradox at the heart of mixed methods research, namely, that mixed methods are assumed to be useful because of the complexity of the social world, yet in spite of this, it is also assumed to be both possible and desirable to integrate data relating to the study of complex, messy social objects. (Uprichard and Dawney 2016: 2)

Spillane et al. (2010) argue that using mixed methods design to influence complex social phenomena, such as educational leadership knowledge and practice in the real world, presents new challenges for education research, and they point to the challenges of verifying inferences from sometimes convergent data. Similarly, Gray (2017) suggests that researchers risk misinterpreting commonalities and differences across data sets when incompatible methods are used.

However, the health researcher Barbour (1999) contends that the key value of mixed methods research is that the integration of qualitative and quantitative dimensions can work to enhance research findings, provided the research design is robust and researchers are critically reflective about the potential pitfalls of mixing methods. The main challenge for researchers engaged in mixed methods research is explicitly to report the 'yield' or insights gained from undertaking qualitative and quantitative approaches within the same study.

Mixed methods research can present challenges when the data sets yield different results, yet discrepant findings may offer interesting insights into the target issue. They could also indicate inadequacies in the research questions or research design which require further data to be gathered and further interpretive activity to be undertaken. For example, a study by Scott and Sutton (2009) in the United States on examining teachers' emotions and reactions to professional development showed significant differences in the data set, making it difficult for meaningful comparison. The first phase of the study consisted of a repeated series of seven questionnaires including pre- and post-questionnaires conducted with fifty teachers four months after the professional development session. The second phase of the study incorporated qualitative interviews which allowed teachers to reflect on the issues of interest. Findings from the quantitative data analysis found no relationships between emotions and changes in teaching practice, while the qualitative data from interviews revealed teachers' mixed emotions related to change. The qualitative interviews in the study enabled teachers to report mixed emotions and revealed the connections between teachers' emotions and practice. In this case, the qualitative data helped to inform and refine the quantitative findings. The use of interviews combined with the standardized survey data counterbalanced the strengths and weaknesses of each individual approach to develop a richer data set. As the authors concluded, 'Without the two-phase, mixed method design, findings from this study could have been misleading' (Scott and Sutton 2009: 168).

At the core of any mixed methods design is triangulation, that is, the process of validating research findings by generating and comparing different data sources from different perspectives on the topic under investigation (Denzin 2012; Fielding 2012). Triangulation entails the corroboration or confirmation of different datasets to assess the credibility of inferences obtained from each approach. The question for researchers using mixed methods is to explore in what ways the results from the quantitative data collection and analysis support or refute the results from the qualitative data collection and analysis, and vice versa. Using two different methods can work to support triangulation by corroborating the findings across a study. However, researchers have argued that triangulation goes beyond methods. Respondent validation, the engagement with the views and perspectives of research participants usually associated with qualitative research, is just as crucial and relevant in quantitative and mixed methods research in ensuring participants' views are represented as fully and validly as possible (Christ 2010).

An essential feature of mixed methods research is that the end product should offer more than the sum of its quantitative and qualitative parts (Bryman 2007b). This approach can accommodate different combinations of data sources and levels of integration. However, a further challenge lies in achieving an optimum balance between the qualitative and quantitative datasets without relegating one method to a secondary role or status. The status of qualitative research in mixed methods continues to be a controversial topic, and Creswell (2007) cautions against qualitative methods being used primarily as a means to enhance the interpretation of quantitative results. Similarly, Denzin (2012) discusses the tendency for there to be a methodological hierarchy in mixed methods research, with quantitative methods at the top, relegating qualitative methods to 'a largely auxiliary role in pursuit of the technocratic aim of accumulating knowledge of "what works"' (p. 81). It is therefore important that both quantitative and qualitative data are designed, collated and analysed equally rigorously so that useful and credible inferences can be made from the combined analyses. Some researchers have argued not just for the inclusion of qualitative methods but for developing a more extensive qualitative approach driven by a social justice agenda in mixed methods designs. Greene (2009) argues for the importance of promoting diversity in mixed methods approaches and promotes the meaningful engagement with difference through mixed methods educational evaluation, while Denzin (2012: 80) asserts that mixed methods 'can and should be used in the service of transformative social justice projects'.

Concluding thoughts

Using a mixed methods design requires far more thought and sophistication than simply fitting together two or more methods in one research study. From the outset, researchers should carefully consider the appropriateness of their methodological approach and articulate a clear purpose for their mixed methods study to establish the rationale for combining quantitative and qualitative methods. When determining whether mixed methods research suits a particular study, important decisions need to be made related to the research questions, purpose, paradigmatic views and research contexts. It is also important to ask whether qualitative and quantitative data should be collected and analysed concurrently, sequentially or iteratively in order to address the research questions most effectively and comprehensively.

The variations in mixed methods research described in this chapter present various strengths and limitations. Ultimately, the key question for researchers is whether a mixed methods design would be the best fit for their research questions and purpose. Pearce (2012) argues that in the age of increasing interdisciplinarity and collaboration between researchers, a mixed methods approach can work to generate new innovative research agendas and new insights into complex social phenomena. If carefully planned and well executed, then mixed method studies can enhance the validity and reliability of findings, and offer scope to explore contradictions that may be found between the quantitative and qualitative results. We suggest that a well-designed and critically reflective mixed methods approach can uncover new knowledge in the field of early childhood education and allow for effective methodologies to mutually inform each other.

Suggestions for further reading

Creswell, J. W. and Plano Clark, V. L. (2011). *Designing and Conducting Mixed Methods Research* (2nd edn). Thousand Oaks, CA: Sage.

Fielding, N. (2012). Triangulation and mixed methods designs: Data integration with new research technologies. *Journal of Mixed Methods Research* 6 (2): 124–36.

Johnson, R. B. and Onwuegbuzie, A. J. (2004). Mixed methods research: A research paradigm whose time has come. *Educational Researcher* 33 (7): 14–26.

Ridenour, C. S. and Newman, I. (2008). *Mixed Methods Research: Exploring the Interactive Continuum*. Carbondale: Southern Illinois University Press.

Tashakkori, A. and Teddlie, C. (2010). *Sage Handbook of Mixed Methods in Social and Behavioral Research* (2nd edn). London: Sage.

Uprichard, E. and Dawney, L. (2016). Data diffraction: Challenging data integration in mixed methods research. *Journal of Mixed Methods Research* 13 (1): 19–32.

Yin, R. K. (2006). Mixed methods research: Are the methods genuinely integrated or merely parallel? *Research in the Schools* 13 (1): 41–7.

CHAPTER NINE

Experimental Research and Randomized Control Trials (RCTs)

This chapter offers critical discussion about using experimental research and RCTs in early childhood research. What counts as 'scientific research' has long been a contentious issue, with views often sharply divided between those who herald experimentation and clinical trials as the 'gold standard' to inform policy and investment in education, while others argue that social science should stay 'close to the complexities of the social world in fostering understanding, reflection and action' (Lather 2006: 783). In this chapter, we briefly consider the historical use of experimentation and RCTs in the medical and life sciences, and the influence of this approach in the development of social science research, particularly education research. We reflect on the enduring influence of the work of psychologists throughout the late nineteenth and twentieth centuries, the more recent influence of neurological studies on early childhood research, and qualitative approaches to experimental research. We consider arguments that question how appropriate experimental methods are for social science research, on the ethics of using experimental and randomized trial approaches in research about young children, and the implications of this methodological approach for early childhood education research, practice and policy development.

What are experimental research and RCTs?

The central goal in experimental research is to establish *causality*, and to identify this, investigators in experimental research deliberately control and manipulate the conditions under which an experiment is conducted. Experimental research often begins with a hypothesis about the relationship between cause and effect in order to demonstrate what outcomes occur when different factors (or variables) are manipulated. Experimental research design therefore needs to be precise and systematic, and is usually reliant on quantitative methods of measurement that are verifiable, so the experiment can be replicated to build further understanding. Broadly speaking, experiments should follow a set procedure which begins by making observations and formulating a hypothesis, then involves designing and conducting an experiment to test the hypothesis, evaluating the results of the experiment, accepting or rejecting the hypothesis, and subsequently making and testing a new hypothesis, if necessary.

An essential feature of experimental research is that researchers make changes to one variable (the *independent variable*), and observe the effects of that change on another variable (the *dependent variable*). The 'ideal' environment for experimental research is therefore a laboratory, where variables can be tightly controlled and manipulated. In a naturalistic environment, it may not be feasible or ethical to control *all* the variables at play, such as the number of children in the classroom, their age distribution and gender, the ambient temperature in the classroom and so on, so it is not possible to carry out true experiments. Experimental research outside the laboratory is therefore often referred to as *quasi-experimental*. For example, a quasi-experimental study might investigate the relationship between the time a teacher spends teaching a particular topic and the resultant student assessment scores. Here, the students' assessment scores would be the dependent variable as that is the variable that is being measured. The length of time spent teaching would be the independent variable, and as part of a quasi-experiment, changes could be made to the time spent teaching, to measure if this has an effect on the dependent variable (i.e. on student assessment scores). A useful way to help remember the relationship between dependent and independent variables is that *the dependent variable depends on the independent variable.*

RCTs are a particular form of experimental or quasi-experimental research, where participants are randomly assigned to different groups, and an intervention is designed to test particular variables. For example, a 'treatment group' (also sometimes referred to as 'experimental group') is subject to an intervention, while a 'control group' does not receive any intervention. Alternatively, one treatment group receives one intervention, while a second treatment group receives a different intervention, so the two approaches can be compared.

The process of randomly assigning participants to different groups is crucial for the outcome of RCT research and can be problematic in naturalistic settings where variables are more difficult to control than in laboratory conditions. For practical reasons, it may only be possible to use pre-existing groups, such as a selection of participants from a heterogeneous class of students, which potentially increases the chance of sampling error. For example, if conducting experimental research about social and economic disadvantage and education outcomes, then it may be difficult to obtain reliable information about family income levels, as this would be regarded as confidential. Great care must therefore be taken to ensure that any differences identified between the groups are due to the intervention – any other small differences are often referred to as random 'noise', but if the differences are significant, then the validity of a study is weakened (see Gray 2017; Styles and Torgerson 2018).

Provided appropriate procedures for randomization are followed, RCT research can be useful to identify what phenomena (or variables) cause a difference in the results between the treatment and control groups, or between two or more treatment groups, with a view to measuring the effects of the intervention and quantifying the results. Pre-tests are sometimes applied at the beginning of experimental and quasi-experimental studies to help identify any traits that may influence the outcome of the experiment. Post-tests are applied at the end of the experiment to calculate the effects of the independent variable on the experimental group, and these are then compared with the results of the same post-tests on the control group.

Experimental research is generally characterized by the systematic processes that researchers follow to ensure the precision of the research procedure, and by the use of statistical means to try to ensure that the only difference between randomly selected groups of people is the independent variable that is the focus of the research. The logic of this approach is that any variation (beyond what might be expected by chance) between the two groups is solely due to the independent variable, so the effects of the intervention can be measured. Following this line of logic, it is argued that using systematic and rigorously designed experimental techniques minimizes the risk of researcher bias and strengthens the internal validity of the findings.

Although some experimental studies fall short of being systematic, this approach is often favoured by education policymakers on the basis that it can offer robust evaluations of teaching and learning strategies. Research Example 9.1 summarizes an experimental study of a reading intervention programme in Ireland, where the researchers used standardized measures and systematic procedures to evaluate the effects of the intervention on randomized experimental and control groups of five- to six-year-old children.

Research Example 9.1: Experimental evaluation of Literacy Lift-Off in Ireland

Literacy learning is a global education priority, and in the Republic of Ireland, great emphasis is placed on the provision of literacy interventions being delivered in class rather than by withdrawing children from class for educational support. The in-class intervention programme 'Literacy Lift-Off' (LLO) was developed in Ireland as an adaptation of the well-known Reading Recovery programme1. While Reading Recovery involves working with individual students outside of the classroom, LLO adopts the principle of whole-class

---

[1]Reading Recovery is an accredited school-based literacy intervention programme for the lowest achieving children aged five or six years that enables them to reach age-expected levels within twenty weeks. It was developed in the 1970s by the New Zealand educator Dr Marie Clay and is now used worldwide. See http://www.ucl.ac.uk/international-literacy/ilc.

intervention. Although already used in many classrooms in Ireland, LLO had not been subject to formal evaluation, and Edel Higgins, Johanna Fitzgerald and Siobhán Howard (2015: 258) identified 'critical scientific gaps in the understanding of the impact of LLO which is being implemented in Irish schools'.

To gauge the effectiveness of LLO in improving students' literacy skills and impacting positively on their reading self-concept, Higgins, Fitzgerald and Howard (2015) designed an experimental study with a sample of ninety-two students aged between five years and six years six months (fifty-two boys and forty girls) attending four senior infant classes in a large suburban primary school in mid-west Ireland. Two class groups were randomly chosen to act as an intervention cohort (n=47) and two class groups were randomly chosen to act as a control cohort (n=45). Although usually in RCTs the focus is on one main outcome, the particular skills tested in this study were multiple, including students' letter identification, word attack skills, word reading, and reading self-concept beliefs. The study was rigorously designed to reduce threats to the validity of the findings. The assessment measures used to evaluate student improvements were standardized and had demonstrated good reliability and validity in previous studies.

All the students completed pre-intervention tests at the beginning of the school year, and classes were then randomly assigned to either the experimental or the control group. Following this random allocation, the class teachers and learning support teachers involved in delivering the intervention received training in LLO, whereas teachers in the control group did not receive training. Four LLO stations were established in the intervention classrooms for familiar reading, letter/word work, writing and new reading. During the intervention period, the intervention teachers were supported in the effective delivery of the LLO scheme by a Reading Recovery–trained expert teacher, and lesson plans were discussed and shared. Post-intervention assessment measures of all children took place in November, and the results for the intervention students were compared with those of the control students who did not receive the LLO intervention.

The results of this experimental study indicated that while both groups showed significant change on all dependent variables from pre-intervention to post-intervention, those in the experimental group showed significantly more improvement on word attack skills and word reading, with the most significant gains in reading self-concept beliefs. The researchers recognized the limitations to their study, particularly as only four groups were compared in only one school setting. Furthermore, there were more learning support teachers in the intervention group than the control group. Despite these shortcomings, the research team argue that the study findings indicate that a whole-class reading recovery programme can be effective in improving literacy skills and reading self-concept. A far larger study sample would be needed to test this hypothesis.

Experimental research, natural sciences and 'the paradigm wars'

Experimental research originated in the natural sciences and can be traced back to the periods of European Renaissance and Enlightenment from the fourteenth to eighteenth centuries. A key assertion of this approach to investigating phenomena is the distinction between *facts* and *values*, where facts describe 'what is' and values include a moral judgement about 'what ought to be'. For example, it is a fact that if a liquid is heated to boiling point, it changes into vapour – there is no moral value to this process. The 'truth' or 'validity' of a particular phenomenon (such as the boiling point of different liquids) can be 'tested' in scientific experiments through careful observation and measurement, and theories can be built based on the facts that become apparent during experimentation.[2]

---

[2]For example, experiments have shown that the boiling point of liquids is not always 100°C but varies according to purity and altitude: seawater boils at a higher temperature than pure water; water boils at a lower temperature at high altitude, where atmospheric pressure is low, and at a higher temperature below sea level, where atmospheric pressure is higher.

This approach to knowledge has often been referred to as a 'positivist paradigm', where certain assumptions are made about what counts as valid knowledge. Although there has been inevitable variation in approaches adopted over the centuries and across disciplines in experimental research, work conducted in this paradigm is united by the core concepts of variables, control, measurement and experiment (Bryman 2007b). From a positivist perspective, 'truth' can only be reliably known through experimentation, measurement and the control of variables (see also Clifford 1876/1999), and scientific research in this paradigm is characterized by the following attributes:

- All knowledge claims can be tested against empirical evidence.

- An explicit account of experimental methods ensures that an experiment can be accurately reproduced to ensure the validity of empirical evidence.

- Phenomena can be measured through quantitative analysis, and causal hypotheses can be tested by manipulating variables.

- Objectivity characterizes the scientific research process, so subjective bias is avoided.

It is widely recognized that great advances have been made in medical and life sciences through scientific experimentation, where variables have been carefully controlled, and precise measurements have been taken to establish cause-and-effect relationships. However, there are profound questions about whether the experimental logic and procedures of the natural sciences are a suitable approach for the study of complex social and psychological phenomena, such as in education environments, where it is not possible to control all variables. There are further debates about whether it is appropriate to herald experimentation as a 'gold standard' or 'an epistemological yardstick' against which 'empirical research in the social sciences must be appraised before it can be treated as valid knowledge' (Bryman 2007a: 12). Complexity theory further raised doubts about the scientific notion of causality in human behaviour (e.g. Cohen and Stewart 1995) and pointed to the impossibility of holding variables constant in dynamic, fluid and open situations, where behaviours are influenced by myriad factors, including, for example, networks, relationships, interactivity, particular social, interpersonal and cultural contexts and dynamic systems.

Despite long-standing debates about the pros and cons of using experiments or quasi-experiments in education research, studies located in a positivist paradigm thrived throughout the 1960s and 1970s, building on scientific approaches used extensively in the field of psychology. By the 1980s, however, the swell of social science research began to turn against experimentation, with accusations that such research was 'at best, inconclusive, at worst, barren' (Tom 1984: 2) and was unable to inform teachers about what to do in the classroom. Social scientists pointed out that human social behaviour is neither stable nor uniform, so it cannot be gauged in the same manner as the material properties found in the natural sciences. The focus turned to looking at variation in outcomes that could be associated with different learning environments and different child/student cohorts. Many education researchers therefore turned to qualitative, interpretive methods, which were considered more appropriate for the study of complex teaching and learning processes, arguing that individuals' intentions, goals, purposes, personal life circumstances and histories are shaped by a multitude of factors that simply cannot be 'controlled' through experimentation.

Throughout the 1980s and 1990s, there followed an extended period of contention or 'paradigm wars' (see Gage 1989), with debates raging between those who favoured experimental approaches and those who favoured interpretive methodologies. These disagreements reflected deep-rooted epistemological differences regarding the nature of 'knowledge', what counts as 'truth', what methods are appropriate to discover the 'truth' about the world, and what role 'belief' plays in shaping knowledge. Although such a polarization of positions was always unlikely to lead to methodological progress, the paradigm wars of the 1980s enabled qualitative enquiry to clear 'a space for itself and became legitimate' (Adams St.Pierre and Roulston 2006: 674). Over more recent decades, there has been a move towards collaboration between experimental and interpretive research, with some recognition that both approaches lend valuable and complementary insights into complex social phenomena (Johnson and Onwuegbuzie 2004). Whereas experimental research tends to address the 'what', 'where', 'when' and 'how much' questions, interpretive research is more able to lend insight into the 'why' and 'how' questions, and these different viewpoints can work well together to design research that aims to improve the educational experiences and life chances of young children.

Experimental methods can help illuminate the causal relationship between two or more seemingly unconnected factors in ways that other research designs do not. For example, a closely defined question such as 'Which of two methods of teaching reading is most effective for children to learn how to decode print?' might lend itself to experimental investigation, whereas a broader question such as 'What are young children's perceptions of reading?' (see Levy 2009) lends itself to an interpretive approach in order to gain children's perspectives. One of the benefits of RCTs is that, if undertaken meticulously, researchers can avoid the danger of incorrectly inferring a causal relationship between two unconnected factors. Assuming that the randomization process for assigning participants to experimental and control groups is effective, the findings can yield valuable information about how effective interventions are in practice.

Experimental research in early childhood education – a journey over time

Experimental research in early childhood education has a long historical tradition dating back most notably to the development of child psychology in the late nineteenth century, where research designs frequently involved experimental methods, which Curtis (2011) has more recently described as the 'modern scientific discipline' (p. 418). For example, in an early publication of 'How to study children', Thorpe (1946) outlined a series of techniques in developmental psychology that are 'in harmony with the attitude and methods of scientific study' (p. 23), including 'observations of spontaneous child activity, controlled experiments, objective tests and measurements, psycho-physiological records, case study investigations'. Thorpe (1946) considered the use of experimental studies in studies of children a novel and pioneering method, despite its recognized challenges:

> Experimentation is a refined type of observation made under controlled conditions. This careful method has only recently been in the study of child behaviour. The results secured from its utilization have, however, been gratifying. It is not easy to experiment with infants and immature children. Yet a number of hypotheses relating to child nature and behaviour have been put to experimental tests. (p. 28)

Early psychology researchers' choices of design and methodology reflected their assumptions concerning the study of children and the nature of knowledge, and their belief that child development is best understood by meticulous experimental methods, with scrupulous recording of the processes of inquiry, data collection and analysis. Experimental techniques, quantitative measurements and clinical tests have historically been used to predict, monitor and assess child development (e.g. Piaget 1929, 1953, 1977), young children's emotional development (e.g. Jersild and Holmes' 1935 study of infant fear) and child behaviours (e.g. Skinner 1938). A fundamental assumption in this work that endures to this day is that careful and inventive experimental designs can illuminate a variety of questions of interest to early childhood education research, policy and practice.

Experimental methods have also been prevalent in evaluation research and in evidencing the benefits of early intervention. Public policy and investment in early childhood education led to these services becoming 'a rapidly growing area of scientific enquiry' (Gettinger, Elliott and Kratochwill 1992: 3), precipitating demands for robust evaluation research and empirical evidence on the efficacy of the services offered, for example, to gauge if particular education programmes were more effective than others in enhancing child outcomes. During the 1980s, experimental research in the United States examined the 'lasting Effects of Early Education' (Lazar et al. 1982), and also measured child outcomes to determine if early childhood education programmes were more effective for some populations than for others. Significantly, when assessing the range of evidence, experimental research was, and often continues to be, judged to be the most rigorous possible test in evaluating the effectiveness of education programmes. A prevalent principle used to justify the preference for experimental research is that it can generate strong empirical evidence as to whether a particular early education intervention makes a difference to young children's learning and development.

In the UK, two more recent examples of quasi-experimental research design include the evaluation of the Sure Start early years intervention programme and its impact on the well-being of three-year-old children and their families (Melhuish et al. 2008), and the effectiveness of the early education pilot programme for two-year-olds (Smith et al. 2009). In the former study by Melhuish and colleagues, a random sampling approach was adopted, where 150 children and families living in Sure Start local areas in England were selected as the evaluation group, along with a comparison group of children and families living in non-Sure Start areas. The final sample included 5,883 three-year-old children and their families from ninety-three disadvantaged Sure Start local areas, with a comparison group of 1,897 three-year-old children and their families from seventy-two similarly deprived areas in England who had not received the Sure Start intervention. The study reported positive impacts of Sure Start on children's social development, with greater effects for children and parents when the programme was tailored effectively to meet the needs of families. Smith et al. (2009) evaluated the pilot intervention programme for two-year-olds, using a similar quasi-experimental design to examine the impact of the pilot programme on parents' experiences and children's cognitive development and social behaviour. This research involved 2,186 eligible children and families who had taken up the pilot and a 'comparison' group of families selected from relatively deprived areas of England where the pilot scheme was not operating. The report showed that parents had largely positive experiences of the pilot programme. They also found positive benefits for child development not just in terms of free early childhood education for two-year-olds but also the additional services and advice that parents received which went beyond early education. The findings from both these quasi-experimental research studies were significant in presenting robust evidence that early intervention can improve the life chances of young children living in deprived areas. These studies in the developed world reflect similar findings of quasi-experimental studies conducted in the global South, as reported in Research Example 9.2.

Research Example 9.2: Evaluating the Madrasa preschool programme in East Africa

Recent decades have witnessed growing recognition by governments, policymakers and communities in the global North and South of the importance of early childhood education. Early childhood development now features in strategic education plans and policy development in many developing countries, including in East Africa (see Mwaura, Sylva and Malmberg 2008). This rise in interest in quality early childhood education in the global South has been fuelled by evidence from empirical studies conducted in the global North that have evidenced the importance of high-quality early childhood education. Interest in early childhood education has also grown in the global South due to a shortage in primary school provision for all children; the increased need for childcare in an era when traditional extended family networks are changing towards more nuclear families; the rise in single parenthood; and the rising trend for women to take up paid employment away from home (Swadener, Kabiru, and Njenga 2000). Furthermore, at the time of the study by Peter Mwaura and colleagues, the World Bank had provided loans totalling US$1,680 million for child development programmes in fifty-two developing countries.

One of the key early childhood community-based initiatives across Kenya, Uganda and Tanzania/Zanzibar is the Madrasa Resource Centre (MRC) Early Childhood Programme, which was initially established in Mombasa in the 1980s to develop high-quality, affordable, culturally appropriate and sustainable early childhood centres in low-income communities. MRC teachers are trained in active learning pedagogy and follow a curriculum that integrates Islamic and secular education, values children as active agents of their own learning and emphasizes the importance of rich learning environments and high-quality teacher–child interaction (Mwaura 2004). In the early 2000s, the researchers Peter Mwaura, Kathy Sylva and Lars-Erik Malmberg received funding from the Aga Khan Foundation to investigate the impact of different types of preschool provision, including MRC, on the cognitive development of young children in the first two years of preschool, and to compare these with outcomes for children who received home provision.

The study used a pre-test/post-test quasi-experimental design with an intervention group (children from the MRC Programme) and two comparison groups (children from non-Madrasa preschools and home children with no preschool experience), along with interviews with parents to establish child age and so on. Children were pre-tested when they started preschool and then post-tested in the last three months of their second year in preschool. For home-educated children, the post-tests were carried out at similar times to the test dates of the children who attended preschool (see Mwaura, Sylva and Malmberg 2008 for details of the larger study involving 906 children and sub-sample of 423 children studied in Kenya, Uganda and Zanzibar). Careful selection criteria for participating preschools were applied (pairs of MRC and non-MRC preschools were chosen from the same community; all had been operational for two or more years and were either community-owned/managed or initiated by government funds for the community). Seventy per cent of child participants were reported to be between four and five years of age, 19 per cent were three-year-olds and 8 per cent were aged over five years but attended preschool for younger children (children's precise ages were not always known).

The children's cognitive attainment was the dependent variable in this study, with pre-test, age, gender, parents' education level and type of preschool provision as independent variables. *British Ability Scales II*, developed in the global North, was used to pre-test children's cognitive ability, along with three indicators of school readiness: language skill, number skill, and non-verbal reasoning and aspects of the *African Child Intelligence Test*. Four graduate assistants were trained to administer the tests and conduct interviews in each country (totalling twelve assistants). The scores of children attending each type of preschool were compared to the scores of children from similar communities who stayed at home. Descriptive statistics and regression analysis were used in data analysis.

The study found positive effects on cognitive achievement for preschool children who attended both types of preschool, as compared to home children, with a higher effect for children attending MRC preschools. Although this study did not investigate the reasons for differences in child outcomes, previous research (Mwaura 2004) had found that MRC preschools offered better quality teaching and learning experiences than the non-Madrasa preschools studied, and this could account for the differences in cognitive outcomes. While acknowledging the study's limitations (imprecise information on child ages, attrition of home children, possible 'Halo effect' of MRC provision and the time frame of the study), Mwaura, Sylva and Malmberg (2008) argue that the study offers evidence on early childhood education in East Africa that is important for its future development, namely that attendance at MRC preschools has a more positive impact on children's cognitive development than attendance at non-MRC preschools, and attendance at either type of programme gives children an intellectual 'boost' compared to remaining at home.

RCTs as the 'gold-standard' for evidence-based education policy

Although many experts would say that one RCT, experimental or quasi-experimental study never delivers categorical evidence,[3]

---

[3]Even in medical research, single drug trials are not considered to constitute categorical evidence. Stronger evidence can be claimed if there is an accumulation of studies in different contexts and conducted by different teams, including, for example, systematic reviews and meta-analyses.

RCT studies are often considered by policymakers to be the 'gold-standard' methodology to enhance policy development in education and the wider social sciences. Despite the debates discussed above, proponents of RCT, experimental and quasi-experimental research have continued to highlight the merits of this approach for testing the effects of innovative educational practices and interventions on student learning. For example, Bryman (2008) recognized that 'experimental research is frequently held up as a touchstone because it engenders considerable confidence in the robustness and trustworthiness of causal findings' (p. 35), and political scientists Jensen, Mukherjee and Bernhard (2014) remarked on the 'rapid acceleration' (p. 290) of experimental methods in their field. The question of how much confidence can be placed in research findings has become particularly important given that RCT, experimental and quasi-experimental approaches have tended to be preferred by social and education policymakers who are often looking for simple 'what works' solutions to complex problems. As Nutley, Powell and Davies (2013) point out, what is often referred to as 'the scientific method' is only the most suitable approach when a particular kind of research question is asked:

> When the research question is 'what works?' different designs are often placed in a hierarchy to determine the standard of evidence in support of a particular practice or programme. These hierarchies have much in common; randomized experiments with clearly defined controls (RCTs) are placed at or near the top of the hierarchy and case study reports are usually at the bottom. (Nutley, Powell and Davies 2013: 10)

This state of affairs is somewhat ironic given that the findings of RCTs, although often strong in their internal validity, tend to be weaker than quasi-experimental methods in terms of their external validity (that is, the reliability of their findings when rolled out to broader populations). Working in the field of public health, Petticrew and Roberts (2003) critique the tendency to conceptualize different methodologies in a hierarchy, arguing that the design of a study is not an appropriate or reliable criterion to gauge the credibility of its research evidence. Instead, they propose a methodological matrix and emphasize the need to match research questions to specific types of research, arguing for a focus on methodological appropriateness, and on 'typologies' rather than 'hierarchies' of evidence to inform and appraise public health evidence:

> The use of RCTs and qualitative methods is therefore less of a choice between extremes than the hierarchy implies, and effective implementation of an intervention ideally requires both sorts of information. (Petticrew and Roberts 2003: 528)

Nonetheless, policymakers' high regard for experimental designs reflects an emphasis on 'evidence-based research and practice', and a tendency to believe that 'what works' in one situation will or should work in another. Indeed, the beginning of the twenty-first century began to see a growing trend in the emphasis of evidence-based policy development and advocacy (Snilstveit, Oliver and Vojtkova 2012; Lohr 2004), in what Lather (2006) describes as the 'repositivization' of education research that reflects the contemporary neoliberal 'rage for accountability' (p. 783). The impetus for 'evidence' has impacted on early childhood research, in the search for solutions to improve the quality of educational services and the care of young children (Pawson 2002; Pring and Thomas 2004; Saracho 2016).

In the UK, the emphasis on evidence-based practice has contributed to a strong 'what works' agenda in education policy development and practice. Since 2010, 'What Works Centres' for education and early intervention have been created with a view to collating and applying 'best evidence' to improve public services (Cabinet Office 2013, 2018). A key purpose of these centres is to provide better quality evidence to support policy formulation and decision-making regarding the care and education of young children. Driven by this evidence-based mandate, the Education Endowment Foundation (EEF) was designated by the UK Government as a What Works Centre, focusing on the use of evidence to improve education outcomes for school-aged children, and subsequently expanded into an early years remit. Driven by cost-benefit analyses of early intervention programmes to improve developmental outcomes for young children, research supported by EEF is derived primarily through quasi-experimental and RCT designs. The notion of RCTs as a rigorous method is implicit in the EEF's rhetoric and further exemplified in one of the organization's lectures on 'Using

Field Experiments to Revolutionize Education' (EEF 2014). An interactive online guidebook has also been developed as a toolkit for practitioners and funders in the delivery of more effective interventions (Early Intervention Foundation 2013). A central assumption in this evidence-based agenda is that collecting data from empirical field experiments, particularly RCTs can improve teaching and learning.

Neuroscience and early childhood education

In addition to the rise in 'What Works Centres', advances in the technologies available to neuroscience and brain imaging have led to rapid growth in experimental research relating to young children's cognitive development. Many education policymakers and educators are keen to tap into this new knowledge to ensure that the teaching and learning strategies used in early childhood education are the most effective to nurture children's development. However, there is currently very little research that directly investigates the relationship between home or classroom-based learning and neuropsychological characteristics.

One area of learning that has received particular attention in the field of neuroscience is cognitive functioning in autism. Clinical observations have contributed to increased understanding of how the behavioural signs of autism appear in the first years of life (Pierce et al. 2011), and recent experimental research has begun to investigate underlying brain dysfunctions that may be a causal factor in behaviours associated with autism (for example, see Eyler, Pierce and Courchesne 2012). Whereas experts working in the field of neuroscience tend to be extremely cautious about the implications of their work for learning, there is always a risk – and an increasing tendency – for highly technical neuroscientific findings to be misinterpreted by non-experts. While research findings across all methodologies are often over-simplified and misrepresented in popular media, Lindell and Kidd (2011) contest that in the present era 'educational consultants and marketers – most of whom lack neuroscientific expertise – have overgeneralized and/or oversimplified distantly related neuroscientific research, with the end result that educators and educational institutions are being encouraged to adopt "brain-based" programs, unaware of the fact that these programs are pseudoscientific' (p. 121).

Qualitative experimental research

Although experimental research is associated primarily with quantitative approaches and numerical or statistical analysis, qualitative experiments also have a tradition in the arts and social sciences. Kleining (1986) proposed that the nature of experimental research lies in systematically manipulating social reality according to scientific rules, and that these rules can follow the principles of qualitative as well as quantitative research. Rather than controlling for, isolating and modifying specific variables with a view to testing hypotheses, as in quantitative research, qualitative experimental enquiry can intervene in – or experiment with – social situations in ways that offer new insights into social phenomena. The aim of qualitative experimentation is therefore not to measure causal relations but to engineer change in social behaviours in order to provoke changed behaviours and therefore allow deeper insights into the object of research. For example, Holly and Ortner (2018) intervened in the social life of five Austrian families by asking all family members to choose one day when they could step outside their usual routines and stop using their mobile phones in family situations or to communicate with other family members. The study design included interviews with family members about their use of mobile phones, followed by the intervention day, and subsequently by reflective interviews about their experiences during the intervention. This small-scale intervention deepened the researchers' (and families') understandings in three main ways: (1) the participants became more aware of their own smartphone practices and were better able to reflect on them; (2) the intervention changed the ways that family members interacted, and participants became more aware of how their lives could be different if they put aside their phones (for example, some families reported that they spoke more to each other during meals and were more attentive to others in the family, or had fewer arguments);

and (3) the experiment enabled the researchers to assess variation in how important smartphones were for different family members and for family life.

Critiques of the 'scientific approach'

While recognizing that experimental research can be powerful in addressing pertinent questions in education, it is also acknowledged that what counts as high quality research evidence is highly contentious and reflects different world views on what counts as valid and valuable knowledge. Reflecting on critiques of experimental, quasi-experimental and RCT methods in education research gives important insights into the challenges that lie ahead for research in this field. Here, we summarize three interrelated areas of critique that have been touched upon throughout the chapter:

- issues of the politicization and hierarchization of research methods (as discussed earlier);
- issues of internal and external validity; and
- issues regarding the ethics of experimental research.

Issues of validity: The first core area of critique concerns the suitability of experimental research for the study of human social behaviours, and the argument that many experimental, quasi-experimental and RCT study designs are flawed in that they produce inconsistent and unreliable results when applied to the social sciences. Despite the commonly held assumption that research conducted through controlled experiments is the 'most reliable' method, it has been contended that because teaching and learning are complex social practices that occur in natural settings such as a school or classroom, they cannot be fully understood from a positivist perspective (see Scott and Usher 2010). Unlike the relatively stable environment of a clinical laboratory setting, in the daily comings and goings of an educational environment it is simply not possible to control external or extraneous variables. This renders problematic any measurement of outcomes or cause-and-effect relationships, as researching children's learning is inherently marked by the complexities of human behaviour and by multiple external factors such as the setting and cultural milieu, and these must be taken into account to ensure the validity of any findings. While statistical controls may make it possible to manipulate data, it is argued that affective variables such as the interpersonal and social contexts of learning, motivational elements and personality characteristics of participants make it impossible to achieve sufficient control over an experiment or quasi-experiment to ensure the validity of the findings. Davies (2003) suggests that some researchers' trust 'in the objectivity of experimental research is embarrassingly naïve' (p. 99), and Hammersley (2001) argues that a research focus on 'evidence-based practice' can undermine the invaluable perspectives of education professionals' perspectives:

> The evidence-based practice movement tends to assume that research can specify not only what *has* been done but also whether it was *good or bad* and what *should* be done; yet it is clear that this necessarily involved value judgments – which research cannot validate on its own .... Equally, this instrumental view of the role of educational research may undermine effective practice because it privileges *research* evidence over evidence from other sources, including that arising from the experience of practitioners. (p. 550, italics in original)

This raises the issue of how experimental research evidence is taken up, and it has been argued that even when evidence about outcomes and effectiveness is clear, local circumstances ultimately dictate how that evidence is translated into practice (Jenson et al. 2014; Morrison 2012; Mutz 2011). Education researchers have long debated the drawbacks of translating experimental evidence into broad-ranging policy with a view to improving care and education provision for children beyond the local level. As Jenson et al. (2014: 296) argue, 'It is precisely the inability to extract generalizable results from experimental research methods that make these methods ill-suited to evaluate predictions from macro level theories that apply to a vast set of countries over an extended time period.' This argument has a long history, for example, in an early study on children's language acquisition, Margaret Davies (1981) cautions against the reliance on statistical inferential evidence from experimental studies that is derived from research that views groups of population as aggregates rather than individuals. Davies argues that groups of children are not homogenous, and many children in a given sample will behave in ways that cannot be isolated as particular variables – to do so will only lead to a lack of deeper understanding.

Advocates of RCTs might argue that, relative to other methods where extraneous variables may bias what is found, the process of randomization in RCTs is an effective way to research the intractable complexity of human behaviour, as there is no reason to think that such extraneous influences are different between the randomized groups that are compared. This necessarily turns the focus of critical attention to the rigour of the randomization processes in RCT research, and to the sampling strategy. Unfortunately, for practical reasons, many RCTs are conducted in (sometimes self-selecting) convenience samples. This seriously questions their generalizability in ways that are often overlooked, and which should be subject to greater scrutiny than is often the case. Ultimately, the validity of experimental research (as any research) lies in the rigour of its design and implementation, and in its self-critique. Particular weaknesses in many experimental or quasi-experimental study designs include the lack of comparison groups, inconsistent use of tests, insufficient scrutiny of the participant sample and processes of randomization, and high levels of attrition in participant samples.

Such critiques highlight the elemental importance of robust research design in experimental research, which is often found to be lacking. As Morrison (2012) cautions, researchers who are 'anxious to show "what works", risk jumping to unwarranted conclusions about the effects of causes and the causes of effects' (p. 15). It can also be argued that the scientific nature of experimental research and the requirement to pre-specify the research design render this approach unable to adapt to the research field as new lines of enquiry emerge during fieldwork. Rather than relying exclusively on results from experimental studies, many have argued that it is essential to supplement the findings of quantitative research with the more sensitive instruments offered by qualitative enquiry to understand why certain approaches work in particular environments but not in others. Educators also play an important role in collecting evidence through their established knowledge and interactions with children, as they are in a unique position to gauge children's understanding, and to rephrase questions or adjust tasks to suit particular children. Overall, while some view experimental research as invaluable to promote educational improvement, others remain cautious. We suggest that, where appropriate, combining large-scale experimental research with smaller-scale qualitative approaches can render both broad and deep insights into educational phenomena.

Issues of politics and ethics: As discussed, there is no doubt that experimental research lends itself to and nurtures the contemporary trend among policymakers and research funding organizations in the global North to favour cost-benefit models of education, and there is a growing trend for such models to be applied in the global South (e.g. Mwaura, Sylva and Malmberg 2008). A great deal of education research has continued to follow the experimental model, partly due to the prevalence and enduring influence of psychology studies in this field. There is also an argument that social researchers feel compelled to adopt experimental methods in order to secure research funding and/or to provide research findings that will be recognized as valid by policymakers (see Bryman 2007a;b, and 'Critiques of the experimental approach' discussed above). A further critique of experimental research is that it has not placed sufficient emphasis on identifying the unequal opportunities for learning experienced by disadvantaged child populations. Others argue that by its very neutrality, experimental research can serve to maintain the status quo of social order/disorder; even if a study aims to inform the reduction of inequality and to identify unequal opportunities for learning, it often fails to take into account the complexity of inequity that is prevalent in all societies. The growth over past decades of critical ethnography, feminist and emancipatory research, for example, has led to calls for all researchers to be ethically responsible not only for understanding events but also for bringing about emancipatory change through their work. Experimental, quasi-experimental research and RCTs can contribute to this goal but not on the basis of single trials, which should never be considered conclusive. Rather, individual trials should be viewed as contributing to a rich body of research carried out and replicated in multiple contexts in order to build confidence in the findings as reliable enough to be used as a basis for change.

Concluding thoughts

In education and the wider social sciences, researchers continue to debate the nature and methods used in experimental research. It is important that in the pursuit of research excellence and quality evidence, researchers and end users of research alike value and respect the methodological diversity and variations in research practice. All methodologies and instruments have their inherent strengths and limitations, but the success of any research lies in its application. The reliability and degree of confidence which researchers place on the research must depend on the degree to which the findings are applicable to the specific situation and, ultimately, whether the results serve to improve the problem it had set out to resolve. Essentially, the merits of experimental research, RCTs or any other method depend on the research aims, the questions a study seeks to address, the rigour of the research design and the context in which the evidence is being used.

Suggestions for further reading

Davies, B. (2003). Death to critique and dissent? The policies and practices of new managerialism and of 'evidence-based practice'. *Gender and Education* 15 (1): 91–103.

Gage, N. L. (1989). The paradigm wars and their aftermath: A 'Historical' sketch of research on teaching since 1989. *Educational Researcher* 18 (7): 4–10.

Jensen, N. M., Mukherjee B. and Bernhard, W. T. (2014). Introduction: Survey and experimental research. *International Political Economy*, *International Interactions* 40 (3): 287–304.

Morrison K. (2012). Searching for causality in the wrong places. *International Journal of Social Research Methodology* 15 (1): 15–30.

Petticrew, M. and Roberts, H. (2003) Evidence, hierarchies, and typologies: Horses for courses. *Journal of Epidemiology and Community Health* 57 (7): 527–9.

Spillane, J. P., Stitziel Pareja, A., Dorner, L., Barnes, C., May, H., Huff, J. and Camburn, E. (2010). Mixing methods in randomized controlled trials (RCTs): Validation, contextualization, triangulation and control. *Educational Assessment, Evaluation and Accountability* 22 (1): 5–28.

Conclusion:

Connecting Past, Present and Future Early Childhood Education Research Methods

In this final chapter we offer our closing reflections on past, present and potential future avenues for early childhood education research methods. We begin by considering the enduring influence of the physical sciences on social science research and the nature of applied research. We then consider recent, refreshing strands in the study of early childhood that point to new possibilities for investigating young children's learning, and we feature innovative approaches to social science enquiry that have been referred to as a post-qualitative research paradigm. We also reflect on global investment during the twenty-first century in improving opportunities for young children's participation in early education, particularly in low- and middle-income countries. Finally, in a bid to ensure that early childhood education research enquiry maintains the highest standards, we briefly revisit the importance of the four tenets of scientific enquiry as systematic, critically reflective, empirical and ethical.

We are cognizant of how the work we do in early childhood education is deeply rooted in many decades of social science research, and this work in turn has been built on several centuries of research in the physical sciences. We value this heritage, and also recognize that many of us are applied researchers, and that our investigative endeavour often has implications for early childhood education practice and policy. So what makes a good applied scientist? The answer has arguably changed little over the past half-century in that 'good applied science usually, though not always, requires greater breadth and a more eclectic attitude toward knowledge' (Brooks 1967: 7), that is, the applied scientist is interested in more than strictly intellectual solutions. In education research, the applied scientist also seeks to understand the knowledge and perspectives of policymakers, practitioners, parents and children. Increasingly, social science researchers act as agents of change in the local, national and international settings that they research, as evaluators and as expert consultants, encouraged also by the requirements of research funding organizations, which increasingly look for impact and tangible outcomes from their investment in academia.

Early childhood education researchers have also begun to engineer change in social science research design, to explore the use of the most recent technological devices for data generation and to disrupt the assumptions of previous methodological frameworks. New theoretical constructs are driving the development of experimentation with research methodology, particularly in the buoyant fields of post-humanism and socio-materialism. Working in the context of early childhood education in Scandinavia, Lenz Taguchi (2010) argues for the development of theoretical concepts and methodological approaches that go beyond the theory/practice divide and open up spaces for new kinds of dialogue across academic disciplines, between academic and practice knowledge, and among children and teachers. Drawing on the works of Barad (1999) and Deleuze and Guattari (1987, 1994), Lenz Taguchi (2010) seeks theoretical perspectives and methodological approaches that support collaborative invention and creation in the classroom through 'intra-active pedagogy'. According to Deleuze (1994), thought is generated by problems, so Lenz Taguchi directs her gaze towards how young children respond to different problems and how they create connections by experimenting in different modes, including different languages, drawing and movement through space. A fundamental principle of intra-active pedagogy is therefore to be responsive to children's problem-solving. But this requires trust – trust in children's inquisitiveness, trust in practitioners' pedagogic responses and trust in pursuing more rhizomatic ways of thinking in place of linear planning.

To pursue these ideas through research, Lenz Taguchi and St.Pierre (2017) offer a 'partly new or re-conceptualized way of doing educational inquiry: a way where concepts – acts of thought – are practices that reorient thinking, undo the theory/practice binary, and open inquiry to new possibilities' (p. 643). In their introduction to a special issue of *Qualitative Inquiry* which features a series of papers reporting on innovative research in this field, Lenz Taguchi and St.Pierre explain how they 'asked authors to begin inquiry with a concept instead of a pre-existing methodology with a predetermined process in which the researcher identifies a problem, conducts a literature review, designs a study using existing research designs (e.g., in qualitative research – case study, ethnography, grounded theory), collects data, analyses data, and writes it up' (p. 646). Instead, authors were asked to allow a concept to orient their research, which might or might not include conventional practices.

Deleuzian theorization (Deleuze 1994; Deleuze and Guattari 1987; 1994) also informs Osgood, Sakr and de Rijke's (2017) investigation of the 'dark' side of young children's online and offline play, and their problematization of commonly held perceptions about children's play as 'good' or 'healthy' or 'bad' and 'unhealthy'. In a groundbreaking special issue on 'dark play', Osgood, Sakr and Rijke (2017) bring together a suite of papers on how material objects operate as agentive non-human actors. For example, Yamada-Rice (2017) reports on a knowledge-exchange network project to inform the development of a video game for hospitalized children, to help them explore the range of emotions they experience about their illness and hospitalization. This study brought together the perspectives of hospital play specialists, academics and representatives from the digital games industry. Four 1-day focus groups were held, with deliberately open provocations and playful activities to prompt the participants' creative thinking. This included a collection of model houses produced by an artist to represent her thoughts on what it would mean to be a child in hospital, inspired by Ingold's (2013) work on thinking through making:

> In the art of inquiry, the conduct of thought goes along with, and continually answers to, the fluxes and flows of the materials with which we work. These materials think in us, as we think through them. (p. 6)

Data from these focus groups were analysed using deductive thematic analysis, which informed the development of a paper prototype of a game, using features and themes identified through the analysis. The next steps before producing the game included plans to consult with children to gain their perspectives on the ideas from the focus groups. This study offers a robust model for future knowledge-exchange projects that are informed by art-and-design-based methods as a means of knowing through making.

The movement in early childhood education towards a re-imagining of pedagogic spaces and practices has led to a shift from a focus on the interpersonal and intra-personal dimensions of interaction towards the *intra-active* relationships between living organisms and the material environment, including artefacts and the spaces and places where children and adults' daily practices are played out. For example, Pacini-Ketchabaw, Kind and Kocher (2017) treat artefacts and materials 'as active and participatory' (p. 2), rather than as static objects, and explore how certain materials make possible different kinds of encounters in the context of an early childhood day-care centre. Pacini-Ketchabaw and colleagues encouraged young children to experiment with five different materials (paper, charcoal, paint, clay and blocks), and through their observations of the children's experimentation, the researchers explored different concepts that emerged as relating to each material: paper and movement; charcoal and encounter; paint and assemblage; clay and ecologies; and blocks in relation to time. Eschewing interpretive logic in their study design, they used experimentation to reveal 'what human and nonhuman bodies can do and produce when they encounter each other' (p. 5) (see encounterswithmaterials.com). The design of this study suggests that experimentation with familiar materials can provoke new ways of thinking about learning in early childhood education settings.

Post-human and new materialist theorization, when combined with innovative uses of digital technology in the research site, can disrupt familiar patterns of thinking and offer original angles on the phenomena under investigation. As part of a study of social inclusion and exclusion in early education settings in a disadvantaged community in the Czech Republic, Petra Vackova (2018) introduced a 360° degree camera in the centre of young children's art-making activity 'in the thick of it, in the constantly changing, affective, socio-material assemblage of people and objects interacting' (np). The subsequent footage heightened her attention to human–non-human interactions and offered a particular perspective on how matter reacted to other matter in unpredictable ways, such as the way liquid paint left traces of movement on paper and in so doing, encouraged the human body to act. Interpreting these data through the lens of new materialist theory (Barad 2007), Vackova was able to demonstrate how affective moments of intra-action during art-making offer possibilities for children's social inclusion and exclusion in early education. Vackova's (2018) and Pacini-Ketchabaw et al.s' (2017) studies both focus on creative activity through the lens of innovative research methods and offer important insights into the cognitive challenge and social opportunities offered by young children's intra-action with and around objects.

Early childhood education researchers are also at the forefront of post-humanist research into how humans and non-humans (animate and inanimate, and visible and invisible) are entangled in the 'more-than-human' twenty-first-century world. Building on Latour's (2004) common worlds approach that asks us to 'remain radically open' and arguing that the survival of the planet requires conceptual and practical innovation, Powell and Somerville (2018) report on their innovative study which brought together new ideas about sustainability and literacy through music in early learning sites in Australia and Finland. Working with children between three and five years of age in 7 early years centres, the project team introduced drums into the playgrounds, and used the ethnographic practice of 'deep hanging out' (Wogan 2004; see Chapter 6, this volume) to observe the children's music-making, and used their iPhones to make video recordings, take photographs and make notes during their observations. The authors describe how the children became immersed in drumming and showed sustained, deep engagement as they drummed – with their feet on the earth and dirt, and their bodies resonating with the vibrations of sound as they engaged in this musical activity for the simple act of enjoyment. Powell and Somerville (2018) argue that the chaotic nature of the children's drumming opened up possibilities for thinking differently about literacy and sustainability through an ontology of sound, where the children could enact emergent literacies in a more-than-human world of music, sound, rhythm and vibration and resonance. Their findings resonate with Taylor and Giugni's (2012) observation that 'it is only when we exercise curiosity to find out more about where we are, and who and what is there with us, that we find hitherto unknown dimensions to our common worlds' (p. 110). Extending this curiosity to how young children experience sounds in their environment, Jon Wargo (2019) has developed innovative ways to capture and analyse children's field recordings in their local communities, and to develop ways by which the richness of the children's fieldwork can be conveyed in non-conventional research reporting.

On a more global scale, early childhood education in the twenty-first century has witnessed increased international commitment to and investment in improving opportunities for young children's participation in early education, particularly in low- and middle-income countries. For example, supranational organizations such as the World Bank Group, Children's Investment Fund Foundation and Department for International Development UK (DFID) have invested heavily in a global Early Learning Partnership (ELP) programme (World Bank 2015). This initiative works across fourteen developing countries to develop programmes, policies and research that deliver sustainable impact on quality early learning. A core agenda of the ELP is tackling global issues in early childhood education such as workforce development and teacher training, impact evaluations of interventions to scale up quality programmes, and measuring early learning quality and educational outcomes. The programme resonates with the global economic policy stance that 'investing in young children is one of the smartest investments that countries can make' (World Bank 2011b: 1). In the early 2000s, the World Bank alone invested over US$3.3 billion in 273 Early Childhood Development and Education programmes (World Bank 2011b). On a programmatic front, in 2018 a consortium of international agencies including UNICEF, the World Bank Group and the World Health Organization (WHO) launched the *Nurturing Care Framework*, which characterizes what effective early childhood development means for children from birth to age three.

These policy frameworks and initiatives make it clear there is now substantial recognition of the importance of early childhood education and development in the wider international community. At the heart of this global landscape are the United Nations

Sustainable Development Goals, which set out a vision for an inclusive and equitable education for all children as part of a transformative global agenda. A key focus for such investment lies in programmes for improving the quality of early childhood education teacher training, yet teaching young children and improving their long-term life chances is complex and dependent on multiple historical, political, religious, ethnic, local and global factors. Given the prominence of early education reform initiatives, critical analysis is needed of the agendas that drive them, and how these agendas frame early childhood and understandings of professionalism (Sahlberg 2015; Urban 2010). As Lash and Castner (2018) argue:

> Across various and sometimes competing points of view, multiple stakeholders (i.e. policymakers, external experts, managerial regulators) promote improving the quality of early education, with an integral part of that being teacher professionalization. What is often overlooked in stakeholders' zealous efforts to allegedly advance the profession and improve young children's education and care is the complexity of teachers' daily practices and the diverse bases of professional knowledge. Yet current policy trends promulgate simplistically narrow appraisals of teachers' work with correspondingly heavy-handed directives. (p. 93)

While global investment in early childhood education is much needed, it is equally important to recognize variations in local perceptions of the purposes of early education and the nature of childhood. How can early childhood education professionals, with their localized and contextualized identities, deliver the kinds of programmes promoted by global agents such as the World Bank and international corporations? There is much work for research to inform how the global early education workforce(s) can 'build individual and collective professional identities that are grounded in diverse local contexts *and* in a broader transnational professional (political) consciousness and collective voice' (Arndt et al. 2018: 98). It is vital that research concerning young children's education scrutinizes the intentions and outcomes from national and international commitments, and offers new empirical insights into how, and whether, young children's development and life opportunities are being optimized.

Concluding thoughts

Throughout this book, we have emphasized the need for early childhood education research methodology to be rooted in a strong theoretical framework, and skilfully tailored to fit the specific aims of individual research studies. Researching early childhood education – in all its diversity and complexity, and the many millions of lives enmeshed in its delivery in the global North and South – requires investigation that is sensitive to the research context, yet is informed by both local and global discourses about childhood and about the purposes of education in a deeply divided world.

As a final point, we re-emphasize that social science research is dependent on the four fundamental tenets that it must be systematic, critically reflective, empirical and ethical:

1. 'Systematic' means that a study design must be rigorous, clear and explained in sufficient detail to be replicable; study aims must be clearly stated with explicit accounts of the theoretical framework; there must be a clear description of the research context and sample; and a clear description of fieldwork methods including the processes of data collection and data analysis.

2. 'Critically reflective' refers to maintaining a reflective and critical frame of mind, and showing clear evidence of this criticality. This involves constant questioning of one's own beliefs, along with reflective consideration of wider societal discourses and 'common-sense' knowledge – whether these stem from religious, social or political beliefs. There is no place for assumptions or 'unturned stones' in social science research.

3. 'Empirical' involves actively setting out to discover information and new data, by making new observations, collecting testimony from witnesses, or re-examining relevant data that already exist.

4. Every scientific study is an 'ethical' project, and all empirical work has an ethical dimension. Conducting ethical research means respecting the rights of all participants (adults, young people and children) throughout all stages of the research process, from the early planning stages through to research dissemination and advocacy. Appropriate permissions must be obtained from *all participants*, including from children – whatever their age. Finally, and perhaps most importantly, research participants must never be 'judged' – human lives are complex, and the researcher can only ever glimpse brief moments in the complexity of issues that motivate human action.

As an early childhood researcher, if your research enquiry is built on these four strong cornerstones, then the work that you contribute to this fascinating field of enquiry will be valued by those that have the pleasure of learning about it.

REFERENCES

Adams St.Pierre, E. and Roulston, K. (2006). The state of qualitative inquiry: A contested science. *International Journal of Qualitative Studies in Education* 19 (6): 673–84.

Adler, P. A. and Adler, P. (eds) (1986). *Sociological Studies of Child Development.* Greenwich Connecticut: JAI Press.

Agar, M. (1980). *The Professional Stranger.* London: Academic Press.

Alanen, L. (1988). Rethinking childhood. *Acta Sociologica* 31 (1): 53–67.

Alderson, P. (2002). Children, healing, suffering and voluntary consent. In G. Bendelow, M. Carpenter, C. Vautier and S. Williams (eds), *Gender, Health and Healing: The Public–Private Divide.* RoutledgeFalmer: London.

Alderson, P. (2012). Rights-respecting research: A commentary on 'the right to be properly researched: Research with children in a messy, real world'. *Children's Geographies* 10 (2): 233–9.

Alderson, P. and Morrow, V. (2004). *Ethics, Social Research and Consulting with Children and Young People.* Ilford: Barnado's.

Als, H., Duffy, F., McAnulty, G., Butler, S. C., Lightbody, L., Kosta, S., Weisenfeld, N. I., Robertson, R., Parad, R. B., Ringer, S. A., Blickman, J. G., Zurakowski, D. and Warfield, S. K. (2012). NIDCAP improves brain function and structure in preterm infants with severe intrauterine growth restriction. *Journal of Perinatology* 32: 797–803.

American Psychological Association (APA) (2010/2016). *Ethical Principles of Psychologists and Code of Conduct.* Available at: https://www.apa.org/ethics/code/index.aspx (Accessed 10.06.2018).

Anderson, B. (2018). Young children playing together: A choice of engagement. *European Early Childhood Education Research Journal* 26 (1): 142–55.

Anderson, L. M., Shinn, C., Fullilove, M. T., Schrimshaw, S. C., Fielding, J. E., Normand, J., Carande-Kulis, V. G. and the Task Force on Community Preventive Services (2003). The effectiveness of early childhood development programs: A systematic review. *American Journal of Preventive Medicine* 24 (3S): 32–46.

Anderson, R. and Shemilt, I. (2010). The role of economic perspectives and evidence in systematic review. In I. Shemilt, M. Mugford, L. Vale,

K. Marsh and C. Donaldson (eds), *Evidence-Based Decisions and Economics – Health Care, Social Welfare, Education and Criminal Justice* (2nd edn, pp. 23–42). Oxford: Wiley-Blackwell.

Andova, E. and Taylor, H. A. (2012). Nodding in dis/agreement: A tale of two cultures. *Cogn Process* 13: 79–82.

Ang, L. (2013). Childhood development on the global agenda: Giving all children equal opportunities for lifelong learning, health and success. *Asia-Pacific Regional Network for Early Childhood Connections* No.7.

Ang, L. (2014). Vital voices for vital years in Singapore: One country's advocacy for change in the early years sector. *International Journal of Early Years Education* 22 (3): 329–41.

Ang, L. (2018). A cross-disciplinary study of early childhood care and education for peacebuilding and global sustainable development in the asia-pacific region. *Asia-Pacific Journal of Research in Early Childhood Education* 12 (4): 1–21.

Ansell, N., Robson, E., Hajdu, F. and Van Blerck, L. (2012). Learning from young people about their lives: Using participatory methods to research the impacts of AIDS in southern Africa. *Children's Geographies* 10 (2): 169–86.

Arnot, M. and Reay, D. (2007). A sociology of pedagogic voice: Power, inequality and pupil consultation. *Discourse: Studies in the Cultural Politics of Education* 28 (3): 311–25.

Arnott, L., Grogan, D. and Duncan, P. (2016). Lessons from using iPads to understand young children's creativity. *Contemporary Issues in Early Childhood* 17 (2): 157–73.

Arnstein, S. R. (1969). Eight rungs on the ladder of citizen participation. *Journal of the American Institute for Planners* 35 (4): 216–24.

Association of Social Anthropologists of the UK and the Commonwealth (ASA) (2011). *Ethical Guidelines for Good Research Practice*. Available at: http://www.theasa.org/downloads/ASA%20ethics%20gui delines%202011.pdf (Accessed 10.06.2018).

Atkinson, P. and Hammersley, M. (2007). *Ethnography: Principles in Practice* (3rd edn). London and New York: Routledge.

Babu, M. S., Gopalaswamy, A. K., Baskar, V. and Dash, U. (2017). *Effects of Interventions and Approaches for Enhancing Poverty Reduction and Development Benefits of 'Within Country Migration' in South Asia: A Systematic Review*. London: EPPI-Centre, Social Science Research Unit, UCL Institute of Education, University College London.

Baker, D., Street, B. and Tomlin, A. (2003). Mathematics as social: Understanding relationships between home and school numeracy practices. *For the Learning of Mathematics* 23 (3): 11–15.

Ban Ki-moon (2015). *Secretary-General's Remarks at Event on Investing in Early Childhood Development as the Foundation for Sustainable*

Development. New York: United Nations. Available at: https://ww
w.un.org/sg/en/content/sg/statement/2015-09-22/secretary-generals
-remarks-event-investing-early-childhood (Accessed 01.06.2017).

Barad, K. (1999). Agential realism: Feminist interventions in
understanding scientific practices. In M. Biagioli (Ed.), *The Science
Studies Reader* (pp. 1–11). New York, NY: Routledge.

Barad, K. (2007). *Meeting the Universe Halfway: Quantum Physics and the
Entanglement of Matter and Meaning*. London: Duke University Press.

Barbour, R. S. (1999). The case for combining qualitative and quantitative
methods in health services research. *Journal of Health Services
Research and Policy* 4: 39–43.

Barker, J. and Weller, S. (2003). 'Is it fun?' Developing children centred
research methods. *International Journal of Sociology and Social Policy*
23 (1/2): 33–58.

Bastian, H., Glasziou, P. and Chalmers, I. (2010). Seventy-five trials and
eleven systematic reviews a day: How will we ever keep up? *PLoS
Medicine* 7 (9): 1–6.

Bateson, G. (1979). *Mind and Nature*. London: Wildwood House.

Bazalgette, C. and Buckingham, D. (2013). Literacy, media and
multimodality: A critical response. *Literacy* 47 (2): 95–102.

Best, M., Knight, P., Lietz, P., Lockwood, C., Nugroho, D. and M. Tobin
(2013). *The Impact of National and International Assessment
Programmes on Education Policy, Particularly Policies Regarding
Resource Allocation and Teaching and Learning Practices in
Developing Countries. Final Report*. London: EPPI-Centre, Social
Science Research Unit, Institute of Education, University of London.
Available at: http://eppi.ioe.ac.uk/cms/Portals/0/PDF%20reviews%
20and%20summaries/Education%20assessment%202013Best%20r
eport.pdf?ver=2013-09-03-141900-363 (Accessed 31.12.2018).

Bezemer, J. and Mavers, D. (2011). Multimodal transcription as academic
practice: A social semiotic perspective. *International Journal of Social
Research Methodology* 14 (3): 191–206.

Blackburn, J., Chambers, R. and Gaventa, J. (2000). *Mainstreaming
Participation in Development. OED Working Paper Series No. 10*.
Washington, DC: The World Bank.

Blackstock, K. L., Kelly, G. J. and Horsey, B. L. (2007). Developing
and applying a framework to evaluate participatory research for
sustainability. *Ecological Economics* 60 (4): 726–42.

Bloor, M. (2016). Addressing social problems through qualitative
research. In D. Silverman (Ed.), *Qualitative Research* (pp. 15–30).
London: Sage.

BMJ (1996). The Declaration of Helsinki (1964). *British Medical Journal*
313: 1448.

Boellstrorff, T., B. Nardi, C. Pearce and T. L. Taylor (2012). *Ethnography and Virtual Worlds – A Handbook of Method*. Princeton: Princeton University Press.

Bombi, A. S., Di Norcia, A., Di Giunta, L., Pastorelli, C. and Lansford, J. E. (2015). Parenting practices and child misbehavior: A mixed-method study of Italian mothers and children. *Parenting: Science and Practice* 15 (3): 207–28.

Brannen, J. (eds) (1992). *Mixing Methods: Qualitative and Quantitative Research*. Aldershot, England: Avebury.

Breathnach, H., Danby, S. and O'Gorman, L. (2017). 'Are you working or playing?' Investigating young children's perspectives of classroom activities. *International Journal of Early Years Education* 25 (4): 439–54.

British Educational Research Association (BERA) (2018). *Ethical Guidelines for Educational Research* (4th edn). Available at: https://www.bera.ac.uk/researchers-resources/publications/ethical-guideline s-for-educational-research-2018 (Accessed 01.10.2018).

British Psychological Society (BPS) (2010). *Code of Human Research Ethics*. Available at: http://www.bps.org.uk/sites/default/files/document s/code_of_human_research_ethics.pdf (Accessed 01.10.2018).

British Psychological Society (BPS) (2013). *Ethics Guidelines for Internet-Mediated Research*. INF206/1.2013. Leicester: Author. Available at: www.bps.org.uk/publications/policy-andguidelines/research-guideli nes-policydocuments/research-guidelines-poli (Accessed 01.10.2018).

Britto, P. R., Yoshikawa, H. and Boller, K. (2011). Quality of early childhood development programs in global contexts. Rationale for investment, conceptual framework and implications for equity. Available at: http://www.mathematicampr.com/publications/pdfs//e arlychildhood/ECD_Global.pdf (Accessed 01.10.2018).

Bronfenbrenner, U. (1979). *The Ecology of Human Development*. Cambridge, MA: Harvard University Press.

Brooker, L. (2011). Taking children seriously: An alternative agenda for research? *Journal of Early Childhood Research* 9 (2): 137–49.

Brooks, H. (1967). *Applied Research: Definitions, Concepts, Themes. The National Academy of Sciences*. Applied Science and Technological Progress: A Report to the Committee on Science and Astronautics, US House of Representatives: 21–55.

Bruner, J. (1997). Celebrating divergence: Piaget and Vygotsky. *Human Development* 40: 63–73.

Brunton, G., Stansfield, C. and Thomas, J. (2012). Finding relevant studies. In D. Gough, S. Oliver and J. Thomas (eds), *An Introduction to Systematic Reviews* (pp. 107–34). London: Sage Publications.

Bryman, A. (1984). The debate about quantitative and qualitative research: A question of method or epistemology? *British Journal of Sociology* 35(1): 75–92.

Bryman, A. (2004). *Quantity and Quality in Social Research* (2nd edn). London: Routledge.

Bryman, A. (2007a). *Quantity and Quality in Social Science Research*. London: Taylor and Francis.

Bryman, A. (2007b). Barriers to integrating quantitative and qualitative research. *Journal of Mixed Methods Research* 1 (1): 8–22.

Bryman, A. (2008). *Social Research Methods* (3rd edn). Oxford: Oxford University Press.

Burls, A. (2009). *What Is Critical Appraisal?* (2nd edn). Newmarket: Hayward Medical Communications. Available at: http://www.band olier.org.uk/painres/download/whatis/What_is_critical_appraisal.pdf (Accessed 15.11.2018).

Burman, E. (2007). *Deconstructing Developmental Psychology*. Hove and New York: Routledge.

Bynner, J. (1980). Experimental research strategy and evaluation research designs. *British Educational Research Journal* 6 (1): 7–19.

Cabinet Office (2013). *What Works Network*. London: Cabinet Office. Available at: https://www.gov.uk/guidance/what-works-network (Accessed 30.11.2018).

Cabinet Office (2014). *What Works? Evidence for Decision-Makers*. London: Cabinet Office. Available at: https://www.gov.uk/government/ uploads/system/uploads/attachment_data/file/378038/What_works_evi dence_for_decision_makers.pdf (Accessed 30.11.2018).

Cabinet Office (2018). *The What Works Network: 5 Years On*. London: Cabinet Office. Available at: https://www.gov.uk/government/publi cations/the-what-works-network-five-years-on (Accessed 30.11.2018).

Caird, J., Sutcliffe, K., Kwan, I., Dickson, K. and Thomas, J. (2015). Mediating policy-relevant evidence at speed: Are systematic reviews of systematic reviews a useful approach? *Evidence and Policy: A Journal of Research, Debate and Practice* 11 (1): 81–97.

Cannella, G. (1997). *Deconstructing Early Childhood Education: Social Justice and Revolution*. New York: Peter Lang.

Cannella, G. and Viruru, R. (2004). *Childhood and Postcolonization: Power, Education, and Contemporary Practice*. London: Routledge/Falmer.

Carr, M. (2000). Seeking children's perspectives about their learning. In A. Smith, N. J. Taylor and M. Gollop (eds), *Children's Voices: Research, Policy and Practice* (pp. 33–45). Auckland: Pearson Education.

Chambers, R. (1982). *Rural Development: Putting the Last First*. Harlow: Longman.

Chambers, R. (1994). The origins and practice of participatory rural appraisal. *World Development* 22 (7): 953–69.

Christ, T. (2010). Teaching mixed methods and action research: Pedagogical, practical and evaluative considerations. In A. Tashakkori and C. Teddlie (eds), *Handbook of Mixed Methods in Social and*

Behavioral Research (2nd edn, pp. 643–76). Thousand Oaks, CA: SAGE.

Christensen, P. (1999). Towards an anthropology of childhood sickness: An ethnographic study of Danish school children. PhD thesis, Hull University. Available at: https://ethos.bl.uk/OrderDetails.do?did= 1&uin=uk.bl.ethos.310242 (Accessed 10.10.2018).

Christensen, P. (2003). Place, space and knowledge: Children in the village and the city. In P. Christensen and M. O'Brien (eds), *Children in the City: Home, Neighborhood and Community* (pp. 13–28). London: Routledge.

Christensen, P. (2004). Children's participation in ethnographic research: Issues of power and representation. *Children & Society* 18 (2): 165–76.

Christensen, P. and James, A. (2017). *Research with Children: Perspectives and Practices* (3rd edn). Abingdon and New York: Routledge.

Christensen, P. and O'Brien, M. (eds) (2003). *Children in the City: Home, Neighborhood and Community*. London: Routledge/Falmer.

Christensen, P. and Prout, A. (2002). Working with ethical symmetry in social research with children. *Childhood* 9 (4): 477–97.

Clark, A. (2005). Ways of seeing: Using the mosaic approach to listen to young children's perspectives. In A. Clark, A. T. Kjørholt and P. Moss (eds), *Beyond Listening: Children's Perspectives on Early Childhood Services* (pp. 29–49). Bristol: Policy Press.

Clark, A. (2011). Breaking methodological boundaries? Exploring visual, participatory methods with adults and young children. *European Early Childhood Education Research Journal* 19 (3): 321–30.

Clark, A. (2017). *Listening to Young Children* (3rd Expanded edn). London and Philadelphia: Jessica Kingsley Publishers.

Clark, A. and Moss, P. (2001). *Listening to Young Children: The Mosaic Approach*. London: Joseph Rowntree Foundation.

Clifford, J. (1986). Introduction: Partial truths. In J. Clifford and G. Marcus (eds), *Writing Culture: The Poetics and Politics of Ethnography* (pp. 1–26). Berkeley, CA: University of California Press.

Clifford, J. and Marcus, G. (eds) (1986). *Writing Culture: The Poetics and Politics of Ethnography*. Berkeley: University of California Press.

Clifford, W. K. (1876/1999). *The Ethics of Belief and Other Essays*. New York: Prometheus Books.

Cochrane Collaboration (2016). Our Vision, Mission and Principles. Available at: http://www.cochrane.org/about-us/our-vision-mission-and-principles (Accessed 15.11.2018).

Cochrane Library (2018). Cochrane Database of Systematic Reviews. Available at: http://www.cochranelibrary.com/cochrane-database-of-sys tematic-reviews/table-of-contents/2007/Issue4 (Accessed 15.11.2018).

Cohen, A. P. and Rapport, N. (1995). *Questions of Consciousness*. Oxon and New York: Routledge.

Cohen, J. and Stewart, I. (1995). *The Collapse of Chaos*. Harmondsworth: Penguin.

Cohen, L., Manion, L. and Morrison, K. (2011). *Research Methods in Education* (7th edn). Abingdon and New York: Routledge.

Collins, A., Miller, J., Coughlin, D. and Kirk, S. (2014). *The Production of Quick Scoping Reviews and Rapid Evidence Assessments: A How to Guide*. London: Joint Water Evidence Group.

Cook, T. D. and Reichardt, C. S. (eds) (1979). *Qualitative and Quantitative Methods in Evaluation Research*. Beverly Hills, CA: Sage.

Cornwall, A. and Jewkes, R. (1995). What is participatory research? *Social Science and Medicine* 41 (12): 1667–76.

Correa-Chávez, M. and Rogoff, B. (2009). Children's attention to interactions directed to others: Guatemalan Mayan and European American Patterns. *American Psychological Association* 45 (3): 630–41.

Corsaro, W. A. (2005). *The Sociology of Childhood* (2nd edn). Thousand Oaks, CA: Pine Forge Press.

Corsaro, W. A. (2017). *The Sociology of Childhood* (5th edn). Thousand Oaks, CA: Sage.

Corwin, Z. B. and Clemens, R. F. (2012). Analysing fieldnotes: A practical guide. In S. Delamont (ed.), *Handbook of Qualitative Research in Education* (pp. 489–502). Cheltenham: Edward Elgar.

Cowan, K. (2014). Multimodal transcription of video: Examining interaction in Early Years classrooms. *Classroom Discourse* 5 (1): 6–21.

Cowan, K. and Flewitt, R. S. (2019). Towards valuing children's learning. In C. Cameron and P. Moss (eds), *Early Childhood Education and Care in England: Towards Transformative Change*. London: UL IOE Press/Trentham Books.

Creswell, J. W. (2003). *Research Designs: Qualitative, Quantitative, and Mixed Methods Approaches* (2nd edn). Thousand Oaks, CA: Sage.

Creswell, J. W. (2008). *Educational Research* (3rd edn.) New York: Pearson Education.

Creswell, J. W. (2010). Mapping the developing landscape of mixed methods research. In A. Tashakkori and C. Teddlie (eds), *Handbook of Mixed Methods in the Social and Behavioural Sciences* (pp. 45–68). Thousand Oaks, CA: Sage.

Creswell, J. W. and Plano Clark, V. L. (2011). *Designing and Conducting Mixed Methods Research* (2nd edn). Thousand Oaks, CA: Sage.

Curran, C., Burchardt, T., Knapp, M., McDaid, D. and Li, B. (2007). Challenges in multidisciplinary systematic reviewing: A study on social exclusion and mental health policy. *Social Policy and Administration* 41 (3): 289–312.

Curtis, S. (2011). 'Tangible as Tissue': Arnold Gesell, infant behavior, and film analysis. *Science in Context* 24 (3): 417–42.

Cutspec, P. A. (2004). Bridging the research-to-practice gap: Evidence-based education. *Centerscope: Evidence-Based Approaches to Early Childhood Development* 2 (2): 1–8.

Dahlberg, G., Moss, P. and Pence, A. (2007). *Beyond Quality in Early Childhood Education and Care: Postmodern Perspectives* (Revised 2nd edn). London: Routledge.

Damon, W., Lerner, R. M. and Eisenberg, N. (eds) (2006). *Handbook of Child Psychology and Developmental Science, Theory and Method* (Volume 1, 6th Revised edn). John Wiley & Sons.

Danby, S. and Farrell, A. (2004). Accounting for young children's competence in educational research: New perspectives on research ethics. *Australian Educational Researcher* 31 (3): 35–50.

Darwin, C. R. (1877). A biographical sketch of an infant. *A Quarterly Review of Psychology and Philosophy* 2 (7): 285–94.

Davies, B. (2003). Death to critique and dissent? The policies and practices of new managerialism and of 'evidence-based practice'. *Gender and Education* 15 (1): 91–103.

Davies, M. (1981). Young children as subjects in developmental research and the possible impact which teachers on advanced courses can make. *Early Years* 2 (1): 9–17.

De Lange, N., Olivier, T., Gledenhuys, J. and Mitchell, C. (2012). Rural school children picturing family life. *Perspectives in Education* 30 (1): 79–89.

Deleuze, G. (1994/1968). *Difference and Repetition* (Trans. P. Patton). New York, NY: Columbia University Press.

Deleuze, G. and Guattari, F. (1987/1980). *A Thousand Plateaus: Capitalism and Schizophrenia* (Trans. B. Massumi). Minneapolis: University of Minnesota Press.

Deleuze, G. and Guattari, F. (1994/1991). *What Is Philosophy?* (Trans. H. Tomlinson and G. Burchell). New York, NY: Columbia University Press.

Dénommé-Welch, S. and Rowsell, J. (2017). Epistemologies of Silence. *Brock Education Journal* 27 (1): 10–25.

Denzin, N. K. (1989). *Interpretive Biography*. London: Sage.

Denzin, N. K. (1997). *Interpretive Ethnography: Ethnographic Practices for the 21st Century*. Thousand Oaks, CA, London and New Delhi: Sage.

Denzin, N. K. (2012). Triangulation 2.0. *Journal of Mixed Methods Research* 6 (2): 80–8.

Denzin, N. K. and Lincoln, Y. S. (2005). *The Sage Handbook of Qualitative Research* (3rd edn). Thousand Oaks, London and New Delhi: Sage.

Department of Health, Education and Welfare (DHEW) National Commission for the Protection of Human Subjects of Biomedical and Behavioral Research (1979). *The Belmont Report.* Washington, DC: United States Government Printing Office.

Derr, V., Corona, Y. and Gülgönen, T. (2019). Children's perceptions of and engagement in urban resilience in the United States and Mexico. *Journal of Planning Education and Research* 39 (1): 7–17.

Dewey, J. (1902). *The Child and the Curriculum.* LLC: Literary Licensing.

Dewey, J. (1938). *Experience and Education.* New York: Colliers.

Dezuanni, M. (2018). Minecraft and children's digital making: Implications for media literacy education. *Learning, Media and Technology* 43 (3): 236–49.

Doak, L. (2019). But I'd rather have raisins! Exploring a hybridized approach to multimodal interaction in the case of a minimally verbal child with autism. *Qualitative Research* 19 (1): 30–54.

Dockett, S. and Perry, B. (2005). Researching with children: Insights from the starting school research project. *Early Child Development and Care* 175 (6): 507–21.

Donaldson, M. (1978). *Children's Minds.* London: Fontana.

Dunn, J. (1989). The family as an educational environment in the pre-school years. In C. W. Desforges (ed.), *Early Childhood Education: The British Journal of Educational Psychology.* Monograph Series No. 4. Edinburgh: Scottish Academic Press.

Dunne, C. (2011). The place of the literature review in grounded theory research. *International Journal of Social Research Methodology* 14 (2): 111–24.

Dyson, A. H. (2001). Writing and children's symbolic repertoires: Development unhinged. In S. B. Neuman and D. Dickinson (eds), *Handbook of Early Literacy Research* (pp. 126–41). New York: Guilford.

Early Intervention Foundation (EIF) (2013). Available at: http://www.eif.org.uk (Accessed 30.11.2018).

Economic and Social Research Council (2016). *ESRC framework for research ethics.* Available at: http://www.esrc.ac.uk/funding/guidance-f or-applicants/research-ethics (Accessed 22.10.2018).

Edunation (2012). A long road ahead for Singapore's early childhood education. *The Singapore Education Magazine* 2012 (4): 12–137.

Education Endowment Foundation (EEF) (2013). About the EEF. Available at: https://educationendowmentfoundation.org.uk/about (Accessed 30.11.2018).

Education Endowment Foundation (EEF) (2014). EEF Blog: Incentives and education – what can we learn from trials in schools? Available at: https://educationendowmentfoundation.org.uk/news/eef-blog-incenti

ves-and-education-what-can-we-learn-from-trials-in-schools (Accessed 30.11.2018).

Edwards, C., Gandini, L. and Forman, G. (2011). *The Hundred Languages of Children: The Reggio Emilia Experience in Transformation* (3rd edn). Westport, USA: Praeger Publishers Inc.

Einarsdóttir, J. (2007). Research with children: Methodological and ethical challenges. *European Early Childhood Education Research Journal* 15 (2): 197–211.

Elwick, S., Bradley, B. and Sumsion, J. (2014). Infants as others: Uncertainties, difficulties and (im)possibilities in researching infants' lives. *International Journal of Qualitative Studies in Education* 27 (2): 196–213.

Elwick, S. and Sumsion, J. (2013). Moving beyond utilitarian perspectives of infant participation in participatory research: Film-mediated research encounters. *International Journal of Early Years Education* 21 (4): 336–47.

Erickson, F. (1984). What makes school ethnography 'Ethnographic?' *Anthropology and Education Quarterly* 15 (1): 51–66.

Erikson, E. H. (1950). *Childhood and Society*. New York: Norton.

Erikson, E. H. (1968). *Identity: Youth and Crisis*. New York: Norton.

Erstad, O., Flewitt, R. S., Pereira, I. and Kümmerling-Meibauer, B. (2019). *The Routledge Handbook of Digital Literacies in Early Childhood*. Oxon and New York: Routledge.

European Union Agency for Fundamental Rights (2016). *Child participation in research*. Available at: http://fra.europa.eu/en/theme/rights-child/child-participation-in-research (Accessed 22.05.2018).

Evans, J. and Benefield, P. (2001). Systematic reviews of educational research: does the medical model fit? *British Educational Research Journal* 27 (5): 527–41.

Eyler, L. T., Pierce, K. and Courchesne, E. (2012). A failure of left temporal cortex to specialize for language is an early emerging and fundamental property of autism. *Brain: A Journal of Neurology* 135: 949–60.

Fanon F. (1952). *Black Skin, White Masks* (1967 translation by Markmann C.). New York: Grove Press.

Fargas-Malet, M., McSherry, D., Larkin, E. and Robinson, C. (2010). Research with children: Methodological issues and innovative techniques. *Journal of Early Childhood Research* 8 (2): 175–92.

Farrell, A., Kagan, S. L. and Tisdall, E. K. (2016). *The SAGE Handbook of Early Childhood Research*. London: SAGE Publications Ltd.

Fielding, N. (2012). Triangulation and mixed methods designs: Data integration with new research technologies. *Journal of Mixed Methods Research* 6 (2): 124–36.

Finnegan, R. (2002). *Communicating: The Multiple Modes of Human Interconnection*. London: Routledge.

Flewitt, R. S. (2003). Is every child's voice heard? Longitudinal case studies of 3-year-old children's communicative strategies at home and in a preschool playgroup. ESRC-funded PhD. Available at: http://eprints.soton.ac.uk/184047 (Accessed 22.05.2018).

Flewitt, R. S. (2005a). Conducting research with young children: Some ethical considerations. *Early Child Development and Care* 175 (6): 553–65.

Flewitt, R. S. (2005b). Is every child's voice heard? Researching the different ways 3-year-old children communicate and make meaning at home and in a preschool playgroup. *Early Years: International Journal of Research and Development* 25 (3): 207–22.

Flewitt, R. S. (2006). Using video to investigate preschool classroom interaction: Education research assumptions and methodological practices. *Visual Communication* 5 (1): 25–50.

Flewitt, R. S. (2011). Bringing ethnography to a multimodal investigation of early literacy in a digital age. *Qualitative Research* 11 (3): 293–310.

Flewitt, R. S. (2012). Multimodal perspectives on early childhood literacies. In J. Larson and J. Marsh (eds), *The SAGE Handbook of Early Childhood Literacy* (2nd edn, pp. 295–309). London: Sage.

Flewitt, R. S. and Cowan, K. (2019). *Valuing Young Children's Signs of Learning: Observation and Digital Documentation of Play in Early Years Classrooms*. Final Report for the Froebel Trust.

Flewitt, R. S., Hampel, R., Hauck, M. and Lancaster, L. (2014). What are multimodal data and transcription? In C. Jewitt (ed.), *The Routledge Handbook of Multimodal Analysis* (2nd edn, pp. 44–59). London: Routledge.

Flewitt, R. S., Jones, P., Potter, J., Domingo, M., Collins, P., Munday, E. and Stenning, K. (2018). 'I enjoyed it because ... you could do whatever you wanted and be creative': Three principles for participatory research and pedagogy. *International Journal of Research & Method in Education* 41 (4): 372–86.

Flewitt, R. S., Messer, D. and Kucirkova, N. (2015). New directions for early literacy in a digital age: The iPad. *Journal of Early Childhood Literacy* 15 (3): 289–310.

Flewitt, R. S., Nind, M. and Payler, J. (2009). 'If she's left with books she'll just eat them': considering inclusive multimodal literacy practices. *Journal of Early Childhood Literacy*, Special Issue on Multimodal Literacy 9 (2): 211–33.

Formosinho, J. and Formosinho, J. (2012). Praxeological research in early childhood: A contribution to a social science of the social. *European Early Childhood Education Research Journal* 20 (4): 471–6.

Foucault, M. (1975). *Discipline and Punish: The Birth of the Prison.*
New York: Random House.

Foucault, M. (2007). *Security, Territory, Population: Lectures at the Collège
de France, 1977–78.* Houndmills, Basingstoke: Palgrave MacMillan.

Freeman, M. (1998). The sociology of childhood and children's rights.
The International Journal of Children's Rights 6: 433–44.

Freire, P. (2000/1970). *Pedagogy of the Oppressed.* New York:
Continuum.

Freud, S. (1973). *An Outline of Psychoanalysis.* London: Hogarth.

Freud, S. (1974). *The Ego and the Id.* London: Hogarth.

Gage, N. L. (1989). The paradigm wars and their aftermath: A 'Historical'
sketch of research on teaching since 1989. *Educational Researcher* 18
(7): 4–10.

Gallacher, L-A. and Gallagher, M. (2008). Methodological immaturity
in childhood research? Thinking through 'participatory methods'.
Childhood 15 (4): 499–516.

Gallagher, M. (2008). 'Power is not an evil': Rethinking power in
participatory methods. *Children's Geographies* 6 (2): 137–50.

Gannan, R., Ciliska, D. and Thomas, H. (2010). Expediating systematic
reviews: Methods and implications of rapid reviews. *Implementation
Science* 5 (56): 2–10.

Gaventa, J. and Cornwall, A. (2006). Challenging the boundaries of the
possible: Participation, knowledge and power. *IDS Bulletin* 37 (6):
122–8.

Geertz, C. (1973). *The Interpretation of Cultures: Selected Essays.*
New York: Basic Books.

Geertz, C. (1984). Anti-Anti-Relativism. *American Anthropologist* 86 (2):
263–78.

Geertz, C. (2002). An inconstant profession: The anthropological life in
interesting times. *The Annual Review of Anthropology.* Available at:
http://anthro.annualreviews.org (Accessed 01.10.2018).

Gesell, A. (1929). The individual in infancy. In C. Murchison (ed.),
Foundations of Experimental Psychology (pp. 628–60). Worcester:
Clark University Press.

Gesell, A. (1934). *An Atlas of Infant Behavior: A Systematic Delineation
of the Forms and Early Growth of Human Behavior Patterns* (With
H. Thompson and C. S. Amatruda). New Haven: Yale University Press.

Gesell, A. and Ilg, F. L. (1946). *The Child from Five to Ten.* New York:
Harper.

Gesell, A. and Ilg, F. L. (1949). *Child Development, an Introduction to the
Study of Human Growth.* New York: Harper.

Gettinger, M., Elliott, S. N. and Kratochwill, T. R. (1992). *Preschool
and Early Childhood Treatment Directions.* Hillsdale, NJ: Lawrence
Erlbaum Associates.

Ghooi, R. B. (2011). The nuremberg code–a critique. *Perspectives in Clinical Research* 2 (2): 71–6.

Gibson, J. J. (1986). *The Ecological Approach to Visual Perception.* Hillsdale, NJ: Erlbaum. (Original work published 1979).

Giroux, H. A. (1983). *Theory and Resistance in Education.* London: Heinemann.

Giroux, H. A. (1989). *Schooling for Democracy.* London: Routledge.

Glassner, B. and Herz. R. (2003). Introduction. In B. Glassner (ed.), *Our Studies, Ourselves: Sociologists' Lives and Work* (pp. 3–9). Cary, NC: Oxford University Press.

Gobo, G. and Molle, A. (2017). *Doing Ethnography* (2nd edn). London, Thousand Oaks, New Delhi: Sage.

Goldacre, B. (2009). *Bad Science.* London: Harper.

Goodfellow, J., Elwick, S., Strategos, T., Sumsion, J., Press, F., Harrison, L. J., McLeod, S. and Bradley, B. S. (2011). *The First Years: New Zealand Journal of Infant and Toddler Education.* Available at: https://research output.csu.edu.au/ws/portalfiles/portal/8820594 (Accessed 01.10.2018).

Goodman, J. (2001). Wise practice: The need to move beyond best practice in early childhood education. *Australian Journal of Early Childhood* 26 (3): 1–6.

Goodwin, C. (2000). Action and embodiment within situated human interaction. *Journal of Pragmatics* 32: 1489–522.

Goodwin, C. (2003a). Pointing as situated practice. In K. Sotaro (ed.), *Pointing: Where Language, Culture and Cognition Meet* (pp. 217–41). New York: Lawrence Erlbaum Associates.

Goodwin, C. (2003b). The semiotic body in its environment. In J. Coupland and R. Gwyn (eds), *Discourses of the Body* (pp. 19–42). New York: Palgrave/Macmillan.

Goodwin, C. (2007). Participation, stance and affect in the organisation of activities. *Discourse & Society* 18 (1): 53–73.

Gough, D. (2007). Weight of evidence: A framework for the appraisal of the quality and relevance of evidence. In J. Furlong and A. Oancea (eds), *Applied and Practice-based Research.* Special Edition of *Research Papers in* Education 22 (2): 213–28.

Gough, D. and Elbourne, D. (2002). Systematic research synthesis to inform policy, practice and democratic debate. *Social Policy and Society* 1 (3): 225–36.

Gough, D., Oliver, S. and Thomas, J. (2012). *An Introduction to Systematic Reviews.* London: Sage Publications.

Government Social Research Unit (GSRU) (2018). Rapid Evidence Assessment Toolkit Index. Available at: http://webarchive.nationalarch ives.gov.uk/20140402164155/http://www.civilservice.gov.uk/networks/ gsr/resources-and-guidance/rapid-evidence-assessment (Accessed 31.12.2018).

Graham, A. and Fitzgerald, R. (2010). Children's participation in research: Some possibilities and constraints in the current Australian research environment. *Journal of Sociology* 46: 133–47.

Gray, C. and Winter, E. (2011). Hearing voices: Participatory research with preschool children with and without disabilities. *European Early Childhood Education Research Journal* 19 (3): 309–20.

Gray, D. E. (2017). *Doing Research in the Real World*. London: Sage.

Green, J. and Bloome. D. (2014). Ethnography and ethnographers of and in education: A situated perspective. In J. Flood, D. Lapp and S. B. Heath (eds), *Handbook of Research on Teaching Literacy Through the Communicative and Visual Arts* (2nd edn, pp. 181–202). New York: Routledge.

Green, L. W., George, M. A. Daniel, M. Frankish, C. J. Herbert, and Bowie, W. R. (2003). Guidelines for participatory research in health promotion. In M. Minkler and N. Wallerstein (eds), *Community-based Participatory Research for Health* (pp. 419–28). San Francisco, CA: Jossey-Bass.

Greene, J. (2009). Meaningfully engaging with difference through mixed methods educational evaluation. In K. Ryan and B. Cousins (eds), *Sage Handbook of Educational Evaluation* (pp. 323–40). Thousand Oaks, CA: Sage.

Greene, J. C., Caracelli, V. J. and Graham, W. F. (1989). Towards a conceptual framework for mixed method evaluation designs. *Educational Evaluation and Policy Analysis* 131: 255–74.

Gregory, E., Long, S. and Volk, D. (eds) (2004). *Many Pathways to Literacy: Learning with Peers, Siblings, Grandparents and in Community Settings*. London: RoutledgeFalmer.

Gregory, E. and Ruby, M. (2011). The 'insider/outsider' dilemma of ethnography: Working with young children and their families in cross-cultural contexts. *Journal of Early Childhood Research* 9 (2): 162–74.

Grieshaber, S. and McArdle, F. (2010). *Trouble with Play*. Berkshire: McGraw-Hill Professional.

Grimshaw, A. (2001). *The Ethnographer's Eye: Ways of Seeing in Anthropology*. Cambridge: Cambridge University Press.

Guishard, M. (2009). The false paths, the endless labors, the turns now this way and now that: Participatory action research, mutual vulnerability, and the politics of inquiry. *The Urban Review* 41 (1): 85–105.

Gülgönen, T. and Corona, Y. (2015). Children's perspectives on their urban environment and their appropriation of public spaces in Mexico City. *Children, Youth and Environments* 25 (2): 208–28.

Gumperz, J. and Berenz, N. (1993). Transcribing conversational exchanges. In J. Edwards and M. Lampert (eds), *Transcription and*

Coding Methods for Language Research (pp. 91–122). Hillsdale, NJ: Lawrence Earlbaum Associates Inc.

Gupta, A. (2006). *Early Childhood Education, Postcolonial Theory, and Teaching Practices in India Balancing Vygotsky and the Veda.* Hampshire, UK: Palgrave Macmillan.

Gutiérrez, K. D. (2008). Developing a sociocritical literacy in the third space. *Reading Research Quarterly* 43 (2): 148–64.

Hackett, A. (2014). Zigging and zooming all over the place: Young children's meaning making and movement in the museum. *Journal of Early Childhood Literacy* 14 (1): 5–27.

Hakyemez-Paul, S., Pihlaja, P. and Silvennoinen, H. (2018). Parental involvement in Finnish day care – what do early childhood educators say? *European Early Childhood Education Research Journal* 26 (2): 258–73.

Hall, G. S. (1893). *The Contents of Children's Minds on Entering School.* New York and Chicago: E.L. Kellog & Co.

Hall, T. (2000). At home with the young homeless. *International Journal of Social Research Methodology* 3(2): 121–33.

Halliday, M. A. K. (1973). *Explorations in the Functions of Language.* London: Edward Arnold.

Halliday, M. A. K. (1978). *Language as Social Semiotic: The Social Interpretation of Language and Meaning.* London: Edward Arnold.

Hammersley, M. (2001). On 'systematic' reviews of research literatures: A 'narrative' response to Evans and Benefield, *British Educational Research Journal* 27 (5): 543–54.

Hammersley M. (2006). Ethnography: Problems and prospects. *Ethnography and Education* 1: 3–14.

Hammersley, M. (2010). Creeping ethical regulation and the strangling of research. *Sociological Research Online* 15 (4): 16.

Hammersley, M. and Atkinson, P. (2007). *Ethnography: Principles in Practice* (3rd edn). London: Routledge.

Hansen. K. and Joshi. H. (2007). *Millennium Cohort Study Second Survey: A Users Guide to Initial Findings.* Centre for Longitudinal Studies, Bedford Group for Lifecourse and Statistical Studies. Economic and Social Research Council/Institute of Education, University of London/National Statistics.

Harcourt, D. (2008). 'Young children's accounts on quality in early childhood classrooms in Singapore'. Doctoral Thesis. Queensland University of Technology. Available at: http://eprints.qut.edu.au/16658 (Accessed 31.12.2018).

Harcourt, D. and Conroy, H. (2005). Informed assent: Ethics and processes when researching with young children. *Early Child Development and Care* 175 (6): 567–77.

Harcourt, D. and Conroy, H. (2011). Informed consent. In D. Harcourt, B. Perry and T. Waller (eds), *Researching Young Children's Perspectives: Debating the Ethics and Dilemmas of Educational Research with Children* (pp. 38–51). London and New York: Sage.

Harcourt, D., Perry, B. and Waller, T. (eds) (2011). *Researching Young Children's Perspectives: Debating the Ethics and Dilemmas of Educational Research with Children*. London and New York: Sage.

Harden, A. and Gough, D. (2012). Quality and relevance appraisal. In D. Gough, S. Oliver and J. Thomas (eds), *An Introduction to Systematic Reviews* (pp. 153–78). London: Sage Publications.

Harden, A. and Thomas, J. (2005). Methodological issues in combining diverse study types in systematic reviews. *International Journal of Social Research Methodology* 8 (3): 257–71.

Harkness, S. and Super, C. M. (1987). The uses of cross-cultural research in child development. In G. J. Whitehurst and R. Vasta (eds), *Annals of Child Development* (Vol. 4, pp. 209–44). Greenwich, CT: JAI Press.

Hart, R. A. (1992). *Children's Participation: From Tokenism to Citizenship*. Available at: https://www.unicef-irc.org/publications/pdf/c hildrens_participation.pdf (Accessed 01.10.2018).

Heath, S. B. (1983). *Ways with Words: Language, Life, and Work In Communities and Classrooms*. New York: Cambridge University Press.

Heath, S. B. and Street, B. (2008). *Ethnography: Approaches to Language and Literacy Research*. New York: Teachers College Press.

Held, V. (2006). *The Ethics of Care: Personal, Political, Global*. New York: Oxford University Press.

Hesse-Biber, S. (2010). Qualitative approaches to mixed methods practice. *Qualitative Inquiry* 16 (6): 455–68.

Higgins, E., Fitzgerald, J. and Howard, S. (2015). 'Literacy Lift-Off': An experimental evaluation of a reading recovery programme on literacy skills and reading self-concept. *Educational Psychology in Practice* 31 (3): 247–64.

Higgins, J. P. T. and Green, S. (eds) (2011). *Cochrane Handbook for Systematic Reviews of Interventions* Version 5.1.0 [updated March 2011]. The Cochrane Collaboration. Available at: http://handbook. cochrane.org (Accessed 31.12.2018.)

Hobbs, M. and Stovall, R. (2015). Supporting mentors of preservice early childhood education teachers: A literature review. *Journal of Early Childhood Teacher Education* 36: 90–9.

Holland, J. and Blackburn, J. (eds) (1998). *Whose Voice? Participatory Research and Policy Change*. London: Intermediate Technology Publications.

Holloway, I. (1997). *Basic Concepts for Qualitative Research*. London: Blackwell Science.

Holly, S. and Ortner, C. (2018). On the Role of Smartphones for Family Relationships. Paper presented to ECREA pre-conference, *7th European Communication Conference Children and Adolescents in a Mobile Media World*, 31.09.2018, Lugano. Summary available at: https://digiliteymethodscorner.wordpress.com/2019/02/13/qualitative-experiment-with-families (Accessed 15.02.2019).

Hopkins, P. E. and Hill, M. (2008). Pre-flight experiences and migration stories: The accounts of unaccompanied asylum-seeking children. *Children's Geographies* 6 (3): 257–68.

Horgan, D. (2017). Child participatory research methods: Attempts to go 'deeper'. *Childhood* 24 (2): 245–59.

Huh, Y. J. (2017). Uncovering young children's transformative digital game play through the exploration of three-year-old children's cases. *Contemporary Issues in Early Childhood* 18 (2): 179–95.

Hull, G. A. and Nelson, M. E. (2005). Locating the semiotic power of multimodality. *Written Communication* 22 (2): 224–61.

Hunter, L., Emerald, E. and Gregory, M. (2013). *Participatory Activist Research in the Globalised World*. Netherlands: Springer.

Hwang, S. K. and Charnley, H. (2010). Honourable sacrifice: A visual ethnography of the family lives of Korean children with autistic siblings. *Children & Society* 24 (6): 437–48.

Hymes, D. (1996). *Ethnography, Linguistics, Narrative Inequality: Towards an Understanding of Voice*. London: Taylor and Francis.

Ingold, T. (2007). *Lines: A Brief History*. London: Routledge.

Ingold, T. (2013). *Making*. London: Routledge.

Institute for Development Studies (1998). *Participatory Monitoring and Evaluation: Learning from Change*. IDS Policy Briefing Issue 12. Brighton: Institute for Development Studies.

International Initiative for Impact Evaluation (3ie). Available at: http://www.3ieimpact.org (Accessed 31.12.2018).

Israel, M. and Hay, I. (2006). *Research Ethics for Social Scientists*. London: Sage.

James, A. and James, A. (2004). *Constructing Childhood: Theory, Policy and Social Practice*. Hampshire, UK: Palgrave Macmillan.

James, A. and Prout, A. (eds) (1990/1997/2015). *Constructing and Reconstructing Childhood: Contemporary Issues in the Sociological Study of Childhood*. London: Falmer/Routledge.

Jenks, C. (1982). *The Sociology of Childhood*. London: Batsford Academic and Educational.

Jensen, N. M., Mukherjee B. and Bernhard, W. T. (2014). Introduction: Survey and experimental research. *International Political Economy, International Interactions* 40 (3): 287–304.

Jersild, A. and Holmes, F. (1935). *Children's Fears, Child Development Monography no.20*. New York Bureau of Publications, Teachers College, Columbia University.

Jewitt, C. (eds) (2014). *Routledge Handbook of Multimodal Analysis*. Abingdon: Routledge.

Jewitt, C., Bezemer, J. and O'Halloran, K. L. (2016). *Introducing multimodality*. London; New York: Routledge.

Johnson, R. B. and Gray, R. (2010). A history of philosophical and theoretical issues for mixed methods research. In A. Tashakkori and C. B. Teddlie (eds), *Handbook of Mixed Methods in Social and Behavioral Research* (pp. 69–94). Thousand Oaks, CA: SAGE Publications, Inc.

Johnson, R. B. and Onwuegbuzie, A. J. (2004). Mixed methods research: A research paradigm whose time has come. *Educational Researcher* 33 (7): 14–26.

Johnson, R. B., Onwuegbuzie, A. J. and Turner, L. A. (2007). Toward a definition of mixed methods research. *Journal of Mixed Methods Research* 1 (2): 112–33.

Jones, L., Osgood, J., Holmes, R. and Urban, M. (2016). Reimagining quality in early childhood. *Contemporary Issues in Early Childhood* 17 (1): 3–7.

Kalantzis, M. and Cope, W. W. (2012). *New Learning: Elements of a Science of Education* (2nd edn). Melbourne: Cambridge University Press.

Kellett, M. (2005). Children as Active Researchers: A New Research Paradigm for the 21st Century? NCRM Methods Review Paper. Available at: http://eprints.ncrm.ac.uk/87 (Accessed 01.10.2018).

Kellett, M. (2014). Images of childhood and their influence on research. In A. Clark, R. S. Flewitt, M. Hammersley and M. Robb (eds), *Understanding Research with Children and Young People* (pp. 15–33). London: Sage.

Kemmis, S. (2006). Participatory action research and the public sphere. *Educational Action Research* 14 (4): 459–76.

Kendon, A. (2004).*Gesture: Visible Action as Utterance*. Cambridge: Cambridge University Press.

King, G., Tucker, M., Desserud, S. and Shillington, M. (2009). The application of a transdisciplinary model for early intervention services. *Infants and Young Children* 22 (3): 211–23.

Kirby, P. and Gibbs, S. (2006). Facilitating participation: Adults' caring support roles within child-to-child projects in schools and after-school settings. *Children & Society* 20 (3): 209–22.

Kleining, G. (1986). Das qualitative experiment [The Qualitative Experiment]. *Kölner Zeitschrift für Soziologie und Sozialpsychologie* 38 (4): 724–50.

Kozinets, R. (2015). *Netnography: Redefined*. London: Sage.

Kress, G. (1997). *Before Writing: Rethinking Paths to Literacy.* London: Routledge.

Kress, G. (2010). *Multimodality: Exploring Contemporary Methods of Communication.* London: Routledge.

Kress, G. and van Leeuwen, T. (1996). *Reading Images: The Grammar of Visual Design.* London: Routledge.

Kress, G. and van Leeuwen, T. (2001). *Multimodal Discourse: The Modes and Media of Contemporary Communication.* London, New York: Edward Arnold; Oxford University Press.

Kress, G., Jewitt, C., Ogborn J. and Tsatsarelis, C. (2001). *Multimodal Teaching and Learning: The Rhetorics of the Science Classroom.* London: Continuum.

Kuby, C. R. and Rowsell, J. (2017). Early literacy and the posthuman: Pedagogies and methodologies. *Journal of Early Childhood Literacy* 17 (3): 285–96.

Kuhn T. (1962). *The Structure of Scientific Revolutions.* Chicago: University of Chicago Press.

Kumpulainen, K., Theron, L., Kahl, C. et al. (2016). Children's positive adjustment to first grade in risk-filled communities: A case study of the role of school ecologies in South Africa and Finland. *School Psychology International* 37 (2): 121–39.

Lancaster, L. (2001). Staring at the page: The functions of gaze in a young child's interpretation of symbolic forms. *Journal of Early Childhood Literacy* 1 (2): 131–52.

Lancaster, L. (2007). Representing the ways of the world: How children under three start to use syntax in graphic signs. *Journal of Early Childhood Literacy* 7 (2): 123–54.

Lash, M. J. and Castner, D. J. (2018). Stories of practice: The lived and sometimes clandestine professional experiences of early childhood educators. *Contemporary Issues in Early Childhood* 19 (2): 93–6.

Lather, P. (2006). Foucauldian scientificity: Rethinking the nexus of qualitative research and educational policy analysis. *International Journal of Qualitative Studies in Education* 19 (6): 783–91.

Latour, B, (2004). *The Politics of Nature: How to Bring Science into Democracy.* London: Harvard University Press.

Lazar, I., Darlington, R., Murray, H., Royce, J., Snipper, A. and Ramey, C. T. (1982). Lasting Effects of early education: A report from the consortium for longitudinal studies. *Monographs of the Society for Research in Child Development* 47 (2/3): i, iii, v–vii, ix–xiv, 1–151.

Leal, P. A. (2010). Participation: The ascendency of a Buzzword in the Neo-liberal Era. In A. Cornwall and D. Eade (eds), *Deconstructing Development Discourse: Buzzwords and Fuzzwords* (pp. 89–100). London: Oxfam.

Lee, L. (1965). *Cider with Rosie.* London: The Hogarth Press.

Lemke, J. (2014). Multimodality, identity, and time. In C. Jewitt (eds), *The Routledge Handbook of Multimodal Analysis* (pp. 165–75). Abingdon: Routledge.

Lenz Taguchi, H. (2010). *Going Beyond the Theory/Practice Divide in Early Childhood Education: Introducing an Intra-Active Pedagogy.* London and New York: Routledge.

Lenz Taguchi, H. and St.Pierre, E. A. (2017). Using concept as method in educational and social science inquiry. *Qualitative Inquiry* 23 (9): 643–8.

Leroy, J. L., Gadsden, P. and Guijarro, M. (2012). The impact of daycare programmes on child health, nutrition and development in developing countries: A systematic review. *Journal of Development Effectiveness* 4 (3): 472–96.

Levine, R. A. and New, R. S. (eds) (2008). *Anthropology and Child Development. A Cross-cultural Reader.* USA: Blackwell Publishing.

Levy, R. (2009). Children's perceptions of reading and the use of reading scheme texts. *Cambridge Journal of Education* 39 (3): 361–77.

Levy, R. (2011). *Young Children Reading at Home and at School.* London: Sage.

Levy, R. and Thompson, P. (2015). Creating 'buddy partnerships' with 5- and 11-year old-boys: A methodological approach to conducting participatory research with young children. *Journal of Early Childhood Research* 13 (2): 137–49.

Lewin, S., Glenton, C. and Oxman, A. D. (2009). Use of qualitative methods alongside randomised controlled trials of complex healthcare interventions: methodological study. *BMJ* 339 (b3496): 1–7.

Lindell, A. K. and Kidd, E. (2011). Why right-brain teaching is half-witted: A critique of the misapplication of neuroscience to education. *Mind, Brain and Education* 5 (3): 121–7.

List, J. A. (2014). Using field experiments to change the template of how we teach economics. *The Journal of Economic Education* 45 (2): 81–9.

Lohr, K. N. (2004). Rating the strength of scientific evidence: Relevance for quality improvement programs. *International Journal for Quality in Health Care* 16 (1): 9–18.

Long, J. W., Ballard, H. L., Fisher, L. A. and Belsky, J. M. (2016). Questions that won't go away in participatory research. *Society & Natural Resources* 29 (2): 250–63.

Lundy, L. (2007). Voice' is not enough: Conceptualising Article 12 of the United Nations convention on the rights of the child. *British Educational Research Journal* 33 (6): 927–42.

MacLure, M. (2005). 'Clarity bordering on stupidity': Where's the quality in systematic review? *Journal of Education Policy* 20 (4): 393–416.

MacNaughton, G. (2005). *Doing Foucault in Early Childhood Studies.* London: Routledge.

MacNaughton, G., Rolfe, S. A. and Siraj-Blatchford, I. (2010). *Doing Early Childhood Research.* Maidenhead and New York: Open University Press.

Malinowski, B. (1913). *The Family Among the Australian Aborigines: A Sociological Study.* London: University of London Press.

Malinowski, B. (2007 [1966, 1935]). *Coral Gardens and their Magic – A Study of the Soil and of Agricultural Rites in the Trobiand Islands. Vol II: The Language of Magic and Gardening* (2nd edn). London: George Allen and Unwin Ltd.

Malone, K. (2013). 'The future lies in our hands': children as researchers and environmental change agents in designing a child-friendly neighbourhood. *Local Environment* 18 (3): 372–95.

Marsh, J. (2012). Children as knowledge brokers of playground games and rhymes in the new media age. *Childhood* 19 (4): 508–22.

Marsh, J. (2014). Online and offline play. In A. Burn and C. Richards (eds), *Children's Games in the New Media Age: Childlore, Media and the Playground* (pp. 109–32). London: Ashgate.

Marsh, J. (2017). The internet of toys: A Posthuman and multimodal analysis of connected play. *Teachers College Record* 119: 1–32.

Mayall, B. (2001). The sociology of childhood in relation to children's rights. *International Journal of Children's Rights* 8 (3): 243–59.

Mayall, B. (2002). *Towards a Sociology for Childhood.* Buckingham: Open University Press.

Maybin, J. (2013). Towards a sociocultural understanding of voice. *Language and Education* 27 (5): 383–97.

McEvoy, O. and Smith, M. (2011). *Listen to Our Voices! Hearing Children and Young People Living in the Care of the State.* Research Report. Dublin: Government Publications. Available at: http://hdl. handle.net/10147/139489 (Accessed 31.12.2018).

McGrath, S. (2010). Education and development: Thirty years of continuity and change. *International Journal of Educational Development* 30: 537–43.

McIntyre A. (2008). *Participatory Action Research.* Thousand Oaks, CA: Sage.

McLaughlin, C., Swartz, S., Cobbett, M. and Kiragu, S. (2015). Inviting Backchat: How schools and communities in Ghana, Swaziland and Kenya support children to contextualise knowledge and create agency through sexuality education. *International Journal of Educational Development* 41: 208–16.

McLeod, A. (2008). *Listening to Children: A Practitioner's Guide.* London: Jessica Kingsley Publishers.

McNeill, D. (1992). *Hand and Mind: What Gestures Reveal about Thought*. Chicago: Chicago University Press.

Mead, M. (1930). *Growing up in New Guinea*. William Morrow.

Mead, M. and Wolfenstein, J. (1955). *Childhood in Contemporary Cultures*. Chicago: University of Chicago Press.

Melhuish E., Belsky J., Leyland A. H., Barnes J. and the National Evaluation of Sure Start Research Team (2008). Effects of fully-established Sure Start Local Programmes on 3-year-old children and their families living in England: A quasi-experimental observational study. *The Lancet* 372: 1641–7.

Melhuish, E., Ereky-Stevens, K., Petrogiannis, K., Ariescu, A., Penderi, E., Rentzou, K., Tawell, A., Slot, P., Broekhuizen, M. and Leseman, P. (2015). A review of research on the effects of Early Childhood Education and Care (ECEC) upon child development. CARE project. Curriculum quality analysis and impact review of European Early Childhood Education and Care (ECEC). (Technical report FP7-SSH-2013-2). European Commission. Available at: http://ece c-care.org/fileadmin/careproject/Publications/reports/new:version_CARE_WP4_D4_1_Review:on_the_effects_of_ECEC.pdf (Accessed 30.10.2018).

Miles, M. B. and Huberman, A. M. (2014). *Qualitative Data Analysis: A Methods Sourcebook* (3rd edn). Thousand Oaks, CA: Sage.

Miller, E. T. (2015). Discourses of whiteness and blackness: An ethnographic study of three young children learning to be white. *Ethnography and Education* 10 (2): 137–53.

Ministry of Community Development, Youth and Sports (MCYS) (2012). Parliamentary Questions. Ensuring quality early childhood education and childcare services. Available at: https://www.ecda.gov.sg/PressR eleases/Pages/Ensuring-quality-early-childhood-education-and-chil dcare-services.aspx (Accessed 31.12.2018).

Moher, D., Liberati, A., Tetzlaff, J. and Altman, D.G. and PRISMA Group (2009). Preferred reporting items for systematic reviews and meta-analyses: The PRISMA statement. *PLoS Med* 6 (7): e1000097.

Moll, L. C., Amanti, C., Neff, D. and Gonzalez, N. (1992). Funds of knowledge for teaching: Using a qualitative approach to connect homes and classrooms. *Theory into Practice* 31 (2): 132–41.

Morelli, G., Rogoff, B. and Angelillo, C. (2003). Cultural variation in children's access to work or involvement in specialized child-focused activities. *International Journal of Behavioral Development* 27 (3): 264–74.

Morrison K. (2012). Searching for causality in the wrong places. *International Journal of Social Research Methodology* 15 (1): 15–30.

Morrow, V. (2008). Dilemmas in children's participation in England. In A. Invernizzi and J. Williams (eds), *Children and Citizenship* (pp. 120–30). London: Sage.

Moss P. (2007). Bringing politics into the nursery: Early childhood education as a democratic practice. *European Early Childhood Education Research Journal* 15 (1): 5–20.

Moss, P. (2016). Why can't we get beyond quality? *Contemporary Issues in Early Childhood* 17 (1): 8–15.

Murphy, E. and Dingwall, M. (2007). Informed consent, anticipatory regulation and ethnographic practice. *Social Science and Medicine* 65: 2223–34.

Mutz, D. C. (2011). *Population-Based Survey Experiments*. Princeton: Princeton University Press.

Mwaura, P. (2004). Secular preschools in Mombasa Madrasas. In R. Zimmermann (ed.), *Stories We Have Lived, Stories We Have Learned about ECD Programmes*. The Netherlands: Bernard Van Leer Foundation.

Mwaura, P. A. M., Sylva, K. and Malmberg, E.-R. (2008). Evaluating the Madrasa preschool programme in East Africa: A quasi-experimental study. *International Journal of Early Years Education* 16 (3): 237–55.

National Children's Bureau (NCB) (2011). *Guidelines for Research with Children and Young People*. London: NCB Research Centre. Available at: https://www.nfer.ac.uk/nfer/schools/developing-young-researchers/NCBguidelines.pdf (Accessed 01.10.2018).

Neumann, M. and Neumann, D. (2017). The use of touch-screen tablets at home and pre-school to foster emergent literacy. *Journal of Early Childhood Literacy* 17 (2): 203–20.

New London Group (1996). A pedagogy of multiliteracies. *Harvard Educational Review* 60: 66–92.

Nind, M. (2011). *What Is Participatory Research?* Thousand Oaks, CA: Sage.

Nind, M., Flewitt, R. and Payler, J. (2010). The social experience of early childhood for children with learning disabilities: Inclusion, competence and agency. *British Journal of Sociology of Education* (31) 6: 653–70.

Nores, M. and Barnett, W. S. (2010). Benefits of early childhood interventions across the world: (under) Investing in the very young. *Economics of Education Review* 29 (2): 271–82.

Norris, S. (2004). *Analyzing Multimodal Interaction*. London: RoutledgeFalmer.

Nugent, C. L. (2018). Sensory-ethnographic observations at three nature kindergartens. *International Journal of Research & Method in Education* 41 (4): 468–79.

Nutley, S., Powell, A. and Davies, H. (2013). *What Counts as Good Evidence?* London: Alliance for Useful Evidence.

O'Neill, J. (2010). One chairperson's experience of ethical review: Balancing principle, convention, relationship and risk in educational research. *International Journal of Research & Method in Education* 33 (3): 229–43.

Oakley, A. (2003). Research evidence, knowledge management and educational practice: Early lessons from a systematic approach. *London Review of Education* 1 (1): 21–33.

Oliver, S., Garner, P., Heywood, P., Jull, J., Dickson, K., Bangpan, M., Ang, L. and Fourman, M. (2017). Transdisciplinary working to shape systematic reviews and interpret the findings. *Environmental Evidence Environmental Evidence* 6 (28): 1–7.

Oliver, S. and Sutcliffe, K. (2017). Describing and analysing studies. In D. Gough, S. Oliver and J. Thomas (eds), *An Introduction to Systematic Reviews* (2nd edn, pp. 135–52). London: Sage Publications.

Oncea, A. and Pring, R. (2008). The importance of being thorough: On systematic accumulations of 'What Works' in education research. *Journal of Philosophy of Education* 42 (S1): 15–39.

Organisation for Economic Co-operation and Development (OECD) (2012). *Starting Strong iii: A Quality Toolbox for Early Childhood Education and Care.* Available at: http://www.oecd.org/education/school/startingstrongiii-aqualitytoolboxforearlychildhoodeducatio nandcare.htm (Accessed 30.10.2018).

Orton-Johnson, K. (2010). Ethics in online research; Evaluating the ESRC framework for research ethics categorisation of risk. *Sociological Research Online* 15 (4): 13.

Osgood, J., Sakr, M. and de Rijke, V. (2017). Dark play in digital playscapes. *Contemporary Issues in Early Childhood* 18 (2): 109–13.

Oxford Department for International Development (2015). *Young Lives: Theory of Change.* Available at: https://www.younglives.org.uk/sites/www.younglives.org.uk/files/YL_Theory_of_Change_2015.pdf (Accessed 31.01.2019).

Pacini-Ketchabaw, V., Kind, S. and Kocher, L. L. M. (2017). *Encounters with Materials in Early Childhood Education.* New York: Routledge.

Pahl, K. (2006). Birds, frogs, blue skies and sheep: an investigation into the cultural notion of affordance in children's meaning making. *English in Education* 40 (1): 20–35.

Pascal, C. and Bertram, T. (2009). Listening to young citizens: The struggle to make real a participatory paradigm in research with young children. *European Early Education Research Journal* 17 (2): 249–62.

Pascal, C. and Bertram, T. (2012). Praxis, ethics and power: Developing praxeology as a participatory paradigm for early childhood research.

European Early Childhood Education Research Journal 20 (4): 477–92.

Pawson, R. (2002). Evidence-based policy: The promise of 'realist synthesis'. *Evaluation* 8 (3): 340–58.

Pawson, R. (2006). *Evidence-based Policy: A Realist Perspective*. London: Sage.

Pearce, L. (2012). Mixed methods inquiry in sociology. *American Behavioral Scientist* 56 (6): 829–48.

Penn, H. (2005). *Understanding Early Childhood: Issues and Controversies*. London: Open University Press.

Penn, H. (2016). Social and political landscapes of childhood. In A. Farrell, S. L. Kagan and E. K. Tisdall (eds), (2016). *The SAGE Handbook of Early Childhood Research* (pp. 469–84). London: SAGE Publications Ltd.

Penn, H., Barreau, S., Butterworth, L., Lloyd, E., Moyles, J., Potter, S. and Sayeed, R. (2004). What is the impact of out-of-home integrated care and education settings on children aged 0–6 and their parents? In Research Evidence in Education Library. London, EPPI-Centre, Social Science Research Unit, Institute of Education. Available at: https://eppi.ioe.ac.uk/cms/Default.aspx?tabid=152 (Accessed 31.12.2018).

Percy-Smith, B. and Thomas, N. (eds) (2010). *Handbook of Children's Participation*. London: Routledge.

Peshkin, A. (1988). In search of subjectivity – one's own. *Educational Researcher* 7: 17–22.

Petticrew, M. and Roberts, H. (2003). Evidence, hierarchies, and typologies: Horses for courses. *Journal of Epidemiology and Community Health* 57 (7): 527–9.

Piaget, J. (1929). *The Child's Conception of the World*. London: Routledge.

Piaget, J. (1953). *The Origins of Intelligence in Children*. London: Routledge and Kegan Paul.

Piaget, J. (1969). *Science of Education and the Psychology of the Child*. Harlow: Longman.

Piaget, J. (1970). Piaget's theory. In P. Mussen (ed.), *Carmichael's Manual of Child Psychology* (Vol. 1, pp. 703–72). New York: John Wiley & Sons.

Piaget, J. (1977). *The Essential Piaget*. Edited by Howard Gruber. New York: Basic Books.

Piaget, J. and Inhelder, B. (1958). *The Growth of Logical Thinking from Childhood to Adolescence*. New York: Basic Books.

Picchio, M., Giandomenico, I. D. and Musatti, T. (2014). The use of documentation in a participatory system of evaluation. *Early Years* 34 (2): 133–45.

Pierce, K., Carter, C., Weinfeld, M., Desmond, J., Hazin, R., Bjork, R. and Gallagher, N. (2011). Detecting, studying, and treating autism early: The one-year well-baby check-up approach. *Journal of Paediatrics* 159: 458–65.

Pink, S. (2013). *Doing Visual Ethnography* (3rd edn). London: Sage.

Plowman, L. and Stephen, C. (2008). The big picture? Video and the representation of interaction. *British Educational Research Journal* 34 (4): 541–65.

Ponterotto, J. G. (2006). Brief note on the origins, evolution, and meaning of the qualitative research concept 'Thick description'. *The Qualitative Report* 11 (3): 538–49.

Pontes Ferreira, M. and Gendron, F. (2011). Community-based participatory research with traditional and indigenous communities of the Americas: Historical context and future directions. *International Journal of Critical Pedagogy* 3 (3): 153–68.

Porter, G., Hampshire, K., Bourdillon, M., Robson, E., Munthai, A., Abane. A. and Mashiri, M. (2010). Children as research collaborators: issues and reflections from a mobility study in sub-Saharan Africa. *American Journal of Community Psychology* 46 (1–2): 215–27.

Powell, M. A., Taylor, N. and Smith, A. B. (2013). Constructions of rural childhood: Challenging dominant perspectives. *Children's Geographies* 11 (1): 117–31.

Powell, S. and Somerville, M. (2018). Drumming in excess and chaos: Music, literacy and sustainability in early years learning. *Journal of Early Childhood Literacy* Online First. 0(0) 1–23. DOI: 10.1177/1468798418792603

Pratt, B. and Loizos, P. (1992). *Choosing Research Methods: Data Collection for Development Workers*. Development Guidelines No. 7. Oxfam.

Pring, R. and Thomas, G. (2004). *Evidence-based Practice in Education*. Maidenhead: Open University Press.

Prosser, J. (2007). Visual methods and the visual culture of schools. *Visual Studies* 22 (1): 13–30.

Prout A. (2005). *The Future of Childhood: Towards the Interdisciplinary Study of Children*. Abingdon: RoutledgeFalmer.

Prout, A. and James, A. (1997). A new paradigm for the sociology of childhood? In A. James and A. Prout (eds), *Constructing and Reconstructing Childhood: Contemporary Issues in the Sociological Study of Childhood* (2nd edn, pp. 7–33). London: Routledge.

Punch, S. (2002). Research with children: The same or different from research with adults? *Childhood* 9 (3): 321–41.

Quennerstedt, A. (2010). Children, but not really humans? Critical reflections on the hampering effect of the '3 ps'. *The International Journal of Children's Rights* 18: 619–35.

Quennerstedt, A. and Quennerstedt, M. (2014). Researching children's rights in education: Sociology of childhood encountering educational theory. *British Journal of Sociology of Education* 35: 115–32.

Qvortrup, J., Bardy, M., Sgritta, G. and Wintersberger, H. (eds) (1994). *Childhood Matters: Social Theory, Practice and Politics.* Avebury Press: Aldershot.

Rao, N., Nirmal Rao, Jin Sun, Jessie M. S. Wong, Brendan Weekes, Patrick Ip, Sheldon Shaeffer, Mary Young, Mark Bray, Eva Chen and Diana Lee (2014). *Early Childhood Development and Cognitive Development in Developing Countries: A Rigorous Literature Review.* Department for International Development. Available at: http://epp i.ioe.ac.uk/cms/Default.aspx?tabid=3465 (Accessed 31.12.2018).

Reason, P. and Bradbury, H. (eds) (2008). *Sage Handbook of Action Research: Participative Inquiry and Practice* (2nd edn). London: Sage Publications.

Reavey, P. (eds) (2011). *Visual Methods in Psychology: Using and Interpreting Images in Qualitative Research.* New York: Routledge.

Ridenour, C. S. and Newman, I. (2008). *Mixed Methods Research: Exploring the Interactive Continuum.* Carbondale: Southern Illinois University Press.

Riley. M. (2009). 'The next link in the chain': Children, agri-cultural practices and the family farm. *Children's Geographies* 7 (3): 245–60.

Rinaldi, C. (2001). A pedagogy of listening: A perspective of listening from Reggio Emilia. *Children in Europe* (1): 2–5.

Rinaldi, C. (2006). *In Dialogue with Reggio Emilia.* London: Routledge.

Roberts-Holmes, G. P. and Bradbury, A. (2017). Primary schools and network governance: A policy analysis of reception baseline. *British Educational Research Journal* 43 (4): 671–82.

Robinson, E. J. and Nurmsoo, E. (2009). When do children learn from unreliable speakers? *Cognitive Development* 24 (1): 16–22.

Rogers, R., Labadie, M. and Pole, K. (2016). Balancing voice and protection in literacy studies with young children. *Journal of Early Childhood Literacy* 16 (1): 34–59.

Rogoff, B. (1990). *Apprenticeship in Thinking.* New York: Oxford University Press.

Rogoff, B. (2003). *The Cultural Nature of Human Development.* New York: Oxford University Press.

Rogoff, B., Paradise, R., Arauiz, R. M. Correa-Chavez, M. and Angelillo, C. (2003). Firsthand learning through intent participation. *Annual Review of Psychology* 54: 175–203.

Rossman, G. B. and Wilson, B. L. (1994). Numbers and words revisited: Being 'shamelessly eclectic'. *Quality and Quantity* 28 (3): 315–27.

Rowe, D. W. and Miller, M. E. (2016). Designing for diverse classrooms: Using iPads and digital cameras to compose eBooks with emergent bilingual/biliterate four-year-olds. *Journal of Early Childhood Literacy* 16 (4): 425–72.

Ryle, G. (1971). *Collected Papers. Volume II Collected Essays, 1929-1968*. London: Hutchinson.

Sahlberg, P. (2015). *Finnish Lessons 2.0: What Can the World Learn from Educational Change in Finland?* (2nd edn). New York: Teachers College Press.

Salamon, A. (2015). Ethical symmetry in participatory research with infants. *Early Child Development and Care* 185 (6): 1016–30.

Sammons, P., Siraj-Blatchford, I., Sylva K., Melhuish, T., Taggart, B. and Elliot, K. (2005). Investigating the effects of pre-school provision: Using mixed methods in the EPPE research. *International Journal Social Research Methodology* 8 (3): 207–24.

Saracho, O. N. (2016). Writing and publishing qualitative studies in early childhood education. *Early Childhood Education Journal* 45: 15–26.

Sarangi, S. and Candlin, C. N. (2003). Trading between reflexivity and relevance: New challenges for applied linguistics. *Applied Linguistics* 24 (3): 271–85.

Sargeant, J. and Harcourt, D. (2012). *Doing Ethical Research with Children*. Maidenhead, UK: Open University Press.

Schieffelin, B. and Ochs, E. (1986). *Language Socialization across Cultures*. New York: Cambridge University Press.

Scott, C. and Sutton, R. (2009). Emotions and change during professional development for teachers a mixed methods study. *Journal of Mixed Methods Research* 3 (2): 151–71.

Scott, D. and Usher R. (2010). *Researching Education: Data, Methods and Theory in Educational Enquiry* (2nd edn). London: Continuum.

Scott, J. (2008). Children as respondents: The challenges for quantitative methods. In P. H. Christensen and A. James (eds), *Research with Children: Perspectives and Practices* (2nd edn, pp. 87–108). Abingdon: Routledge.

Scribner, S. and Cole, M. (1981). *The Psychology of Literacy*. Cambridge, MA: Harvard University Press.

Seale, J., Nind, M., Tilley, L. and Chapman, R. (2015). Negotiating a third space for participatory research with people with learning disabilities: An examination of boundaries and spatial practices. *Innovation: The European Journal of Social Science Research* 28 (4): 483–97.

Semenec, P. (2018). Re-imagining research with children through an engagement with contemporary art. *Childhood* 25 (1): 63–77.

Sharav, V. (2003). Children in clinical research: A conflict of moral values. *American Journal of Bioethics* 3 (1): 1–99.

Shaw, C., Brady, L.-M. and Davey, C. (2011). *National Children's Bureau Guidelines for Research with Children and Young People.* Available at: https://www.researchgate.net/publication/260060346_NCB_Guidelines_ for_Research_With_Children_and_Young_People (Accessed 31.12.2018).

Shea, B., Andersson, N. and Henry, D. (2009). Increasing the demand for childhood vaccination in developing countries: A systematic review. *BMC International Health and Human Rights 9* (Suppl 1): S5.

Shea, B. J., Reeves, B. C., Wells, G., Thuku, M., Hamel, C., Moran, J., Moher, D., Tugwell, P., Welch, V., Kristjansson, E. and Henry, D. A. (2017). AMSTAR 2: A critical appraisal tool for systematic reviews that include randomised or non-randomised studies of healthcare interventions, or both. *BMJ* (Sep. 21) 358: j4008.

Shier, H. (2001). Pathways to participation: Openings, opportunities and obligations. *Children and Society* 15: 107–17.

Shweder, R. A. (2007). The resolute irresolution of Clifford Geertz. *Common Knowledge* 13 (2–3): 191–205.

Siegel, M. (2006). Rereading the signs: Multimodal transformations in the field of literacy education. *Language Arts* 84 (1): 65–77.

Sikes, P. and Piper, H. (2010). Editorial: ethical research, academic freedom and the role of ethics committees and review procedures in educational research. *International Journal of Research and Method in Education* 33 (3): 205–13.

Simons, H. and Usher, R. (2000). *Situated Ethics in Educational Research.* London: Routledge/Falmer.

Singapore Statement on Research Integrity (2010). Available at: https:// www.jsps.go.jp/english/e-kousei/data/singapore_statement_EN.pdf (Accessed 31.12.2018).

Siraj, I. and Mayo, A. (2014). *Social Class and Educational Inequality: The Impact of Parents and Schools.* Cambridge University Press.

Siraj-Blatchford, I. (2010). Learning in the home and at school: How working class children 'succeed against the odds'. *British Educational Research Journal* 36 (3): 463–82.

Siraj-Blatchford, I., Mayo, A., Melhuish, E. C., Taggart, B., Sammons, P. and Sylva, K. (2011). *Performing against the Odds: Developmental Trajectories of Children In the EPPSE 3–16 study.* London: Department for Education / Institute of Education, University of London.

Siraj-Blatchford, I., Sylva, K., Muttock, S., Gilden, R. and Bell, D. (2002). *Researching Effective Pedagogy in the Early Years* (Research Report RR356). London: Department for Education and Skills. Available at: http://dera.ioe.ac.uk/4650/1/RR356.pdf (Accessed 30.12.2018).

Siraj-Blatchford, I., Taggart, B., Sylva, K., Sammons, P. and Melhuish, E. (2008). Towards the transformation of practice in early childhood education: The effective provision of pre-school education (EPPE) project. *Cambridge Journal of Education* 38 (1): 23–36.

Skinner, B. F. (1938). *The Behavior of Organisms: An Experimental Analysis*. New York: Appleton-Century.

Sligo, J. L., Nairn, K. M. and McGee, R. O. (2018). Rethinking integration in mixed methods research using data from different eras: Lessons from a project about teenage vocational behaviour. *International Journal of Social Research Methodology* 21 (1): 63–75.

Smith, F. and Barker, J. (2000). Contested spaces: Children's experiences of out of school care in England and Wales. *Childhood* 7 (3): 315–33.

Smith, H. V. (2018). Cooking the books: What counts as literacy for young children in a public library? *Literacy* 52 (1): 31–8.

Smith, M. (2006). The whole is greater: Combining qualitative and quantitative approaches in the evaluation studies. In A. Bryman (ed.), *Mixed Methods* (Vol. 3, pp. 253–72). London: Sage.

Smith, R., Purdon, S., Schneider, V., La Valle, I., Wollny, I., Owen R. Bryson, C., Mathers, S., Sylva, K. and Lloyd, E. (2009). *Early Education Pilot for Two Year Old Children: Evaluation*, Research Report DCSF-RR134. London: Department for Children, Schools and Families.

Snilstveit, B., Oliver, S. and Vojtkova, M. (2012). Narrative approaches to systematic review and synthesis of evidence for international development policy and practice. *Journal of Development Effectiveness* 4: 409–29.

Spillane, J. P., Stitziel Pareja, A., Dorner, L., Barnes, C., May, H., Huff, J. and Camburn, E. (2010). Mixing methods in randomized controlled trials (RCTs): Validation, contextualization, triangulation and control. *Educational Assessment, Evaluation and Accountability* 22 (1): 5–28.

Stephenson, A. (2009). Horses in the sandpit: Photography, prolonged involvement and 'stepping back' as strategies for listening to children's voices. *Early Child Development and Care* 179 (2): 13–41.

Stewart R. (2014). Changing the world one systematic review at a time: A new development methodology for making a difference. *Development Southern Africa* 31 (4): 581–90.

Streeck, J. (1993). Gesture as communication: its coordination with gaze and speech. *Communication Monographs* 60 (4): 275–99.

Street, B. V. (1984). *Literacy in Theory and Practice*. Cambridge: Cambridge University Press.

Styles, B. and Torgerson, C. (2018). Randomised controlled trials (RCTs) in education research – methodological debates, questions, challenges. *Educational Research* 60 (3): 255–64.

Sumsion, J. and Goodfellow, J. (2012). 'Looking and listening-in': A methodological approach to generating insights into infants' experiences of early childhood education and care settings. *European Early Childhood Education Research Journal* 20 (3): 313–27.

Sumsion, J., Harrison, L. J., Press, F., McLeod, S., Goodfellow, J. and Bradley, B. S. (2011). Researching infants' experiences of early childhood education and care. In D. Harcourt, B. Perry and T. Waller (eds), *Researching Young Children's Perspectives: Debating the Ethics and Dilemmas of Educational Research with Children* (pp. 113–27). London and New York: Sage.

Super, C. M. and Harkness, S. (1986). The developmental niche: A conceptualization at the interface of child and culture. *International Journal of Behavioral Development* 9: 545–69.

Swadener, B. B., Kabiru, M. and Njenga, A. (2000). *Does the Village Still Raise the Child? A Collaborative Study of Changing Child Rearing and Early Education in Kenya.* Albany, NY: State University of New York Press.

Sylva, K., Melhuish, E., Sammons, P., Siraj-Blatchford, I. and Taggart, B. (2004). *The Effective Provision of Pre-school Education (EPPE) Project: Findings from Pre-school to End of Key Stage 1.* Nottingham: Department for Education and Skills.

Sylva, K., Melhuish, E., Sammons, P., Siraj-Blatchford, I. and Taggart, B. (2010). *Early Childhood Matters: Evidence from the Effective Pre-school and Primary Education Project.* London: Routledge.

Sylva, K., Melhuish, E., Sammons, P., Siraj-Blatchford, I. and Taggart, B. (2011). Pre-school quality and educational outcomes at age 11: Low quality has little benefit. *Journal of Early Childhood Research* 9: 109–24.

Sylva, K., Melhuish, E., Sammons, P., Siraj-Blatchford, I. and Taggart, B. (2012). *Effective Pre-school, Primary and Secondary Education 3-14 Project (EPPSE 3-14): Final Report from the Key Stage 3 Phase: Influences on Students' Development from Age 11–14*, Research Report DfE-RR202, London: Department for Education.

Tangen, R. (2008). Listening to children's voices in educational research: Some theoretical and methodological problems. *European Journal of Special Needs Education* 23 (2): 157–66.

Tashakkori, A. and Teddlie, C. (eds) (2003). *Handbook of Mixed Methods in Social and Behavioral Research.* Thousand Oaks, CA: Sage.

Tashakkori, A. and Teddlie, C. (2010). *Sage Handbook of Mixed Methods in Social and Behavioral Research* (2nd edn). London: Sage.

Taylor, A. and Giugni, M. (2012). Common worlds: Reconceptualising inclusion in early childhood communities. *Contemporary Issues in Early Childhood* 13 (2): 108–19.

Taylor, D. and Dorsey-Gaines, C. (1988). *Growing Up Literate: Learning from Inner-City Families.* Portsmouth: Heinemann.

Taylor, R. E. (2006). Actions speak as loud as words; A multimodal analysis of boys' talk in the classroom. *English in Education* 40 (3): 66–82.

Thomas, J., Newman, M. and Oliver, S. (2013). Rapid evidence assessments of research to inform social policy: Taking stock and moving forward. *Evidence and Policy: A Journal of Research, Debate and Practice* 9 (1): 5–27.

Thomas, N. (2017). Turning the tables: Children as researchers. In P. Christensen and A. James (eds), *Research with Children: Perspectives and Practices* (3rd edn, pp. 160–79). Abingdon and New York: Routledge.

Thomson, P. (eds) (2008). *Doing Visual Research with Children and Young People*. London: Routledge.

Thorpe, L. P. (1946). *Child Psychology and Development*. New York: The Ronald Press Company.

Tisdall, E. K. M. and Davis. J. (2004). Making a difference? Bringing children and young people's views into policy-making. *Children and Society* 18 (2): 131–42.

Tisdall, E. K. M. and Punch, S. (2012). Not so 'new?' Looking critically at childhood studies. *Children's Geographies* 10 (3): 249–64.

Tobin, J., Wu, D. Y. H. and Davidson, D. H. (1991). *Preschool in Three Cultures: Japan, China and the United States*. New Haven and London: Yale University Press.

Todayonline (2012). *Make Preschool Education Free: Proposal among Wide-ranging Reforms Suggested to Improve early Childhood Education Here*. Todayonline: Singapore.

Tom, A. (1984). *Teaching as a Moral Craft*. New York: Longman.

UNESCO (2004). *The Plurality of Literacy and its Implications for Policies and Programmes*. Paris, France: UNESCO.

UNESCO (2015). *Education for All*. Global Monitoring Report. Available at: http://unesdoc.unesco.org/images/0023/002322/232205e.pdf (Accessed 01.10.2018).

UNESCO Institute of Statistics (2013). Toward Universal Learning: Recommendations from the Learning Metrics Task Force. Summary Report. Available at: http://www.uis.unesco.org/Education/Documents/lmtf-summary-rpt-en.pdf (Accessed 01.10.2018).

UNICEF (2017) *The State of the World's Children: Children in a Digital World*. New York: UNICEF. Available at: https://www.unicef.org/publications/files/SOWC_2017_ENG_WEB.pdf (Accessed 31.01.2019).

United Nations (1989). *The United Nations Convention on the Rights of the Child*. Available at: https://www.unicef.org.uk/wp-content/uploads/2010/05/UNCRC_united_nations_convention_on_the_rights_of_the_child.pdf (Accessed 01.10.2018).

United Nations (2015). *Transforming Our World. The 2030 Agenda for Sustainable Development* A/RES/70/1. Available at: https://sustainabled evelopment.un.org/content/documents/21252030%20Agenda%20for%20Sustainable%20Development%20web.pdf (Accessed 01.10.2018).

Universities UK concordat to support research integrity (2012). Available at: https://www.universitiesuk.ac.uk/policy-and-analysis/reports/Docu ments/2012/the-concordat-to-support-research-integrity.pdf (Accessed 31.12.2018).

Uprichard, E. (2008). Children as 'being and becomings': Children, childhood and temporality. *Children & Society* 22 (4): 303–13.

Uprichard, E. and Dawney, L. (2016). Data diffraction: Challenging data integration in mixed methods research. *Journal of Mixed Methods Research* 13 (1): 19–32.

Urban, M. (2010). Rethinking professionalism in early childhood: Untested feasibilities and critical ecologies. *Contemporary Issues in Early Childhood* 11 (1): 1–7.

Vackova, P. (2018). How a 360° camera unveiled ethnography as a relational practice in early years artmaking settings. Available at: https ://digiliteymethodscorner.wordpress.com/2018/12/12/how-a-360-came ra-unveiled-ethnography-as-a-relational-practice-in-early-years-artmak ing-settings (Accessed 30.12.2018).

Van Leeuwen, T. (2004). *Introducing Social Semiotics: An Introductory Textbook*. London: Routledge.

Veale, A. (2005). Creative methodologies in participatory research with children. In S. Greene and D. Hogan (eds), *Researching Children's Experience: Approaches and Methods* (pp. 253–72). London: Sage.

Viruru, R. (2001). *Early Childhood Education: Postcolonial Perspectives from India*. New Delhi and London, Sage Publications.

Vygotsky, L. S. (1962). *Thought and Language*. Cambridge, MA: MIT Press.

Vygotsky, L. S. (1978). *Mind in Society: The Development of Higher Psychological Processes*. Cambridge, MA: Harvard University Press.

Waite, S., Boyask, R. and Lawson, H. (2010). Aligning person-centred methods and young people's conceptualisations of diversity. *International Journal of Research and Method in Education* 33 (1): 69–83.

Waksler, F. (1991). Studying children: Phenomenological insights. In F. Waksler (ed.), *Studying the Social Worlds of Children: Sociological Readings* (pp. 60–70). London: Falmer Press.

Walkerdine, V. (1984). Developmental Psychology and the child-centred pedagogy: The insertion of Piaget into early education. In J. Henriques, W. Hollway, C. Urwin, C. Venn and V. Walkerdine (eds), *Changing the*

Subject: Psychology, Social Regulation and Subjectivity (pp. 153–202). London: Methuen.

Waller, T. (2014). Voices in the park: Researching the participation of young children in outdoor play in early years settings. *Management in Education* 28 (4): 161–6.

Waller, T. and Bitou, A. (2011). Research 'with' children: Three challenges for participatory research in early childhood. *European Early Childhood Education Research Journal* 19 (1): 5–20.

Wargo, J. (2019). *Sonification and the Field Recording.* Available at: https://digiliteymethodscorner.wordpress.com/2019/04/22/sound-and-sonic-methodologies (Accessed 01.06.2019).

Wells, K. (2009). *Childhood in a Global Perspective.* Cambridge, UK: Polity.

Whiting, B. (1963). *Six Cultures: Studies of Child-Rearing.* New York: Wiley.

Wickenden, M. and Kembhavi-Tam, G. (2014). Ask us too! Doing participatory research with disabled children in the global south. *Childhood* 21 (3): 400–17.

Wiles, R. (2013). *What Are Qualitative Research Ethics?* London and New York: Bloomsbury Academic.

Wiles, R., Coffey, A., Robison, J. and Prosser, J. (2012). Ethical regulation and visual methods: Making visual research impossible or developing good practice? *Sociological Research Online* 17 (1): 8.

Wogan, P. (2004). Deep hanging out: Reflections on fieldwork and multisited Andean ethnography. *Identities* 11 (1): 129–39.

Wohlwend, K. E. (2009). Early adopters: Playing new literacies and pretending new technologies in print-centric classrooms. *Journal of Early Childhood Literacy* 9 (2): 117–40.

Wohlwend, K. E. (2017). Who gets to play? Access, popular media and participatory literacies. *Early Years* 1 (37): 62–76.

Wohlwend, K. E. and Rowsell, J. (2017). App maps: Evaluating children's iPad software for 21st century literacy learning. In N. Kucirkova and G. Falloon (eds), *Apps, Technology, and Younger Learners: International Evidence for Teaching* (pp. 73–88). London: Routledge.

Wolfe, S. and Flewitt, R. S. (2010). New technologies, new multimodal literacy practices and young children's metacognitive development. *Cambridge Journal of Education* 40 (4): 387–99.

Wood, D., Bruner, J. and Ross, G. (1976). The role of tutoring in problem solving. *Journal of Child Psychology* 17: 89–100.

World Bank (2011a). *Investing in Young Children.* Washington: The World Bank.

World Bank (2011b). *Learning for All Investing in People's Knowledge and Skills to Promote Development. World Bank Group Education Strategy 2020.* Washington: The World Bank. Available at: http://siteresources.worldbank.org/EDUCATION/Resources/ESSU/Education_Strategy_4_12_2011.pdf (Accessed 01.10.2018).

World Bank (2015a). *Early Childhood Development*. Available at: http://www.worldbank.org/en/topic/earlychildhooddevelopment/overview (Accessed 01.10.2018).

World Bank (2015b). *Early Learning Programme*. Available at: http://www.worldbank.org/en/topic/education/brief/early-learning-partnership (Accessed 10.01.2019).

World Health Organisation, United Nations Children's Fund and World Bank Group (2018). *Nurturing Care Framework for Early Childhood Development: A Framework for Helping Children Survive and Thrive to Transform Health and Human Potential*. Geneva: World Health Organisation Licence: CC BY-NC-SA 3.0 IGO.

World Medical Association (WMA) (2013). *Declaration of Helsinki*. Available at: https://www.wma.net/what-we-do/medical-ethics/declaration-of-helsinki (Accessed 01.10.2018).

Worthington, M. and van Oers, B. (2017). Children's social literacies: Meaning making and the emergence of graphical signs and texts in pretence. *Journal of Early Childhood Literacy* 17 (2): 147–75.

Xie, S. and Li, H. (2018). Perspectives on readiness for preschool: A mixed-methods study of Chinese parents, teachers, and principals. *Children and Youth Services Review* 95: 19–31.

Yale University and ACEV partnership (2012). *Ecology of Peace: Formative Childhoods and Peace Building. A Conceptual Framework*. Available at: https://medicine.yale.edu/childstudy/fcpb/research/publications/briefnote_online_FINAL_171407_28959_v2.pdf (Accessed 31.12.2018).

Yamada-Rice, D. (2017). Designing play for dark times. *Contemporary Issues in Early Childhood* 18 (2): 196–212.

Yelland, N. J. (2018). A pedagogy of multiliteracies: Young children and multimodal learning with tablets. *British Journal of Educational Technology* 49 (5): 847–58.

Yin, R. K. (2006). Mixed methods research: Are the methods genuinely integrated or merely parallel? *Research in the Schools* 13 (1): 41–7.

INDEX